JOY
IN MUDVILLE

D1560114

JOY
IN MUDVILLE

Being a Complete Account of the

Unparalleled History of the New York Mets

from Their Most Perturbed Beginnings

to Their Amazing Rise to Glory and Renown

GEORGE VECSEY

The McCall Publishing Company
NEW YORK

To David Spencer Vecsey

Born on September 24, 1969, the day the Mets clinched their division title. All his life the Mets have been winners. He's not going to believe this, but . . .

CONTENTS

PHOTOGRAPHS FOLLOWING PAGE 128

JOY
IN MUDVILLE

1

JOY IN MUDVILLE

◆

THEY SPILLED OVER the barricades like extras in a Genghis Khan movie, all hot-eyed and eager for plunder. The Mets had just won the 1969 World Series, and the fans wanted to take home a talisman piece of Shea Stadium, to secure good fortune for the rest of their lives.

For half an hour they sacked the stadium, clawing at home plate with their fingernails, ripping out great chunks of sod for souvenirs, ransacking the swivel chairs from the box seats. Others pranced merrily over the infield, waving their forefingers in the air, performing for the television cameras, chanting "one-one-one" like some mystical incantation. There always had been something mystical about Met fans, the way they kept the faith.

The New York Mets had justifiably been called the Worst Team in the History of Baseball. In their first seven lean years, they had won 394 games and lost 737 for a staggeringly poor percentage of .348. They had finished a total of 288½ games out of first place in those seven years.

The Mets were absolutely awful. They didn't try to be. They just were. Anybody can fumble a grounder or give up a long home run, but the Mets were champions at it. They had a first baseman named Marvelous Marv Throneberry, who chased runners to the wrong base when he was in the field and forgot to touch the bases when he was running them. They had a pitcher who gave up a home run on his first pitch as a Met. Most Met pitchers waited at least until their second or third pitch.

Fortunately, there were people who saw the Mets in perspective, right from that dreadful start. Casey Stengel, the manager, used to laugh "It's a joke" when the Mets blew another game. A new breed of New York fans were just plain happy to have a National League team again and would have flipped their wigs for just a Little League team—which, in effect, they did. And a sensitive band of sportswriters sensed this spirit of the people that was more important than winning or losing.

The fans endured the losing for seven years and were prepared for another hundred years of it. New York was getting used to losing. The city had been evacuated by too much of its middle class; it was barren in finances and in spirit. Its mayor was running for reelection as an underdog against two "law and order" candidates. It was a city that badly needed bread and circuses —maybe even a miracle.

Now on October 17, the miracle happened. The Mets had stormed through an unbelievable season to capture the World Series, and the people were piling into the street to celebrate. Tons of paper were streaming out of office windows. People were dancing in the streets, holding hands with strangers, reaching back to their childhood for ways to express their joy.

Over on the East Side, the pastor of St. Agnes Church told his curate to ring the bell in honor of this most secular occasion. It was like the closing minutes of some old Bing Crosby movie, the kind of ending that had become impossible in our world of war and ghettoes.

Yet for a few brief weeks in 1969, the Mets reminded people of love and hope, sentiments that were neither very stylish nor realistic in 1969. If the Mets could win the World Series, people said, anything was possible. It was a joke, sure. But perhaps the Mets' victory had been planned for a long time, maybe for a million years, just so in this one crazy season they could send us all out into the streets, to hold hands and dance in a circle.

2

HOLY WAR ON THE
SUBWAY

◆

SOMEDAY WHEN THE Mets are hailed as the greatest dynasty in sports, the fusing process of history will make millions of fans assume that New York baseball sprang full-grown out of Shea Stadium sometime in the middle 1960s. The truth is that New Yorkers had been conditioned to love the Mets even before there was a Mets. The seeds of mad devotion and ironic appreciation had been planted for generations and needed only the bright sunshine of the new Mets in 1962 to make them flourish.

Actually, the Mets began back in the nineteenth century when Brooklyn was still a separate city, when teams alternately called the Trolley Dodgers or Bridegrooms or Superbas reigned across the river, and other teams named the Giants and Highlanders ruled in New York.

There was even a New York Mets before. In 1883, the one-year-old American Association expanded to eight teams, accepting Columbus and the New York Mets. The Mets finished fourth in their first season, and one imaginative writer claimed he heard manager Jim Mutrie lament even then: "Can't anyone here play this game?"

As the Mets prepared for 1884, few people expected them to

go higher than fourth. But the durable Tim Keefe hurled 492 innings for a 37–18 record while strong-armed Jack Lynch was 37–14 for 487 innings, and the Mets beat out Columbus by 6½ games.

The Mets then took on the Providence Grays in the first postseason series in baseball history and lost to Old Hoss Radbourne, 6–0, 3–1, and 12–2, in three straight days. In 1885, the Mets finished next to last and went out of business three years later.

In the early 1900s, the major leagues became more stable. The Highlanders became the New York Yankees of the American League, a nondescript outfit that would obviously never go anywhere. The real action in town was in the National League, represented by the Brooklyn Dodgers and the New York Giants.

The Giants won ten pennants and finished second eight more times by 1924, and they were the prestige team in town. Wealthy families parked their horse-and-buggies—and later their horseless carriages—behind the outfield at the oval-shaped Polo Grounds, a baseball park situated alongside the Harlem River in uptown Manhattan. Politicians and show people and millionaires vied for the best seats to watch Christy Mathewson, manager John McGraw, Bill Terry, Carl Hubbell, and Mel Ott.

One of the families that patronized the Giants was the Whitney family, which had built a few railroads and could afford to take the afternoon off to watch a game now and then. Sometime around 1910, Mrs. Helen Hay Whitney brought her daughter, Joan, to the family box behind first base and taught little Joan how to mark down the game on her scorecard.

The Dodgers did not draw the same carriage trade to their games at old Washington Park in South Brooklyn or later at Ebbets Field on Bedford Avenue. Brooklyn was the other side of the river, the other side of the tracks, the dark side of the moon as far as New Yorkers were concerned. Only the dead knew Brooklyn, according to Thomas Wolfe, who spent several lonely years in the borough of churches and cemeteries.

Actually, Brooklyn was a collection of middle-class neighborhoods in those days, but it was scorned from afar by New Yorkers. If a playwright wanted a sure laugh, he invented a character who came from Brooklyn, talked in "dems and doses," and ate with his hands so he would not stab himself with a fork. New Yorkers told Brooklyn jokes the way people told Polish and Italian jokes in the 1960s.

The Dodgers, of course, contributed to this mystique by their fumbling brand of baseball. If Babe Herman did not get hit on the head with a fly ball, then three Dodgers would wind up on third base at the same time. Or perhaps a bright-eyed young slicker named Casey Stengel would tip his cap to the fans and have a sparrow fly out.

The club was nicknamed "The Robins" because of the manager, rotund Wilbert Robinson—"Uncle Robby." Uncle Robby was a democratic soul who willingly debated his own strategy with fans after each loss. Sometimes he would sit in the taxi, with the meter running, while fans assailed his wisdom. His wife—known as "Ma" —would often take the side of the fans until Uncle Robby growled to the cabbie: "Get the hell out of here."

Thus, a tradition of the fans' involvement was created in this Athenian democracy known as Brooklyn. In later years this expressive strain would reassert itself in the form of advice written on bedsheets.

As tough as they were on their own kind, Dodger and Giant fans were tougher on the other team. In the old eight-team National League, teams played each other twenty-two times—eleven at home, eleven away. In New York, this meant twenty-two days a year when the subway was packed with holy crusaders, eager pilgrims carrying their lunches in brown paper bags, running the scales to warm up their voices. The rivalry was also carried out in taverns throughout the metropolitan area. The intensity was more akin to the soccer rivalries in neighboring cities of Italy or England than to American sports, where rivalries are conducted over thousands of miles. Dodger and Giant fans were close enough to get their hands on each other—and frequently did.

The Dodger fans did the suffering in the first four decades of the twentieth century as the Giants won thirteen pennants and the Dodgers won only three. Meanwhile, over in the Bronx, the Yankees became the most powerful organization in baseball, winning the pennant almost every year, often beating the National

League in the World Series. Except for those few days every
October, Dodger and Giant fans ignored the Yankees.

Early in the 1940s, the teams reversed directions as the proud
Giants went downhill and the Dodgers were rebuilt by Larry
MacPhail and Branch Rickey with a farm system that began to
produce many fine young players. The Dodgers won the pennant
in 1941 and then lost a play-off in 1946, when their young pros-
pects came back from the war. By then the Dodgers had a new
source of heroes. In 1946, the religious and pragmatic Branch
Rickey signed Jackie Robinson, the first Negro to be given a
major-league contract in the twentieth century (although several
Negroes had probably masqueraded as Indians or other such dark
minorities).

Looking back, it seems incredible that baseball did not permit
Negroes into its structure before 1946. But the sport had its roots
in the minor leagues and drew many of its players from the South,
and club owners were afraid of the consequences of bringing
Negroes into the all-white structure. By signing the former football star from UCLA, Rickey instantly transformed the Dodgers
into more than a baseball team representing the borough of
Brooklyn. To many people with any awareness of baseball, the
Dodgers now stood for something progressive and hopeful.

In 1947, Jack Roosevelt Robinson was the National League
Rookie of the Year and helped the Dodgers win the pennant.
They missed in 1948 but bounced back in 1949 with the help of
Don Newcombe, a strapping Negro right-hander, and Roy Cam-
panella, a chunky Negro-Italian catcher.

The Dodgers also had heroes like shortstop Pee Wee Reese,
right fielder Carl Furillo, third baseman Billy Cox, the combustible
center fielder Duke Snider, and the huge, graceful first baseman
Gil Hodges. Hodges was prone to taking too many third strikes,
but he was a slugger and a beautiful fielder as well as a thorough
gentleman, so the fans endured his one bad habit.

With all these good players, the Dodgers settled into the golden
decade of Brooklyn baseball, often packing the compact old ball
park. The Dodger fans were appreciative of success but they
never thought of themselves as winners, as Yankee fans undoubtedly did. Dodger fans retained the nervous energy and the flip-

pant insecurity of the underdog, a trait that would be very evident in a future generation.

One of the trademarks of a Dodger fan was personal involvement in the game. Baseball wasn't just nine men on the field, it was all the *yoots* from Queens and Brooklyn who hung out of the center-field bleachers throwing pink rubber balls (*Spaldeens*) and imaginative oaths at the visiting outfielders.

Back around 1950, there were a bunch of us from P.S. 35, in Hollis, Queens, who felt we were never given enough credit for a Dodger victory. We were snarling at the Philadelphia Phillie outfielders, hoping to distract them.

The blond center fielder of the Phillies, Richie Ashburn, knew how to handle us. He winked at us, waved at us, tossed our rubber balls back into the stands, thereby demonstrating an affinity for New York fans that would come in handy ten years later, when he would help invent Marv Throneberry.

But the brawny right fielder of the Phillies, Del Ennis, was not as friendly. He turned his back to us, so we began to concentrate on unnerving him. Late in the game, a Dodger lofted a fly to deep right field. With us shouting "miss it, miss it," Ennis did indeed muff the fly ball as two vital Dodger runs crossed the plate.

The next day we all bought copies of the *Daily News* to see if Dick Young, our favorite writer, would acknowledge our role in the error. But Young gave Ennis all the credit for the error, which is one of the few good stories that Dick Young ever missed.

That was Brooklyn. That, and meeting your friends under the "Rotunda" behind home plate, chatting with Jackie Robinson when injuries forced him to kill time in the grandstand, watching the players emerge from the dingy tunnel from the dugout, having Don Newcombe mutter "get outta here" to the autograph seekers.

Meanwhile, the Giants had their own rooters who always seemed to glory more in what Ott had done twenty years before than in what was happening under their noses. The Giants did try to climb out of the mire with some ponderous cavemen named Johnny Mize, Willard Marshall, Walker Cooper, and Sid Gordon. They hit 221 homers in 1947, a major-league record, but still finished fourth behind the Dodgers. They hit 131 of those homers in their Polo Grounds, with its short foul lines to right and left field and its deep center field. The Giants therefore produced the ultimate in American democracy. All hitters were equal, but some more than others. It made life very tough for a Dodger fan when some inconspicuous Giant could flick a 250-foot "Chinese home run."

The year was around 1950 and it was a holiday. Two wonderful friends of my father, Jim and Joe McGuinness, were taking me to a Giant-Dodger game in the Polo Grounds. They were Giant fans, of course, and they smoked cigars, and they seemed illogically cocky about a team that had not won a pennant since 1937. They were also lovely men and very nice to take me to a game. We were sitting in the left-field grandstand, upstairs. We had a fine view of the whole field except for the left fielder. He was somewhere below us, in the shadows of the overhanging grandstand.

The teams were tied, 1–1, going into the bottom of the ninth. Willie "the Knuck" Ramsdell was throwing his knuckle ball in relief for the Dodgers. No way the Giants could score. The Giant batter was named Jack Conway, a man I never heard of before that day, or since. Conway was obviously fooled by Willie the Knuck and blooped a fly ball to left field. Reese even drifted back for a possible play. The ball soared to our eye level. It glistened in the sun. Then it began to fall. Suddenly people began to shout. The next thing I saw was Furillo and Hodges running for the clubhouse in center field. The scoreboard had a big "1" for the Giants in the ninth. But how?

"The ball must have ticked the overhang," Jim McGuinness told me, lighting a cigar.

"Tough way to lose a game, on a little pop-up like that," Joe McGuinness said.

I sulked all the way home. In a later year, Bobby Bragan of the Milwaukee Braves would label the Polo Grounds a "chamber of horrors."

Soon after Rickey signed Robinson, the Giants became pragmatic idealists too. They signed Monte Irvin and Hank Thompson and a young Alabaman named Willie Mays, and they started to improve.

The Yankees, however, refused to hire Negro players, which would hurt them in later years. But it didn't seem that way in 1949, when old Casey Stengel came back from the Pacific Coast League to give the Yankees a dash of excitement.

Then came 1951, a great year for New York baseball, a pivotal year for the evolution of a future Met mentality. In 1951 the Yankees came up with a moody young lion named Mickey Mantle, a country boy who hit long home runs and kicked his batting helmet when he didn't. With Mantle destined to replace the aging monument, Joe DiMaggio, the Yankees were sure to remain the grim bunch of executioners they always had been.

The Dodgers had their own center fielder in the temperamental Snider, who could smash home runs and make magnificent catches and still grumble about the undeserving Dodger fans.

Also in 1951, Willie Mays arrived in the Polo Grounds while the Giants were skulking far behind the Dodgers. Under the cajoling of Leo Durocher, who had a fine eye for genius, Mays sparked the Giants to a second-half rally. Trailing the Dodgers by thirteen and a half games in the middle of August, the Giants finished in a tie on the last day of the season. The Yankees, naturally, had long since captured their championship.

Thus the world stood still in 1951 to watch the Dodgers and the Giants, the Sharks and the Jets, the Montagues and the Capulets, play off for the National League pennant. The Giants won the first game, the Dodgers won the second, and in the third and final game, the Dodgers took an early lead.

As we were dismissed from class at Junior High 157 in Rego Park, the Yankee fans dispassionately watched the Giant and Dodger fans.

"If the Dodgers lose this one," a Yankee fan said to me, "I don't see how you can show your face in school tomorrow."

By the time we got out of the subway, it was the eighth inning. By the time we got off the bus, it was the ninth inning. Then all of a sudden, Bobby Thomson hit a three-run homer and the Giants won the pennant, 5–3.

Did Dodger fans hide their faces for the next week or two? No. In fact, when the World Series opened the next day, Dodger fans were either overtly or secretly rooting for the Giants. Having viewed the death struggle between the two teams, Dodger fans (and perhaps Giant fans) were now suitably purged to appreciate the other side.

In that World Series of 1951, Mays and Irvin and Sal "the Barber" Maglie seemed like heroes to some Dodger fans as they battled the lucky Yankees, who needed a day of rain to alleviate their pitching problems and assure them of another World Series victory. But the memory of rooting for the hated Giants and the hated Durocher in the hated black and orange uniform did not fade. In the years that followed, there was an increased tolerance between Giant and Dodger fans, while the Yankees continued to stomp with hobnailed boots on the face of the American League. For all New York fans, it was the best of times. The worst of times was soon to come.

3

MA AND PA

◆

IN THE SUMMER OF 1957, a press conference was called at the New York Giants' executive offices at 100 West Forty-second Street. Horace Stoneham, the principal owner of the Giants, announced that the team of John McGraw and Willie Mays was moving to San Francisco for the 1958 season.

"It's a tough wrench," Stoneham said. "I'm very sentimental about the Giants and New York City. But conditions were such we had to accept now or they might not be so favorable again."

Stoneham had been very democratic about moving the franchise, however. He had let the Giants' board of directors take a vote. Stoneham's son voted to move. Stoneham's nephew voted to move. Stoneham's brother-in-law voted to move. Four others voted to move. Only one man voted against the move. His name was M. Donald Grant.

M. Donald Grant voted no because he was representing one of the minority owners of the Giants, Mrs. Charles Shipman Payson, who had begun life with the name Joan Whitney. Mrs. Payson owned around 10 per cent of the New York Giants, and she had no need of a few hundred thousand dollars in dividends for moving the club to San Francisco. She would rather have the Giants in New York.

"It just tears my heart to see them go," said M. Donald Grant. "I've been a Giant rooter all my life. Then, too, as a businessman, I think they would do better staying here. I would rather have a National League franchise here than in any other city."

The loss of a New York team was not totally unexpected. The Dodgers, unable to draw huge crowds into cramped old Ebbets Field, had been casting about for a new home. There was talk of building a stadium at Boro Hall or over the Long Island Rail Road terminal at Atlantic Avenue or even out in the wilds of Queens County, on the site of the 1939 World's Fair.

Some people suspected that Walter O'Malley, the lawyer who had gained control of the Dodgers, had his eye on Los Angeles, but O'Malley assured them this was not so. "My roots are in Brooklyn," he said.

The season ended gloomily in the Polo Grounds, where the Giants lost, 9–3, to the Pirates. The widow of John McGraw made a pilgrimage that day and said, "It would have broken John's heart."

After the game, some angry fans congregated below Stoneham's office, cursing and shaking their fists at the king in his counting house. But it is doubtful if Stoneham heard, or cared.

A few days later, O'Malley let his own shoe drop. He had milked a few extra admissions out of the Brooklyn fans but now that the season was over—surprise—the Dodgers were moving to Los Angeles. New York City was now without a National League baseball team.

In New York, Giant and Dodger fans screamed in unison that they did not deserve this total desertion. But Warren Giles, the portly red-faced president of the National League, who lived and worked in Cincinnati, said he did not think the National League necessarily needed a franchise in New York. Mr. Giles, of course, had his salary paid by the owners—and O'Malley and Stoneham were the two most powerful owners in the league.

Faced with some long and barren baseball seasons, many people began action to find another team. In Brooklyn, lawyer George D. McLaughlin felt particularly compelled since he had gotten Walter O'Malley involved with the Dodgers in the first place. McLaughlin needed some help, and he called up a younger

lawyer he had befriended several years before, a husky and athletic New Yorker named William A. Shea.

Bill Shea began contacting other National League teams, hoping to lure one of them to New York. In 1958, Mayor Robert Wagner—under criticism for having the Dodgers and Giants walk out
—appointed Shea as chairman of a baseball committee. Thus began
a four-year crusade that would interrupt Shea's career as a cor-
poration lawyer, keep him away from his family, and cause him
to spend his own money too often.

Shea started by co-operating with several Congressional com-
mittees that were investigating antitrust violations in sports.

As a focal point for the disenfranchised, Shea then became
involved in a proposed third baseball league, the Continental
League, which, on July 28, 1959, announced franchises in New
York, Houston, Toronto, Denver, and Minneapolis-St. Paul. Other
franchises would be awarded in the future.

The proposed New York team would play in a municipal stadium to be built on the World's Fair site by Mayor Wagner and
his projects man, Robert Moses. The proposed owners of the new
club would be Joan Whitney Payson and Dwight Davis, whose
father had donated the Davis Cup to tennis and whose rugged
working week now consisted of "clipping coupons."

"If the major leagues co-operate with us," Shea said, "we won't
have a bit of trouble getting players. There are enough good
players around right now to staff a new league.

"Actually, the supply of young players can be unlimited," Shea
continued. "They haven't been coming up now because they
haven't been given the opportunities. The risk of a big-league
career with only sixteen teams has been too great. The big leagues
keep too many old players around now simply to profit from their
names and reputations. The young players have to wait too long
for their chance. With twenty-four big-league teams—or maybe
more—they'll get their chance.

"After a year or two, people will realize what can be done.
This is the sort of thing which America does best. No one ever
heard of an atomic scientist fifteen years ago. Now they're coming out of the woodwork. You can't tell me that a nation of

a hundred and sixty million can't produce two hundred more big-league ball players."

The owners of the sixteen major-league clubs tried to ignore the Continental League, but they couldn't. They feared that Congressional investigations would endanger the "reserve clause" that bound a player to his club forever. Then they looked at the areas clamoring for admission to the Continental League and decided there were some juicy franchises to be had out there, as well as some juicy admission fees. And by admitting four new clubs from four different states, they could actually curry the favor of eight senators. Expansion suddenly seemed like such a good idea that the owners began to think they dreamed it up themselves.

In August of 1960, the American League announced a new franchise in Los Angeles, a new franchise in Washington, and the shifting of the old Washington franchise to Minnesota. The National League announced a new franchise in Houston and a new franchise in New York City. The owner of the new franchise would be Mrs. Charles Shipman Payson. Somewhere along the line. Dwight Davis was aced right off the court without even a trophy.

There was a great deal of interest in Mrs. Payson since she would become the only female majority owner in the major leagues. People wanted to know if she had bought the team with Green Stamps or scrimped on the family budget or what. Women owners were rare in sports, but this lady could afford her new acquisition.

Most sports owners were usually written about in *Sports Illustrated* or *Sport Magazine*, but Mrs. Payson's background was *Fortune* all the way. A 1957 *Fortune* survey had called her one of the richest women in the world, estimating her value at between $100 and $200 million. Her father's will had been $200 million in 1929, the largest will ever probated at that time. The Whitney family had an estate in Manhasset, Long Island, had built hospitals, owned a racing stable, owned homes all over the world. A baseball team to Mrs. Payson was like a new car is to other people.

Joan Whitney was born in 1903 in New York and educated at Miss Chapin's School and Barnard College. The Whitney family loved sports. Her father had been captain of the 1898 Yale crew, enjoyed golf on his private course on Long Island, swam at the family indoor pool, and donated the $7.5 million Payne Whitney Gymnasium at Yale.

Joan's mother was Helen Hay Whitney, the daughter of a former Secretary of State. Mrs. Whitney helped found Greentree Stable, and the pink and black colors were seen on Twenty Grand in the winner's circle at the 1931 Kentucky Derby. She frequently gave her horses names from baseball—Shutout, One Hitter. It was not unusual to see Mrs. Whitney watching a big race at Belmont while listening to an early radio broadcast of a Giant baseball game.

Mrs. Whitney often invited famous athletes to the family mansion. Abe Simon once trained for a prize fight at Greentree and Mrs. Whitney shook his hand in the ring. "Pardon my glove," he said to her. Another time Babe Ruth came to lunch, and Mrs. Whitney tested his fielding ability by pitching hard-boiled eggs to him at the other end of the table. She later ordered the entire household to eat only Wheaties for breakfast so she could cast her box-top votes for Joe DiMaggio as the most popular major leaguer.

Joan's first sporting memories were of betting a quarter a race at Saratoga and winning frequently. She also spent many afternoons with her mother at the Polo Grounds.

It was not surprising that Joan should find a husband from the same background as hers. She married "tall, red-haired Charles Shipman Payson, scion of an old Portland, Maine, family," as the newspapers used to say. Mr. Payson, himself a former Yale crewman, was not without his means.

"Charlie's a businessman," Mrs. Payson once said. "I don't know exactly what he does. He's just a businessman. I remember once I asked Father what he did and he said: 'I'm a businessman.' Well, that's what Charlie is."

The Paysons had five children. The oldest, Daniel Carroll died at the age of eighteen in the Battle of the Bulge. Three girls were followed by another son, John.

In 1950, at a luncheon in Hobe Sound, Florida, Mrs. Payson met M. Donald Grant, a former hotel employee who had moved up to a senior partnership in Fahnestock & Co. Grant confided that he had always wanted to manage a baseball team. Mrs. Payson confided that she had always wanted to own one. That was interesting, Grant said. He happened to own one share of stock in the New York Giants. It wasn't much, he agreed, but it did get him into stockholder meetings. Mrs. Payson, a Giant fan all her life, asked Grant if she could buy his one share of stock. By 1957, Grant had rounded up 10 per cent of the New York Giants for the chubby little lady, who in turn appointed him to represent her on the Giants' board of directors. He wasn't a manager, but he was getting close.

Mrs. Payson and Grant were good sports about the 8–1 vote that moved the Giants to San Francisco. Mrs. Payson offered to buy the Giants from Stoneham, but he refused. So in the spring of 1958, when the Giants opened at Seals Stadium, she flew out to the Coast to root for them.

Once back in New York, she found that life was not the same. She still had her stable, her art gallery, her private railroad car, her homes in Maine, Kentucky, Florida, Long Island, and Upper Fifth Avenue. She still had her Gauguins, Renoirs, and Van Goghs on the wall, and she had a certain attachment to the Republican Party (she had donated $65,000 to the G.O.P. in 1956). But now she had to fly 3000 miles if she wanted to watch her favorite baseball team. Even for a Whitney, that can be a drag.

So when she had a chance to buy the new New York franchise, Mrs. Payson eagerly paid $3 million for 85 per cent of the stock. A business associate named G. Herbert Walker bought 6 per cent and Grant bought 5 per cent.

Some people have suggested that Mrs. Payson bought the new team as a possible tax loss. But the Whitneys have a magic touch about money. In 1938, Joan and her brother, Jock, later an ambassador to the Court of St. James's, purchased the film rights to a novel named *Gone With the Wind*. They didn't do that for money, either.

Oh, yes. When the National League reminded Mrs. Payson that she could not own stock in two clubs at the same time, she didn't bother to sell her stock in the Giants. Instead, she gave it away to New York Hospital.

Now they had a ball club, these two old Giant fans who had respectively wanted to own and manage a club. Mrs. Payson had no intention of running the club herself, because she was too involved with her children and her husband ("my present husband," she still called him after thirty years of marriage).

So she and Grant (who would eventually be respectfully called "Ma and Pa" by their players) began looking for an experienced baseball executive who could build a team in New York. Their search soon narrowed down to one man, George M. Weiss, the man who had maintained the Yankee dynasty in the 1940s and 1950s.

Weiss was currently at liberty in Greenwich, Connecticut, spending his time reading his scrapbooks from the 1937 Newark Bears. He had been fired by the Yankees on November 3, 1960, in the second phase of their "youth movement" that had also claimed Casey Stengel on October 18, 1960.

A shy man who ran his business with proper Prussian authoritarianism, Weiss missed working, and he probably even missed some of his baseball associates. He was not used to hanging around the house. His vivacious wife, Hazel, was not used to him hanging around either. In early 1961 somebody asked Hazel Weiss how she liked having her man home in retirement. "I married George for better or for worse—but not for lunch," she said.

People snickered at this view of the solemn man, but not at his record or his knowledge. On March 14, 1961, they appointed George M. Weiss president of the still-unnamed New York Metropolitan Baseball Club.

Weiss had the title of president because he had left the Yankees with an agreement that he not take another job as general manager. This semantic difference seemed to satisfy Weiss, and there wasn't much the Yankees could do. But obviously Weiss was hired to be the general manager—to run the new baseball franchise.

The next step in building the club was to find a nickname for it. Fans had been submitting names like "Empire Staters" and "Meadowlarks" (for Flushing Meadow, where the team would play). There were also some dreadful amalgamations like "Do-Gints" and "Gi-odgers." A committee of reporters had screened the nominations down to a final ten.

On May 8, 1961, the names were submitted to Mrs. Payson. "Mets," she said. "I like this one." And since she had somewhat more invested in the new project than anybody else, Mets it was.

Now they needed a manager. All summer long as they scouted the National League, they analyzed their needs. The Mets would be in a building situation for several years, so they would need a patient teacher. But the Mets would also be bucking for publicity and affection in the biggest of big cities, so they needed a man who could make headlines. Mrs. Payson and Grant had their pro-Giant sympathies and might have preferred a Leo Durocher or an Eddie Stanky.

But Weiss had memories of perhaps the best move he ever made—bringing an old Pacific Coast League manager back to New York in 1949. That man had given the Yankees twelve exciting seasons, plus ten pennants. His name was Casey Stengel and he, too, was presently at liberty.

4

THE SLICKEST MANAGER
IN BASEBALL

◆

GRANDVIEW AVENUE RUNS vertically from the San Fernando Free-
way to the top of a brown mountain above Glendale, California.
Halfway up that mountain is a spacious home, complete with
guest house and swimming pool and a citrus grove out back. In
1924, the home was given to Edna Lawson by her father upon
the occasion of her marrying a baseball player by the name of
Charles Dillon Stengel.

In that spacious home, on the second floor with a view of the
mountain, is a bedroom with authentic Japanese furniture, including beds, dressing tables, fans, mirrors, rugs, drapes, and bric-
a-brac. When Casey and Edna Stengel accompanied the New
York Yankees to Japan in the 1950s, they purchased the stunning
assortment and had it shipped back to Glendale.

In time, Edna developed a theory about that authentic Japanese bedroom. She felt that a man who was born in 1890 eventually ought to spend a few years in that bedroom before he got
too old to appreciate the splendor of it.

The New York Yankees, so it turned out, shared Mrs. Stengel's
desire for Casey to spend his seventies in a Japanese bedroom.
On October 18, 1960, after Casey had led the Yankees to their

tenth pennant in twelve years under him, he was discharged by the ownership of the Yankees.

The ownership made a mistake, however—a rather basic one. They let Casey appear at the announcement of his "retirement." Perhaps Dan Topping, the swarthy playboy owner, anticipated that Casey would give some flannel-mouthed rationalization of his departure. But Casey had a favorite saying that predicted how he would behave at this peculiar ceremony: "I can make a living telling the truth," he often said.

So when the Yankees held a press conference in Le Salon Bleu of the Savoy Hilton Hotel on Manhattan's Fifth Avenue, there was the old soothsayer himself, holding a glass of bourbon, ready to dispense with formality.

Reporter: Casey, the Associated Press says you've been fired.

Casey: Well, what does the U.P. (United Press) say?

Reporter: Were you fired?

Casey: Quit, fired, quit, discharged, use whatever you damn please. I don't care. You don't see me crying, do you?

Thus having charmed the reporters and mugged for the television cameras for presumably the last time as a baseball manager, Casey went back to his Japanese bedroom and his tall, pretty, intelligent, and sensitive Edna. Any other man in America might have given up his World Series rings for the privilege of retiring to the good life in Glendale.

Casey put in some time in his office at the Valley National Bank, where he was a vice-president, and he made speeches at civic luncheons, and he hobnobbed with baseball people on the West Coast. But by the summer of 1961, Edna could tell that her seventy-one-year-old husband still missed the late hours, the constant public recognition, the authority, the excitement of managing. Now "the Slickest Manager in Baseball"—as Casey liked to call himself—was bored.

He had been in baseball since 1910 and he wanted no other life. People had written that he would have made an excellent teacher or politician or lawyer or whatever, but Casey Stengel was basically a jock. He had been a powerful young athlete, 5 feet, 10 inches tall and 175 pounds. Much has been written about his elfish qualities, and certainly he was mentally and spiritually quick. But he was also a physical man who, in his final years with the Yankees, could walk proudly through the clubhouse without his clothes on, a strong-legged, barrel-chested man with unwrinkled skin, the body of a forty-year-old.

Of course, he had the seamy face and ears of an elephant—a cartoonist's dream. He was also one tough old man. When he pounded his chest it sounded like a drum, and when he grabbed your shoulder you didn't move away. At times like that, reporters and players alike would marvel at this tough old bird. Whatever their feelings about him as a manager, the players respected him as a man. And they marveled at the kind of tough young man he must have been.

Charles Dillon Stengel was born in Kansas City, Missouri, on July 30, 1890. His parents were Louis Stengel, of German descent, and Jennie Jordan Stengel, of Irish descent. He had a brother, Grant, and a sister, Louise, and people used to joke that when his parents saw flop-eared young Charley, they gave up the idea of any more children.

Young Charley attended Central High, where people knew him as "Dutch" Stengel, the fellow who was always fighting during basketball games. Then he started at the Western Dental School, spending three years trying to be a left-handed dentist. But one day he raised a patient all the way to the ceiling while he absent-mindedly thought about turning a double into a triple. So he knew he shouldn't be a dentist, and he took off for Kankakee of the Northern Association. The league folded in July, and for the next fifty years Casey would grumble that they owed him two weeks' salary.

He stuck with baseball and reached the major leagues in 1912, reporting to the Brooklyn Dodgers at old Washington Park. Some country boys were destroyed by their first excursion to the big city but young Dutch Stengel was turned on by the whole scene. He was not even upset when the older players refused to let him into the cage for batting practice. Instead, he had calling cards printed and he distributed them to his teammates.

MY NAME IS CHARLES DILLON "DUTCH" STENGEL. I WOULD LIKE TO TAKE BATTING PRACTICE, the card announced. This thoroughly

charmed the roughnecks, who let him take a swing or two as a
reward for his audacity.

Before long, Dutch was one of the old-timers himself. Only now
his nickname was "Casey" because of his home town. But there
was very little Kansas City left in him when he was in Brooklyn.
He became like a native, and enjoyed nothing more than taking
the latest rube from the country for his first ride on the subway.

"Yes, here we are on the IRT—or is it the BMT?" Casey would
muse as they rattled through Brooklyn. Then Casey would give
explicit directions to the rube about how to get back to civiliza-
tion in case they should get parted. After which Casey would
step casually out of the train just before the doors closed. Casey
would wave grandly at the rube as the train thundered into the
bowels of Brooklyn.

Casey also became famous as a clown during his Dodger days.
His most memorable moment came when he tipped his hat to
his razzing admirers and a sparrow flew out. Leon Cadore, a
Dodger pitcher, had found the bird in the bullpen. Casey was
protecting the seemingly injured bird by keeping him under his
cap. But the bird made a miraculous recovery and soared away
as the fans applauded.

After five years in Brooklyn, Casey himself flew away to Pittsburgh and Philadelphia before joining the New York Giants in
1922. Here he ran into John J. McGraw himself, who utilized
Stengel as a part-time player. Casey undoubtedly screamed like
crazy when McGraw alternated him with a right-handed hitter,
but in later years Casey would also platoon players like Hank
Bauer and Gene Woodling—and they would scream like crazy
too.

The platoon system was exactly the way to handle Stengel,
because in 1922 he batted .368 in 84 games, and the Giants won
the pennant. In 1923, he batted .339 in 75 games and they won
the pennant again.

It seems ironic, in the long view, that one of Casey's weaknesses was his fielding. In his later years he would harangue
players at least to improve their defense. But he had only ade-
quate range and a mediocre arm and he was often removed for

defensive purposes in the late innings, a tactic Casey would repeat with his players in the future.

The early shower did give Casey an advantage in one important aspect of the game, however. It gave him a head start on the pretty girls in the stands. Baseball in those days was always conducted in the middle of the afternoon, giving bankers, stockbrokers, musicians, gamblers, bartenders, and actresses a chance to enjoy sunshine and baseball together.

One day in the summer of 1923, Casey spotted a tall and pretty girl sitting in the stands with Van Meusel, the wife of the Giant right fielder.

Edna has always maintained that she had a tentative date to meet Long George Kelly, the stylish Giant first baseman, but perhaps she has said this to tease the man she married.

At any rate, Long George Kelly was playing first base while Casey was excused for the last two innings. Casey saw no point in following the game from the dugout, not when there was such a pretty girl in the stands. He rushed to the clubhouse for a shower and climbed into his jaunty big-city suit. Then he dashed into the grandstand and casually happened to sit near Mrs. Meusel and her attractive friend.

Dutch Stengel did not have to pass out calling cards to pretty girls, the way he did to teammates in batting practice. While Long George Kelly was still playing first base, Casey Stengel asked Edna Lawson to go dancing with him that night.

Then it was the World Series of 1923 and the Yankees and Giants were tied, 4–4, late in the first game. Suffering from a bruised heel, Casey amazed himself by clouting a line drive toward the clubhouse in deep center field. Casey's normal pace was slowed down by the injury, and he huffed past third base and staggered home with the winning run, an inside-the-park home run.

The next morning, Edna's father was reading an account of the game in the newspaper. Sports reporting was much better in the good old days because writers had such vivid imaginations. They did not bother asking questions in the clubhouse. They just wrote about the game the way it appeared in their fertile minds.

The writers had a wonderful time with Casey's 360-foot tour of the bases. They described him tripping over his gray beard, crawling on all fours, losing his shoes, taking several minutes to round the bases, needing a stretcher to reach the dugout, needing artificial respiration in the clubhouse, the whole bit. Mr. Lawson read these reports carefully. Then he said to his daughter: "Edna, I guess you'd better marry him before he dies of old age."

Casey, who was all of thirty-three years old, also hit a homer to win the third game of the Series. Then he and Edna made plans to be married, which they were on August 18, 1924, in Belleville, Illinois. Mr. Lawson donated the house halfway up the mountain on Grandview, but Casey and Edna didn't spend much time there. Instead they moved to Boston in 1924, Worcester in 1925, and Toledo in 1926. Casey eventually became player, owner, and manager in Toledo.

In 1934 he became manager of the Dodgers, replacing the beloved Uncle Robby. The Dodgers had the same collection of clowns and Casey tried to get some laughs out of the team. But after he finished sixth, fifth, and seventh, he was paid off for the final year on his contract and released.

Casey was hardly a national figure at this time, but he did have enough of a reputation that the Boston Braves hired him as manager in 1938, where he went through the Dodger experience all over again. In six years the Braves never got above fifth place and Casey was fired after 1943. And so Casey was hardly a hero in Boston either. One year he was run down by a taxi during a rainstorm and lay in the hospital for weeks waiting for his broken leg to mend. A cranky Boston sports columnist nominated the cabby to be Boston's "sports personality of the year."

So Casey went back to the minor leagues at the age of fifty-three, seemingly out of the national spotlight forever. He worked in Milwaukee and Kansas City before moving to the Oakland Oaks of the Pacific Coast League.

This was a wonderful time in the Coast League. Oakland and San Francisco played holiday doubleheaders, crossing the Bay in a ferry as they switched ball parks between games. When the Oaks traveled to Southern California, Casey and Edna could live at home in Glendale and drive to the games in Los Angeles and

Hollywood and San Diego. If this was the minor leagues, Edna had no complaint. She was near her family and her own interests in banking and real estate. The dreary seasons in Boston and Brooklyn were far behind.

But when Casey's Oaks won the championship in 1948, he became a valuable property again. In New York, the Yankees had just lost the pennant and Bucky Harris was fired. The general manager of the Yankees was George Weiss, who had been Casey's boss at Kansas City in 1945. Weiss asked Casey to manage the Yankees in 1949, and Casey could not refuse. He wanted one more try at the major leagues.

Once again they closed up the house in Glendale, this time taking up residence in the Essex House on Central Park South in Manhattan. And this time Casey was in the right place at the right time. He was managing the best club in baseball, with Joe DiMaggio and Tommy Henrich, Vic Raschi and Allie Reynolds. When the old Yankees wore out, George Weiss reached out and got him a Mickey Mantle or a Whitey Ford.

Any manager would have loved to handle the Yankees, and many managers would have won a lot of pennants. But Casey Stengel won ten pennants in twelve years, which is almost perfect, and he did it fearlessly, with frequent lineup changes and resourceful strategy, always backed up by the basic superiority of the Yankee organization.

The Yankee management and the dour Yankee fans would have been satisfied with mere victory, but Stengel gave them more than they knew. He gave the Yankees a feeling of electricity, a sense of excitement they never had before. He was not afraid to do anything. He played the old Joe DiMaggio at first base one day, just to see what would happen. He batted a powerful pitcher, Don Larsen, in the seventh position in the batting order. The Yankee fan could go to the ball park expecting the desired victory but also expecting that something else might happen, something beyond victory. Or the next day the fan might read in the paper that Stengel was snapping at some of his younger players.

"Lumpe looks good," Stengel might grumble, "until I play him."

Operating in the communications center of the country, Stengel became familiar to all sports fans in the United States. They knew of his new language form, Stengelese. They knew he was a brilliant old guy, but sometimes you couldn't understand him. They also suspected he planned it that way.

In 1958, Senator Estes Kefauver called Stengel to Washington to testify in front of a congressional committee investigating baseball.

"At my age," he testified, "and I have been in baseball, well, I will say I am possibly the oldest man who is working in baseball. I would say that when they start an annuity for the ball players to better their conditions, it should have been done and I think it has been done."

And Kefauver replied: "Mr. Stengel, I am not sure that I made my question clear."

Clear questions, however, did not guarantee clear answers. Casey was only specific when he wanted to be, and one of those days was October 18, 1960, the day the Yankees fired him.

"I'm taking a jet home," Casey snapped at the reporters, with a stunned Dan Topping within earshot. "And I'm charging it to the club. A man gets his transportation home even if they don't want him."

So he went home to the house on Grandview and he sat around for a month or two. When Weiss was appointed president of the new club, certainly Stengel had thoughts about going east. And when the Mets made their official offer in late September of 1961, Casey took only a few days to accept.

On September 29, 1961, the Mets announced in New York that their manager would be seventy-one-year-old Casey Stengel. Back at his bank office in Glendale, Casey held a press conference.

"I guess they want high-class people back there," he said. "You can say I'm happy to be going back to the Polar Grounds and the salary—well, it's wonderful."

In the course of his conversation, Casey managed to call his new team "The Knickerbockers," but people knew what he meant. The Old Man looked excited as he recalled the offer from Mrs. Payson and Grant. "They're enthusiastic and ambitious," he said.

"I was pleased to think they wanted me over so many men now available in baseball."

What did Casey think about managing an expansion team? "You're gonna have troubles in the baseball business every day, no matter who you're with," he said. "Myself, I'll expect to win every day. I hope not to get sick worrying about it if I don't. The main thing is to keep up the spirit of your men. Keep your head up and feel you're gonna win the next one."

Did Casey have any ideas for players? "I wouldn't doubt that people in Brooklyn and New York would like to see Hodges," he said. "I think we should have some men from both the old Dodgers and Giants."

Then Casey flew east for the World Series, which, as usual, was opening at Yankee Stadium. He popped around the Series headquarters, drawing huge crowds of reporters and baseball officials, and the Yankee ownership must have gulped at seeing this healthy old ghost from Series past.

Casey sat with the new Met management as the Yankees beat the Cincinnati Reds in the opening game. But on the second day, a stirring antiestablishment note was sounded as the Reds beat the Yankees, and a dashing little Venezuelan named Elio Chacon sneaked home while the Yankee pitcher wasn't looking.

During the last inning, Casey got up to beat the crowd out of the ball park. The fans, perhaps encouraged by the Yankee loss, started waving at the Old Man, cheering as he strutted down the aisle behind home plate. Casey waved his hand at the fans, his wrinkles curving upward in delight. He was back in business now. People were still cheering the Slickest Manager in Baseball —maybe more than ever.

5

I WANT TO THANK ALL THOSE GENEROUS...

◆

IN HIS FIFTY YEARS of baseball, George Martin Weiss had developed the reputation of being one of the shrewdest, most cold-blooded of all baseball executives. The son of a New Haven, Connecticut, grocer, he had jumped from manager of the Hillhouse High varsity to organizer of the Colonial semipros, bringing in Ty Cobb and Walter Johnson on Sunday when they could not play major-league games because of the "Blue Laws."

In 1919 Weiss had borrowed $5000 to purchase the New Haven franchise in the Eastern League. He soon had his investment back after selling a number of his better players to a higher league, often for as much as $20,000.

The calculating man moved up to Baltimore of the International League in 1929 and developed his skills, selling men to the major leagues for as much as $40,000. Then he moved into the Yankee farm system, where he channeled the Charlie Kellers and Phil Rizzutos to the varsity.

After moving across the river from Newark to the Yankees in 1947, Weiss helped perpetuate the dynasty by operating a shuttle system between the Yankees and the Kansas City Athletics. Any time the Yankees needed a starting pitcher or a right fielder or whatever, Weiss would ship off eight or ten of the top farmhands who couldn't quite make the Yankees.

Thus in fifty years of baseball, George M. Weiss had rarely known frustration, had always enjoyed the upper hand, had always dealt from strength. In October of 1961, his streak ended.

As part of the agreement for entering the National League, the Mets and the Houston Colt 45s had to spend $1,800,000 each. This modest initiation fee included a pool of major-league talent from the existing eight clubs, and it seemed safe to assume that George M. Weiss would find a way to come up with talent.

But the National League owners had been fighting each other for a generation, and they were not about to help the man who had once run the most successful organization in baseball.

The National League owners had a distinct advantage in this miserly enterprise, having observed the American League's expansion after the 1960 season. The kindly Brother-in-Law League, acting in haste, had frozen all rosters during the season before the clubs could hide all the promising youngsters in their farm systems.

Thus the new Los Angeles Angels had come up with promising youngsters like Dean Chance, Jim Fregosi, Bob Rodgers, and Bo Belinsky from the other American League rosters. The Angels were helped by friendly Chub Feeney of the San Francisco Giants and kindly Buzzie Bavasi of the Los Angeles Dodgers, who made their scouting reports available to the new club in return for observing the expansion process.

By October of 1961, the National League executives had juggled their rosters to protect themselves in the draft. The existing clubs could protect only seven of their top fifteen farmhands on their forty-man roster. So rather than elevating promising youngsters to the major-league roster, they loaded up their forty-man rosters with older minor leaguers who would never make the majors—except for expansion, of course.

The existing clubs could also protect only the top eighteen men on their twenty-five-man roster. So they carefully loaded their varsities with fringe players in 1961, even if it hurt them in spots. In Philadelphia, wily young Gene Mauch kept a catcher named Choo Choo Coleman despite his .128 average, displaying him like a poker player casually showing off a card in his hand.

On October 10, 1961, the Mets and the Colts were shown lists of available players. In later years, Weiss would more or less admit that he had been stunned by the lack of talent. But he couldn't go screaming to Senator Kefauver. All he could do was pick. Baseball was a business, run for profit by the owners. The threat of antitrust legislation had scared the owners into expansion, but that didn't mean they had to create two equitable teams. Zounds! The thought of parity for New York and Houston sounded almost like communism to the owners.

Still, Weiss had certain options as he prepared to pick his players. He could concentrate on younger men who "hadn't failed yet," in Stengel's words, or he could go for the older hands.

Weiss knew that Mrs. Payson was hoping to come up with as many old Dodgers and Giants as possible, even to the point of paying almost any price for Willie Mays if he had been available. But Mrs. Payson had said that Weiss "would shoot me if I interfered," and both she and Grant knew better. Perhaps her one indulgence was Elio Chacon, the little daredevil who had sneaked home against the Yankees in the 1961 World Series. But mostly Weiss was on his own, and his instincts told him to go for older players.

The reasoning was that the Mets were going to operate in New York City, in the wake of the old Dodgers and Giants. The Mets had to draw from these frustrated National League fans and the best way to draw them into the ball park was with familiar names. The Mets were following the same theory that Broadway shows use: have your tryouts on the road, but when you open up on the Great White Way, you'd better have a star—or at least some familiar names.

So with a comment "you've got to have a catcher," Weiss plucked Hobie Landrith, a spunky little catcher from the Giants. When that October day was over, the Mets picked twenty-two players. Technically, some cost more than others. But all came under the mandatory $1,800,000 price tag. The new Mets were:

For $125,000 each—pitchers Jay Hook (Cincinnati) and Robert L. Miller (St. Louis); infielder Don Zimmer (Chicago); outfielder Lee Walls (Philadelphia).

For $75,000—pitchers Craig Anderson (St. Louis), Roger Craig (Los Angeles), Ray Daviault (San Francisco), and Alvin Jackson (Pittsburgh); catchers Landrith, Chris Cannizzaro (St. Louis), and Coleman; first basemen Ed Bouchee (Chicago) and Gil Hodges (Los Angeles); infielders Chacon, Felix Mantilla (Milwaukee), and Sammy Drake (Chicago); outfielders Gus Bell (Cincinnati), Joe Christopher (Pittsburgh), John DeMerit (Milwaukee), and Bobby Gene Smith (Philadelphia).

For $50,000—pitcher Sherman Jones (Cincinnati) and outfielder Jim Hickman (St. Louis).

These twenty-two were not actually the first Met players. Ted Lepcio, a former Red Sox bonus player, had been signed as a free agent late in the season. He would never play a game for them, but he could always say he was the first Met.

After the draft, Weiss tried to promote some established major-league players. This gave the other clubs a chance to make more money from the new clubs. Weiss acquired Billy Loes, an erratic ex-Dodger right-hander who had once claimed to have lost a ground ball in the sun during a World Series game, and Johnny Antonelli, a former Giant left-hander. Upon being claimed by the Mets, Loes promptly retired to go into the restaurant business and Antonelli promptly retired to go into the tire business. But who can say they were not original Mets?

The next Met was a brawny slugger named Frank Thomas, purchased from the Milwaukee Braves. Thomas had been playing in organized baseball since 1948 and had never been with a pennant winner. In fourteen previous seasons, he had finished in the first division only four times—a rather ominous sign for the new club. He had played with the Pirates, Reds, Cubs, and Braves, hitting 223 homers in 1307 games, but clubs seemed to win pennants before they got him or after they traded him away.

Next the Mets obtained Richie Ashburn, the fiery outfielder who had wound up in Chicago after many fine years in Philadelphia. Then Lee Walls, one of their draft choices, was sent along with approximately $100,000 for Charlie Neal, an old Brooklyn hand who had mysteriously faded after starring in the 1959 World Series.

Two relief pitchers were picked up—Clem Labine, the old

Dodger right-hander who had shuttled around to other clubs, and Ken MacKenzie, a left-hander from Yale and the Milwaukee Braves.

As the Mets stockpiled some recognizable names, the fans in New York began remembering them in their prime.

—Remember how Labine stopped the Giants in that second playoff in 1951?

—Remember how Neal decked Don Hoak in that fight with Cincinnati?

—Remember how Ashburn threw out Cal Abrams in the last game in 1950?

—Remember when Bell's homer broke Maglie's scoreless streak?

—Remember how Hodges hit those four homers in one game?

—Remember Craig pitching the Dodgers to the 1959 pennant?

But all the memories were in the past tense, and most of the talent was that way too.

George M. Weiss had gone to the well and come back empty. In later years he would be criticized frequently for not going for younger players as Houston did. But there were not many good players available, young or old, and Weiss felt the Mets had to come up with familiar faces.

One man always understood that Weiss had done his best. In later years Casey might fight with Weiss about specific players, but he always defended Weiss's role in the expansion choices.

"Yes," Stengel would say bitingly, "I want to thank all those generous club owners for making these fine players available to New York and to my Amazing Mets."

The club also recruited three men at this time who would have the impossible job of making the Mets sound competitive. They were the troika of broadcasters, hired specifically to promote the club and the sponsor's product, and they would become personally identified with the Mets.

The new announcers were big Ralph Kiner, the former slugger for the Pittsburgh Pirates; Bob Murphy, a chunky Oklahoman who had broadcast for the Red Sox and Orioles; and Lindsey Nelson, a glib Tennessee native who was more familiar for his football broadcasting. The trio lent a touch of class to the Met entourage. Kiner was knowledgeable about his game, and he was quietly available to the players for batting advice. Nelson, whose peacock wardrobe of bright jackets and shirts and ties made him a natural for color television, was charming and well traveled and had even been known to read a hard-cover book from time to time.

These three men were supposed to stress the positive at all times, avoid the negative as much as possible, and not root openly for the Mets. All three of these tasks would become almost impossible in the very near future.

6

SPRING FEVER

◆

ST. PETERSBURG SPRAWLS QUIETLY on the west coast of Florida, in the section daringly called "The Suncoast." St. Petersburg is not the neon lights and power boats and fur stoles of the Miami-Fort Lauderdale area. The Suncoast is where middle-class folks come when they retire from the frozen north.

They sit on the park benches downtown or they buy into retirement apartments or trailer parks. They spread suntan lotion on their dry noses and they pull yachting caps down on their heads. Then they wait for something to happen.

On February 17, 1962, something happened in St. Petersburg. It was a one-man brass band, a Pied Piper blowing his horn for a new baseball team. Casey Stengel, seventy-one years old and coming out of a one-year retirement, showed up on the Suncoast. It was even sunny.

The folks were used to rooting for the Yankees, who had trained in St. Petersburg for many years until leaving for Fort Lauderdale in 1962. But St. Petersburg still had the St. Louis Cardinals and now it had this new team—the uh, Mets.

The fans may not have known the Mets but they knew the manager. Casey had been a favorite in St. Petersburg for years, turning the dull training camps into a sideshow when he felt like it. Also, the elderly folks had great respect for somebody who, like themselves, had survived six or seven decades on this silly planet.

Casey arrived in Florida on two hours of sleep after the long flight from Los Angeles, but two hours was enough for him. He had work to do. He had to begin plugging the New York Mets, making them a national institution. His first assignment was to promote his own book, *Casey at the Bat*, at an autograph party in a bookstore. The shop was packed, and the old folks brought money.

"Casey, I'm a Detroit Tiger fan but I like to see young fellows like you get ahead," said seventy-five-year-old John DeWilde of Holland, Michigan. This sentiment inspired Casey to write a long inscription on the flyleaf of the man's book. "I'm writing a novel for you," Casey said. "More here than in the book."

To most people he would write: "Casey Stengel—Join the Mets."

If Casey was solicitous to the older folks, he was downright aggressive to the youngsters. Casey seemed to sense right away that he must build a broad base of appeal for the Mets—and the place to start was with the young. He was like St. Augustine or Karl Marx or whoever it was who called for the hearts and minds of the seven-year-olds. Only Casey was looking for the affections of the "Youth of America," that vast silent majority he knew was out there somewhere.

A twelve-year-old Little Leaguer named Billy Knieren presented his copy for autographing. "See me in a year," Casey announced. "Give me your address. We'll sign you for the Mets. A bonus, too. We don't fool around."

Before he was finished signing, Casey promised more bonuses than even Mrs. Payson could afford. His conspiratorial winks and his strong handshakes and his flourishing personalized autographs drew people into the Met fold. Any guerrilla force, any government propaganda team, would have done well to study Casey's tactics.

A couple of hundred folks even showed up on February 18 at Miller Huggins Field on the near north side of St. Petersburg for the Mets' first minor workout. About a dozen pitchers ran in the outfield while Casey charmed the folks in the stands.

"Yes," he announced, "we have a special window on the side of our office where we are selling World Series tickets for this October. Make sure you get yours now."

Somebody asked Casey how the Mets would be run. "Can't say how the Mets will be run. They never been run yet."

But the real opening day was February 19. The pitchers and catchers began arriving by plane at Tampa or driving in from all over the country. The players assembled at the Colonial Inn, a modern low-slung motel alongside the Gulf of Mexico, half an hour from downtown. In the lobby a sign declared: "Stengelese Spoken Here."

The Yankees had always stayed at the musty old Soreno downtown, and Weiss naturally maintained his quarters there, where old-timers sat and rocked on the front porch, wearing spats and dinner jackets.

But Casey had an unerring instinct for sunshine and kind breezes and he now avoided the funereal Soreno. He had no attachment to the past. He went where the crowds went. He gravitated to brightness and newness. He was forever young.

At 9:45 in the morning on February 19, Casey called his new men together in the clubhouse at Huggins Field and told them: "Bust your asses for me and I'll get you more money." Then he snapped, "All right," and the twenty-two pitchers and catchers romped out to the playing field.

The players did little more than throw the ball on the first day. Roger Craig, the gangling pitcher from the Dodgers, who resembled the old-time movie actor named Slim Summerville, was the first Met to throw from the mound. And Ken MacKenzie, who looked more like Wally Cox than a left-hander from Yale, was the first Met to suffer an injury, a cramped calf muscle.

Casey and Weiss sat on the newly painted benches in front of the clubhouses and even Weiss seemed to smile at their new team. Retirement was for the thousand folks in the stands, not for these two old Yankees.

This day also marked the debut of the Mets' first official fan, a hulking New Yorker named Looie Kleppel. "You want I should go to Candlestick Park?" the former Polo Grounds denizen barked in his piercing voice. "The Mets are my team now. I give them my voice. I will support them all the way." His was a voice the players would hear many times in the future, at work and in their nightmares.

Normally, a placid nonevent like the first workout of the spring would have been minor news back in New York, with the traditional hard-news baseball reporters concentrating on the three pitchers who had not yet signed contracts. But the men covering the first Met camp were by and large the best reporters on each sports section in the metropolitan area, and they realized that something special was happening.

They were not the traditional Yankee-type reporter, who could be stereotyped as somebody whose basic concern with baseball was the makeup of the squad and the winning of games. If such a reporter had covered the Mets, he would have suffered a nervous breakdown in two days.

The Met reporters were more visionary, more tolerant, some because they missed the Dodgers and Giants and would have been glad to cover a junior high school team, others because they were new to baseball and saw it from a fresh perspective.

The roster of reporters in the first Met camp were: Dick Young of the New York *Daily News*, Jack Lang of the Long Island *Press*, Barney Kremenko of the *Journal American*, Leonard Shecter of the *Post*, Bill Dougherty of the Newark *News*, Stan Isaacs of *Newsday*, Bob Lipsyte of the *Times*, Gus Steiger of the *Mirror*, Harold Rosenthal of the *Herald Tribune*, and Joe King of the *World Telegram and Sun*. Together they gave an honest and refreshing view of this strange new club.

Dick Young had become identified with the Brooklyn Dodgers in 1946 at the start of the golden decade. As the Dodgers alternately won and lost pennants, Young quarreled with managers, shouted with ball players, kept management honest, and entertained his 2,000,000 readers with fearless and blunt fact and opinion.

In 1951, as the Dodgers folded and the Giants roared to their miraculous victory, Young had written: "The tree that grows in Brooklyn is an apple tree." (In baseball, when a player tightens up under pressure, he "chokes up" or "feels that apple" in his throat.)

When the Dodgers went west, Young roared as if the wily
O'Malley had picked his pocket. And in a real sense, O'Malley
had robbed Young and other reporters of their youth and their
identification.

For four years, Young thrashed around without a ball club,
widening his scope as a reporter but missing the close identification with one team. When the Mets were formed, he was forty-
five years old and bursting with energy, a wiser and more
tolerant man. He did not expect the new team to be the Brooklyn Dodgers. It was enough that they were the Mets.

"You don't spank a child until it reaches the age of reason,"
said Young, who had eight children of his own. "Usually, a child
reaches the age of reason when it's seven."

If Young was the natural leader of the press corps, his friend
Jack Lang was the quartermaster—perhaps a Sancho Panza to
Young's Don Quixote. A chunky man in his early forties, Lang
did not have the writing flair of his friend, but he was a source
of delightful negative information. He kept a little black book
full of negative statistics, called "Neggies," and delighted in
springing them in a crowded press box while Met officials
smoldered.

Stan Isaacs of the fine young Long Island paper, *Newsday*,
was more concerned with man's behavior than with his batting
average. Writing in his humorous column "Out of Left Field,"
Isaacs became the first writer to appreciate fully the Mets as a
people's team, as a worthy combination of the old Dodger and
Giant complexes.

Bob Lipsyte was a young Columbia University graduate who
had been doing night rewrite at the *Times*, dreaming of writing
the great American novel until somebody had recognized his
ability and sent him to cover this amazing new team. Lipsyte was
not familiar with baseball. For all he knew, all ball clubs were
funny like the Mets: tired old players ate soup in the clubhouse;
eccentric geniuses like Casey Stengel told anecdotes until four in
the morning.

By describing the humorous flavor of the Mets, Lipsyte gave
the new club its proper recognition in the so-called paper of
record. If the Mets had been described in standard runs-hits-and-

errors form in the *Times*, it would have taken much longer for many fans to catch on. But this excellent young writer helped give the Mets their official *New York Times* stamp of approval. Thump. Next case.

Harold Rosenthal, witty and cynical, was in somewhat of a predicament since Mrs. Payson's brother, Jock Whitney, owned the *Tribune*. But Harold did his best to explain the Mets without incurring the wrath of the Whitneys.

Leonard Shecter was a former copyreader who had been born again after breaking away from the desk in his thirties. Shecter was a fearless questioner who could be caustic toward the Big Brokers from the Bronx, but he had recurring dreams about Casey as a father figure, and he was kind to the Mets.

The *Journal American* sent down Barney Kremenko, a tall red-headed dynamo straight out of *Guys and Dolls*. Barney had spent his early manhood dealing gin rummy for Leo Durocher and other Giants. He was a hard-news man, always looking for the financial angle, for the big scoop, and everybody enjoyed matching wits with "Big Barn."

This assortment of journalistic talent was vastly superior to the talent of the Mets in that first spring. Fortunately, these men brought great compassion and enthusiasm with them. Also fortunately, they had Casey Stengel.

Most of these reporters had known Casey in his years with the Yankees, knew him to be a brilliant baseball man, knew him to be shrewd, aggressive, and a winner. They also knew he had the power to cloud men's minds.

"We knew what he was doing," Dick Young has said. "He was using diversionary tactics. We did not mind because we knew what the situation was."

Together the reporters gave the Mets a public exposure the club could not have purchased for a million dollars. And back north, the fans read Lipsyte at the breakfast table or Shecter on the subway, chuckled at Casey's latest wisecrack or the latest misadventure in Wonderland. The people were conditioned to expect a bad, funny ball club, whose merit was in merely existing —never mind winning.

The power of the press also produced the First Met Legend

in the first week of camp. Isaacs and Lipsyte happened to over-hear a young man in the Colonial Inn tell the clerk he was join-ing the Mets for a tryout. The clerk was so impressed that he gave John Pappas a special team rate of ten dollars a day instead of the twenty-two dollar winter rate.

The next day the young man badgered Johnny Murphy, the director of scouting, for a tryout. He said he was a pitcher. He hadn't qualified for his high school team a few years back, but now he was in shape to pitch.

"I've been throwing up north for four days," the young man said.

"It's been snowing up north," said the very dubious Murphy.

"Not under the Triborough Bridge," the young man replied.

Murphy stared at the young man. He was of medium height and slender, and in his shiny continental suit he did not look like a baseball player.

"If we did it for you, a million guys would show up here," said Murphy as politely as possible.

"I don't see a million guys out there," the young man said, also politely.

Murphy wondered if the young man was being insolent. The executive would have liked an excuse to banish him, but there was something intense and sincere about him. Finally Murphy agreed to watch the young man pitch—providing the young man came up with his own field and his own catcher.

Everything might have been forgotten except that Isaacs and Lipsyte both wrote about this young man from Astoria, Queens. The reporters suggested that the Mets would be heartless if they let this earnest young man leave camp without a tryout. Besides, who knows? Maybe he could really pitch.

John Pappas was not about to quit now. He had not traveled for sixty-six dollars on the night jet, taking a vacation from City College, to be rebuffed. So he found a catcher and he found a field and he told Murphy he would be available on the afternoon of the twenty-third.

Murphy was a gentleman, a former Fordham University star who had become the Yankees' great relief pitcher, "Fireman Johnny." A gracious man who enjoyed French cooking and good Beaujolais wine, he could never be unpleasant to anybody.

"They're making more of a fuss over this than they are about John Glenn," Murphy said, referring to the astronaut who had orbited the earth three times the day before.

That afternoon, John Murphy stood behind the pitching mound in a public park and watched John Pappas throw for eighteen minutes. At the first pitch, Isaacs and Lipsyte sighed. It was obvious that John Pappas was not exactly the next Bob Feller. He was not even the next Roger Craig.

"In my humble opinion, there is nothing there," Murphy said. "He is as poor as anybody I've ever seen—and I've seen thousands." Then he gently advised John Pappas to go back to college and find himself another dream.

"At least I tried," John Pappas said. "I'm only sorry they didn't give me a chance to hit. I'm not a bad hitter and I play the outfield, too."

The reporters wrote another story about the failure of the first Met pheenom. The sensitive front office of George M. Weiss was afraid this publicity would make the Mets look like amateurs, but the reaction could not have been better. Every shivering fan back in New York now realized that the Mets were the people's team.

While John Pappas was on his way back to Astoria, the infielders and outfielders began checking in. In any corner of the Met clubhouse, there was somebody's old hero—Charlie Neal, Gil Hodges, Richie Ashburn—talking about finding the sweet stroke of his youth. What if most of them should find one more good year in their system? Why couldn't the Mets go all the way? Bear in mind, this is standard talk for any clubhouse on the first day of March. Perhaps it's the hot Florida sun.

After a day of this brave talk, the Mets eagerly awaited their first intrasquad game on March 2. The lineups were announced by Dr. Stengel (he called everybody else "Doctor"), and the first Met batter of all time was scheduled to be Sammy Drake, the little infielder from the Cubs. But when the appointed time arrived on March 2, Sammy Drake was nowhere in sight.

Joe Ginsberg, the gentle lumbering catcher, was ordered to hit for the AWOL infielder. But after Ginsberg took a few pitches, Sammy Drake was spotted emerging from the Met clubhouse, buttoning his pants and hitching his belt. While he should have

been in the batter's box, he had been in the men's room. The visit
had obviously been worth it, however, since Drake lashed a triple
on his very first pitch. The real star of the scrimmage was Neil
Chrisley, an itinerant outfielder with a career average of .209. He
had three hits, drove in three runs, made a nice catch in the field
—and was dropped a few weeks later after reality caught up with
him.

On March 10 the Mets made their first appearance in the public
arena, taking on the Cardinals at Al Lang Field. Jay Hook, Clem
Labine, and Craig Anderson allowed twelve hits as the Mets were
defeated, 8–0. Afterward a fan was heard to shout "same old
Mets," perhaps the first public wisecrack and the forerunner of a
million others.

The Mets broke their one-game losing streak with a 4–3 victory over the Cardinals as Ashburn doubled and Chacon singled
in a ninth-inning rally.

Then the Mets actually won two more games. A youngster
named Evans Killeen pitched four hitless innings in relief. Killeen was a Long Island boy who had been a Kansas City bonus
boy at one time. On the morning after his promising debut, he
reached into his shaving kit and cut a finger on his right hand.
By the time the wound healed, he was pitching for the farm club
and he would never rejoin the Mets. He was the first in a long
strand of one-day marvels who would further frustrate the Mets
fans.

Then there was Dawes Hamilt, a young minor-league infielder
who was discovered by the sizable New York press to be of Jewish descent. Dan Parker of the *Mirror* watched Hamilt hit two
triples in the first intrasquad games and predicted that this nice
Jewish boy would be very popular at the Polo Grounds. But
Hamilt, of course, never even came close.

On March 18, Mrs. Payson motored over from Hobe Sound,
near Palm Beach, to watch the Mets play at St. Petersburg. Craig
set an early pattern of bad luck when he lost a four-hitter to the
Phillies, 3–2. It was the fourth straight Met loss.

"I will save the scorecard, like I saved the scorecard of the
game when Bobby Thomson hit that home run against Ralph

Branca in the Polo Grounds," she said. "I'm sorry the Mets lost —but they didn't play badly."

On March 22 the Mets took on the Yankees for the first time. The Yankees took the exhibition casually, chatting with Stengel and the old Dodgers and Giants. To the Yankees, spring training was merely conditioning for the pennant race, but the Mets had something to prove. In a World Series atmosphere, with even the 6277 old-timers getting excited, the Mets held the Yankees to a 3–3 tie going into the bottom of the ninth.

Then Joe Christopher hit a triple past Hector Lopez in left field, and Ashburn whacked a pinch single to win the game.

"The Mets were amazing," Casey chortled as he danced a little jig on his way from the field. "If ever it was good to be good, this was the time. If you beat the Yankees, you should beat many clubs. . . . There is some ability in these players if we can get it out of them. . . ."

Asked if he expected to get a congratulatory telegram from Dan Topping, Casey snapped: "Yes, he's gonna take me back in about eight years."

And an old-timer behind the backstop shouted: "You're the best, Casey, you're the best."

"When we meet in the World Series this fall, then it will matter," Casey advised his fellow senior citizen.

There were sadder days ahead, however. On March 26 the Mets played the Orioles down in Miami. Jay Hook, the handsome young pitcher with the engineering degree from Northwestern, was allowed to take one of the most prolonged beatings any pitcher has ever received in Florida or anywhere. Casey kept him on the mound for six innings. In the first five innings Hook allowed eight runs and eight hits. But then in the sixth inning he lost his speed, and the Orioles tagged him for nine more hits and eight more runs.

When he was finally removed from the game, Hook sobbed in the dugout, then marched into the clubhouse and began dismantling the room, chair by chair, locker by locker.

Later, the young pitcher sat red-eyed and subdued and told reporters: "How can I feel? No, I'm not mad."

Casey explained the merciless bombing this way: "I'm trying

to make him a nine-inning pitcher. He wasn't mad at me, he was mad at himself."

The Yankees had known that Casey was capable of treating a player harshly, and the Mets were not completely surprised. The reporters happened to know that Casey and Edna, who were themselves childless, were capable of great affection for certain players. On the Yankees, Tony Kubek had been a particular favorite for his youthful, earnest appearance. Casey and Edna would often speak fondly of Jay Hook and his pretty wife and their darling little children. Thus, Casey's treatment of Hook could be seen as a legitimate attempt to give the pitcher some work—even if it didn't seem that high-minded at the time.

As sad as Hook appeared that afternoon in Miami, there were others who would soon be sadder. The Mets began lopping men off the squad, epic names like Ted Lepcio, Neil Chrisley, Howie Nunn, Butterball Botz. But perhaps the saddest of all was a young pitcher named Aubrey Gatewood, who felt he had pitched pretty well.

"I'd like to keep you," the Old Man explained. "But I got some experienced pitchers here and we may be fighting for the pennant so I got to go with experience."

The pennant? Gatewood looked at Casey and decided the Old Man was serious. Well, then, there was no disgrace in being cut from a pennant contender.

The Mets did indeed win twelve and lose fourteen of their spring exhibitions, and Weiss did say, "We demonstrated we belong somewhere in the league," whatever that meant.

Mrs. Payson looked at that mediocre record and she asked Dick Young: "Couldn't we beat out the Cubs and the Phillies?"

"Absolutely not," Young replied.

"Well, can't we please expect to finish ahead of the other new team, Houston?"

"No, I told you to expect nothing," Young said.

"All right then, I'll settle for tenth place," Mrs. Payson said. In the months to come she would appreciate the honesty of Dick Young, a modern-day Tiresias who had foreseen all and predicted a dismal last place.

7

HISTORY'S NEGGIES

◆

THE METS MADE THEIR FIRST APPEARANCE in New York on the evening of April 8, 1962, in a setting that was suitably ramshackle and temporary.

They landed at LaGuardia Airport, whose terminal building was under construction, and their introduction to the big city was picking their way through boards and wheelbarrows and piles of debris.

This feeling of newness and rawness lasted through the next day when they visited the old Polo Grounds, where they would be playing until their new stadium in Queens was ready. The old stadium had been renovated at a cost of $400,000. There were new lights, a new bat rack, a new water cooler, and even a paint job. The Mets had gone so far as to purchase an American flag with fifty stars on it to replace the forty-eight-star job that the New York Titans, a football team of no small imcompetence, had used in the fall of 1960.

For some of the older players, it was exciting to be back in the old ball park under the mica schist of Coogan's Bluff. But for the younger players, there was a feeling of impermanence, of not knowing where they were, or where they might be the next week.

The Mets took a workout on April 9, taking dead aim on the

Howard Clothes signs in the left- and right-field corners. The batter who hit those signs most often during the season would win a $7000 power boat, the signs advertised. Little did the players know that the ultimate winner was, at this moment, a reserve first baseman with the Baltimore Orioles. Marv Throneberry was still in the unknown future.

After the workout they flew west to open the season in St. Louis. In the air, they learned that their brawny left fielder, Frank Thomas, was quite a bit more valuable than they had imagined. Thomas liked to serve the meals to his teammates during a flight, and his big hands never fumbled a tray. Players ate sooner when "Big Donkey" put on a borrowed stewardess apron. Soon they were calling him "Mary"—behind his back, of course.

The Mets should have gotten the clue on their first visit to the Chase Hotel in St. Louis. They rushed in from the rain, picked up the keys to their rooms, and crowded into an elevator, sixteen of them at once. Naturally the elevator stalled between floors, trapping the players for half an hour. They were freed just in time to be rained out of their first game.

They did play the next night, however, making April 11 an historic date in Met history. On that night, Roger Craig balked home the first run of official Met history. The Cardinals also made sixteen hits and stole three bases while the Mets made three errors and grounded into two double plays. Hodges hit a homer but the Mets lost, 11–4. They were on their way.

Back in New York on April 12, they were accorded a ticker-tape parade, drawing an estimated 40,000 fans on the one-mile route from Bowling Green to City Hall. The players traveled the same route that Lindberghs and Eisenhowers had once taken. They flung autographed plastic baseballs at the new faithful and speculated about parades to come—if they should become winners.

Then it was Friday, April 13, and what better day for the Mets to play their first home game? It was a damp, chilly, typical New York April day, but it seemed like the finest summer holiday to the fans who headed for the old ball park.

People walked up from the subway, craning their necks to get the first glimpse of the old landmark. Men parked their cars across the river near Yankee Stadium and chatted with each other, strangers, as they walked back across the bridges. There was a feeling of community among these fans, the kind of closeness that New Yorkers usually permit themselves only in a severe snowstorm or a blackout.

There was an air of surprise, of unexpected good fortune, as if something precious from the past had been born again. It was as if all these men in their heavy early-spring jackets had suddenly grown five years younger. Or it was as if a married man, now living in the suburbs, had visited his favorite old tavern in the old neighborhood and found all his buddies still drinking there.

Old Giants fans became emotional as they approached the old ball park, rattling on about Matty and Ottie and Willie. Dodger fans remembered Stanky and Durocher leaping like schoolboys as Thomson rounded third base. Old Dodger fans changed the subject to: "Hey, whose limousine is that? Mrs. What's-Her-Name?"

Inside there were 12,447 fans on this raw April day. (The Mets had already sold 2000 season tickets. In the last fumbling year of Horace Stoneham's Giants, there had been 900 season tickets sold.) The fans endured the speeches from the politicians, preferring to watch each other or wander around the old joint. And up in the left-field stands, the first banner in Met history appeared on a bedsheet: LEONIA, N.J., LOVES HOT ROD KANEHL.

The Mets found it a source of wonder that the itinerant minor-leaguer, Rod Kanehl, had been lionized by New York.

"Hey, Hot Rod, how come you've got fans in this town when you've never been here in your life?" they asked him.

"My fame preceded me," the brash Kanehl said.

The Mets were cheered when they were introduced, and the biggest cheers were for Stengel and Hodges. Stengel was not so popular a few minutes later. The fans wanted Hodges to start at first base, but Gil had a pulled leg muscle and Stengel did not want to use him against a right-handed pitcher on the muddy field. At the last moment, Jim Marshall trotted out to first base and the fans jeered.

There was more noise in the second inning when ancient Gus Bell staggered under a fly ball in right field, turning it into a double. The next batter hit another fly ball between Bell and Ashburn. The two gray-heads wobbled under this one, and it fell for a triple. The fans booed the old players, and the tainted runs helped the Pirates beat the Mets, 4-3, as Tom Sturdivant bested Sherman "Roadblock" Jones.

Mrs. Payson wasn't particularly disappointed when the Mets lost their opener, but she did hope to see the Mets win before she left on a vacation to the Greek islands. However, the Mets lost twice more to Pittsburgh, once to Houston, and twice more to St. Louis, and Mrs. Payson began her vacation, asking the Met office to wire her after every game.

The club then went on the road and lost two more in Pittsburgh, giving them no victories and nine losses and tying a league record for most consecutive losses at the start of a season. The Pirates had won ten straight themselves.

But on the night of April 23, the law of averages produced a stunning 9-1 victory for the Mets. The winning pitcher was none other than Jay Hook, the friendly and intelligent young man who had been allowed to take such a beating down in Miami. True to Casey's hopes, Hook went all nine innings this night and Stengel shouted: "I may pitch Hook every day. I don't see how we ever lost a game."

And Joe Ginsberg shouted: "Break up the Mets."

Overconfidence may have hurt them, however, for they soon lost their next three games. And over in Greece, Mrs. Payson amended her order just slightly. From now on, she merely wanted a cable when the Mets won. The international cable service promptly went into a mild recession.

The Mets were in their own recession, falling to a 3-16 record as Weiss and Stengel battled over player changes. Weiss wanted to farm out Stengel's "Little Scavenger," Rod Kanehl, the darling of Leonia, N.J.

Stengel wanted to send out John DeMerit, a tall and quiet outfielder who had once received a huge bonus from the Milwaukee Braves. Stengel was mad because he felt his old friend wanted to keep DeMerit over Kanehl because DeMerit had cost more money. Weiss hated bookkeeping losses just as much as losses on the field.

"He says I've got to get rid of the guy who busts his ass for me, but the other guy you don't know if he's awake," Stengel would snarl after a noisy meeting with Weiss. Casey would not mention the two players by name, but reporters who were hip to Stengelese could fit the pieces together while newcomers sat and blinked. It was something like reading *Finnegan's Wake* without the *Key*.

Stengel won this battle. Kanehl stayed and DeMerit was dropped. Soon other player changes were made. Herb Moford, Clem Labine, Ginsberg, Bobby Gene Smith, all went the way of the dodo. New hopes were imported, like Harry Chiti, Dave Hillman, and Sammy Taylor.

There was another battle shaping up in the press box at this time. The older reporters were sure they had never seen so many wild pitches, passed balls, strikeouts, and errors in their lives. But when the reporters glanced at the daily statistic sheets, they found no mention of such "negative statistics." The Met management did not care to record its own ineptitude.

Dick Young, the harsh-voiced leader of the press corps, registered his protest to Tom Meany, the old newspaperman who had been hired as publicity man. But Meany had his orders from above. The man to see was Julie Adler, who served as liaison man from Grant and Weiss to the world outside.

"Julie, you've got to get them to include negatives on the stat sheet," Young remembers screaming. But the answer was that the Mets would become historians when there was something positive in their history.

"But this is history," Young argued. "We're starting from scratch. How are you ever going to appreciate the past when we finally improve? In ten years when we win the pennant, wouldn't it be nice to look back to 1962 and see all the errors we used to make?"

The Met front office said no. It would not be nice to look back at all the errors they used to make. So Jack Lang, the man from the Long Island *Press*, bought himself a little black book and began recording negative statistics. But first he asked to borrow the club's official box scores for the first few games.

"Don't show them to him," Adler ordered an assistant. "He'll only write a negative story."

Lang soon became a source for many fine stories, since he was not selfish with his facts. He delighted in notifying the press box: "This is the eleventh straight game in which the Mets have made an error," or, "That strikeout by Ed Bouchee gives Met pinch hitters an average of .056."

One of the early negative stories was poor Don Zimmer, the eager ex-Dodger, who went hitless in his first thirty-four at-bats. When he finally got a base hit, he bent down and patted the base. A few days later, now that he had reestablished his market value, he was traded to Cincinnati for Cliff Cook, a third base-man, and Robert Gerald Miller, a left-handed pitcher who refused to go to the minor leagues and temporarily retired to the auto-mobile business.

For a couple of weeks, there was some positive news. The Mets won a doubleheader from the Milwaukee Braves on a couple of fluke "Chinese home runs" that could happen only in the Polo Grounds. Then the Mets went out to Milwaukee and won three more, raising their record to 12–19.

After that last victory in Milwaukee, the Mets took an all-night airplane to Houston, including a stop in Dallas. Casey, feeling like a winning manager at last, chattered at his coaches all night. Then the club arrived in the muggy, oily dawn of Houston, the players gasping for breath in the strangulating climate, shading the sun from their eyes. Stengel, as chipper as ever, bought break-fast for reporters, found a morning newspaper, and slowly headed for the elevators.

"If any of the Houston reporters want to see me," he snapped, "tell them I'm being embalmed."

When Casey and his players emerged from their deep sleep in Houston, it was the Mets who should have been embalmed. They lost two straight to their fellow expansion club, establishing a long-term jinx against Houston. Then they gratefully left the mosquitoes and the humidity and flew to the West Coast for their first encounter with the Dodgers and Giants.

The Met players had no feeling of a crusade against the O'Mal-leys and the Stonehams, even if the reporters did. After all, if the Giants and Dodgers hadn't left New York, most of the Mets would still be in the minor leagues.

The Mets lost three straight to the Dodgers, then lost a day game in San Francisco, stretching their losing streak to six. On May 27, they were scheduled to play a noon doubleheader at Candlestick Park, a frightening prospect to everybody who enjoyed staying out late in the City by the Bay.

"Noon?" gasped one of the Met party. "I won't be done throwing up by then." It was a line that would live on in Met legend, with only the name shielded.

At high noon the Mets were indeed out on the field trying to break their losing streak. The hardworking Roger Craig tried everything. He tried throwing close to Orlando Cepeda, the dangerous first baseman. Then he tried picking Willie Mays off second base.

Somehow, Elio Chacon had managed to spot the signal for the pick-off and he even held on to Craig's fine throw. But Mays barreled back into the base, knocking Chacon backward as the umpire signaled Mays safe.

Chacon was mad because he thought Mays was out. He was also mad because Mays had slid into him. So Chacon, a welterweight, began pummeling Mays, a heavyweight. It was a dangerous thing to do. Mays picked up Chacon like a sack of flour and seemed prepared to throw him over the right-field fence in the direction of Lower San Francisco Bay.

Meanwhile, Cepeda began berating Craig for throwing too close to him and the two men began swinging near the pitching mound.

The fights were quickly broken up before any damage could be done, but both Mays and Cepeda were judged the winners on points.

The next morning on Long Island, readers of *Newsday* found a story by Jack Mann that began: "San Francisco—The Mets can't fight either."

The "either" told it all. The Mets lost seventeen straight, dropping their record to 12–36 and cutting down on the talk of a pennant. No matter what Casey had told Aubrey Gatewood back in spring training, it was quite apparent that if the Mets were going to succeed in New York City, it would have to be as something other than a champion.

8

PASSION IN THE BLEACHERS

◆

FORTUNATELY FOR THE METS, the fans had taken their cue from the enlightened press and were less concerned with winning than with having a National League team of their own. The winning could always come later.

For four years these fans had crawled into an emotional cellar, brooding over the loss of their loved ones. Some of them, guiltily, had patronized Yankee Stadium like a drinker who will take 3.2 beer if Chivas Regal is not available. But few National League fans felt any thrill at watching the rest of the American League fall tamely at the Yankees' feet every summer. Also, the sombre atmosphere in Yankee Stadium—which Weiss had helped maintain—was hardly conducive to enjoying baseball.

But now the National League was back in town and the Mets were the beloved home team right from the start. They did not have to prove themselves as athletes or gentlemen. The very fact of their existence brought them love.

Beyond loving the Mets, the fans could once again see the Dodgers and Giants nine times a year, could watch Stan Musial come to terrorize his favorite road city, could see Ernie Banks, Frank Robinson, and Roberto Clemente for the first time since

1957. The fans were also assured of seeing brushback pitches, a trademark of the jugular National League, as well as nasty slides and harsh arguments between managers and umpires. The National League had been gone too long.

The fans did not fill up the Polo Grounds for every game, but there was an instant hard core that brought excitement to the stadium. There were usually 5000 fans for midweek games and there were often 20,000 for weekend games, enough to develop the mystique of mass support. If the crowds had been poor at the beginning—let's say under 2000 too often—then there would have been trouble.

But there were enough. Mostly they came from New York City, taking the subways from Brooklyn and midtown and the Bronx, taking buses, walking in from Harlem. Suburban fans came more slowly, discouraged by the limited parking at the stadium that was built on the side of a hill, next to a river.

The white middle-class fans from the suburbs also hesitated to visit the Polo Grounds because it was in Harlem. They were afraid of whatever it was that had driven them out of the city in the first place. But gradually word got around that the Polo Grounds was next door to a middle-class housing project whose residents did not, in fact, slash tires or perform muggings after night games. Whites also noticed Sugar Hill, the area above Coogan's Bluff, where well-to-do black professionals had their own doormen and sports cars. In time, whites got over their hang-ups about driving to this part of Harlem and the attendance started to rise.

The stadium itself did not encourage new fans, particularly women. It was an old plant, despite the $400,000 the Mets had spent on modernization, and the pigeons had made the stadium their private Guernica for years. The seats were built for the smaller beams of another generation and the narrow aisles often led nowhere. It was almost impossible to get from some sections to other sections; it was easier to go outside and start again.

But the Polo Grounds did breed intimacy among the fans and between players and fans. Many customers could lean out of the overhanging upper deck and noisily advise the players of their strengths and weaknesses. In the distance of center field, bleacher fans could concentrate on the comings and goings from the clubhouses. The pitcher who was drilled from the game had to climb fourteen wooden steps to his clubhouse while fans told him how he should have thrown a fastball instead of a curve.

The Polo Grounds was a fan's paradise but the players had mixed feelings. When they won, they were glad the fans were so close. When they lost, they would have appreciated a barrier between themselves and the fans.

There was a new way of communicating in 1962, however, and this method did not require a sense of hearing. This was the banner craze, started by some anonymous Rod Kanehl fans from New Jersey, continued by expressive rooters from everywhere.

Many of the early banners said LET'S GO METS and some of them extolled the virtues of THE NEW BREED, which encompassed both the players and the fans. Other banners were shorter (PRAY!) or longer (WE DON'T WANT TO SET THE WORLD ON FIRE—WE JUST WANT TO FINISH NINTH).

Many of the first banners were followed by men in blue uniforms trying to wrest the banners away. George Weiss felt that banners were unbecoming in such a holy place as a ball park, and the guards were instructed to confiscate the banners on the grounds that they obstructed people's vision.

Up in the press box, an old tin submarine poised above and behind home plate, and Dick Young peered through his ever-present binoculars that were usually used by the rest of the reporters to spot pretty girls.

"Hey, look, the cops are trying to take that banner away from those kids," Young screamed, putting the noon whistles to shame with his velocity.

The press made such a fuss about the attempted confiscation that the fans reacted with more and more banners in the days that followed. Weiss was put directly against the wall. Either he would have to relax his stand against banners or be remembered for trying to run a concentration camp on Eighth Avenue. Reluctantly, Weiss gave in. The guards were told to lay off the banners, the fans became more inventive, and the era of the banner was upon us.

Within a year, the Mets would be holding a Banner Day with the blessing of M. Donald Grant and Weiss. Big Julie Adler would be the grand marshal of the banner parade. The Met players would unfurl a banner that said WE LOVE YOU FANS. But the image would always persist of George Weiss on Banner Day, muttering: "These people . . . these noisy people with their bedsheets . . . Where do they come from? . . . Why don't they keep quiet?"

The fans were incredibly hip in all ways. One afternoon I was wandering through the sunny left-field grandstand when Frank Thomas muffed a fly ball just below us. But suddenly the scoreboard noted that the batter had been credited with a hit by the presumably anonymous official scorer.

Just next to me, a mustached young man in a City College sweat shirt grumbled: "That goddamn Shecter." This young man, undoubtedly cutting Psych II to take in a ball game, not only cared about the niceties of official scoring but also knew that Leonard Shecter of the *Post* was the official scorer that day.

The joy was contagious in those early days. People who would sneer at each other in the subways or in a bar began talking to each other in the Polo Grounds. They had something wonderful in common—they loved the Mets. They were the "New Breed," whether they were whites buying the standard rubber hot dog or youngsters carrying sandwiches or Negroes wisely bringing their own fried chicken. I have been in every ball park in the major leagues but have never seen as many chicken bones as there were in those first seasons in the Polo Grounds.

The emotional first year in the Polo Grounds uplifted the spirits of many citizens. For one married couple it did even better. It got them excited enough to attempt an act of physical love in the ball park, which they would normally have enjoyed in the privacy of their home or perhaps in their car. Certain prudish fans at this Sunday doubleheader became suspicious of what was happening under the beach blanket and they called the stadium police. The amorous couple was evicted from the stadium despite the protest of the woman that "we're married—and we're Met fans." The couple was told that passion was indeed rampant in the Polo Grounds—but only to a point.

Yet others found more acceptable ways of expressing their love of the Mets. Looie Kleppel and Mother of the Mets were the best of all the merry anarchists who discovered the Mets. They were the twin sirens of the Harlem River, the Scylla and Charybdis of 155th Street. To navigate them safely required all the nerve a wayfaring player could muster.

Looie and Mother of the Mets were not friends. They traded charges about the misappropriation of funds after a collection for a watch for Willie Mays back in the 1950s. Whatever the reason, when the Mets were formed Looie took one side of the bleachers and Mother of the Mets took the other. Together they formed stereophonic sound but they were strictly soloists and never a duet.

Looie was a bulky man in his early sixties, wearing rumpled dark clothing and always a hat. He had been a piano mover until a back condition put him out of work. With nothing else to do, he had taken residence in the bleachers of the Polo Grounds, his owl eyes glowing in the darkness under his hat, his walking stick resting against a seat, his knapsack loaded with memorabilia, including a book called *Bleacherites Never Forget* that had never quite made print.

He had been a Giant fan since 1910, enjoying the McGraw era, suffering through the postwar Dodger period. "For thirteen years I took verbal shafts, hip and thigh, from Brooklyn fans," Looie would announce in his singsong radio broadcast style. But in 1951, the Giants began a miracle and Looie went West to help. On September 14, he shook Bobby Thomson's hand in Chicago and told him that would bring him luck. A few weeks later, Thomson hit the homer which Looie took some credit for.

In 1957 the Giants broke Looie's heart by leaving town and he did everything but cast a spell on them. In 1959, while the Giants blew the pennant in Chicago, Looie went to Wrigley Field to taunt them. This was a surprise to out-of-town players, who had always assumed that Looie had been paid by the Giants.

In his book, *The Long Season*, pitcher Jim Brosnan of the Cincinnati Reds wrote: "A huge almost gross Negro wearing a dirt-stained panama hat sat at the gate on a portable camp stool. . . . Some players suspected Stoneham hired him to agitate the opposition bullpen."

Looie resented this claim on two grounds. He was not prejudiced but he liked to point out that he was Caucasian. His skin became darker because of his winters in Florida, he said. Other players called him "Dirty Looie," but not to his face. They knew better than to unleash the fury of the winds. Looie also resented being called a paid agitator.

"I don't agitate. I don't ride. I simply give the players the benefit of my knowledge of the game. My professional services as a fan are not for hire. I'm a free-lance rooter, tied down to no one team."

Now he was tied down to the Mets. He picked them up in spring training in 1962, living in a boardinghouse in downtown St. Petersburg. He advised them all spring, then rode the Seaboard Railroad home to New York, his lungs in fine shape to open the season.

"The Mets are going to be the No. 1 team in New York, as the Giants were," Looie announced in the spring. "The Mets are going to continue in the McGraw tradition because Stengel is like McGraw. Stengel was a fighting ball player and has the happy facility of imparting his desire to the men who play under him."

But if the Mets were going to be winners, they would have to listen to the True Believer. Looie had the answer for Ray Daviault's hanging curve ball. Looie knew how Felix Mantilla could handle a ground ball. If only they would listen to him.

The players had plenty of opportunity. As they walked down the clubhouse steps, they hunched their shoulders, anticipating that voice.

"Hickman," Looie would shout. "Hickman, listen to me. You've got to swing at the first pitch, Hickman. A big boy like you, you could be a star. I taught Whitey Lockman. Ask Monte Irvin what I did for him. Hickman, are you listening to me?"

And Jim Hickman, still unsure of himself in his first nervous months in the big city, would glance sideways, mutter a nervous "Hello, Looie" as he passed. This was like paying dues because Looie threatened to "roast you like a potato" if you ignored him. Nobody wanted to have his inadequacies echoed off Sugar Hill and back across the Harlem River.

"Hickman . . ."

Mother of the Mets had a different style, preaching to her own congregation. She was a big-boned Negro woman who had spent her years working for a wealthy family, and she now seemed comfortable in retirement. She called herself "Mother of the Mets" but her real name, she said, was Sadie James.

Sadie was not the technical and historical wizard that Looie was. Her interests were feminine and subjective. As a true Mother of the Mets, she was all soul.

"Brown," she would begin. (The name has been changed to protect the not-so-innocent.) "Brown, I saw you in that place on 135th Street last night. You'd better stay out of there, Brown, that's a rough bunch in there. They carry knives and there's all kinds of winos and addicts in there. Also, Brown, you'd better stick to beer when you've got a game the next day."

This motherly advice would be broadcast to the players—visiting and home—as they clumped down the wooden steps.

Looie and Sadie both had the kind of noisy charisma that attracted knots of gaping youngsters. Little boys from the North Bronx or Rego Park or Leonia, N.J., followed these sages of the bleachers, absorbing the wisdom of the ages.

Sadie tended to mother her young followers, drawing them together. She also brought congratulation cards for players or reporters whose wives had given birth. She thought of the Mets as her family, and she frequently lamented: "What am I going to do when my boys move to that new stadium?"

The "boys" themselves marveled at the reception they were receiving in New York. Some of them had been jeered in other cities for being merely mediocre, but now they were being applauded in supposedly the most critical city in the country for being collectively and colossally abysmal.

The Met phenomenon attracted a number or psychologists, armchair and legitimate. One New York headshrinker had this to say about the Mets and their army of fanatics:

"All phallic games—games in which a ball is thrown and caught —are sublimated desires of sexual wishes. They represent the infantile wish to overcome the father and win the mother. The Met fan . . . is the kind of person who is wrecked by success because of his unconscious fears of displacing the father."

The players weren't sure about this theory, but some of them knew they didn't like being applauded for losing. To Richie Ashburn, a Goldwater Republican from Nebraska, the Met mystique sounded like creeping socialism.

"I don't think it's a moral victory to get the tying run to second base against the Dodgers," he snorted. "What good is that. Winning is the only thing. They shouldn't settle for losing good."

But then the right-wing right fielder added some praise for the fans: "These people are behind us. We can't dog it. Lord knows, we've tested their faith. They could make it real miserable for us."

Jay Hook, the engineer, dabbled in sociology one night while staring up at the hot-eyed fans in the grandstand. "These people are the real fans," Hook theorized. "They can't afford a big night out but they'll pay to get into the park and have their fun cheering. They enjoy themselves. They aren't tourists, like you see in some ball parks.

"I've never seen fans like this," Hook continued. "When I get knocked out early, I sit in the stands and listen to them. We can be down, 9–0, but they'll be cheering for a rally. They know the game, too. We've really got the best of the old Bums and Giants, don't we?"

There was still plenty of vestigial affection for the Dodgers and Giants, as indicated when the California teams finally came to New York at the end of May.

The Dodgers came first, wearing unfamiliar gray road uniforms with "Los Angeles" written across the front. Hefty, graying Duke Snider was cheered wildly just for carrying the lineup card to home plate before the game. Leo Durocher, now a Dodger coach, snarled at all the New York press once again. Maury Wills hit homers left-handed and right-handed. And the Dodgers won three straight.

Then the Giants came in, bringing manager Alvin Dark and coaches Larry Jansen, Whitey Lockman, and Wes Westrum and a center fielder named Mays, who for some obscure reason was presented with a ten-foot salami. The Giants won all four games, dropping the Mets twenty-three games out of first place, but the Polo Grounds had been almost filled for each of the six dates with the Dodgers and Giants. The surge of emotion seemed to guarantee that the Mets could exist in New York and the surge of fans seemed to guarantee they might even make a profit. There was at least enough money to pay for the following advertisement on June 6, 1962:

How Cold Is New York?

Never in sports history has there been such a heart-warming demonstration of loyalty and affection as we have received from the Met fans, the New Breed. They are the new Miracle of Coogan's Bluff.

Once and for all the myth has been shattered that New York is a cynical sports city, settling only for a winner. Our Met fans have proved that New York is the warmest, the most sympathetic, the most tolerant city in the nation and we are grateful.

The Met fans have shown that they appreciate the battling of Casey Stengel and his team against tremendous odds. The Met fans have shown an understanding of unstinting efforts, regardless of expense, to bring National League baseball back to New York under the best conditions possible.

We thank all of those who came to the Polo Grounds to see us play. We thank the press and the other media of communication, but above all, we thank the Met fans. Our fans, you see, have shown that they love us and we love them.

THE BOARD OF DIRECTORS

Mrs. Charles S. Payson	*G. Herbert Walker, Jr.*
Frederick H. Trask	*James M. Carlisle*
George M. Weiss	*M. Donald Grant*
PRESIDENT	CHAIRMAN

9

MARVIN EUGENE
THRONEBERRY

◆

IN THOSE FIRST MAD WEEKS, it became apparent that the Mets were becoming mass folk heroes in the New York area. All the component parts were there—the passion for the return of the National League, the awfulness of the team, the diverting tactics of Casey Stengel, the involvement of the press, and finally the realization by the fans that something very special was happening here. With this giddy feeling prevailing in the Polo Grounds, it was now time for the first individual folk hero—even if he was not willing to accept such a reverse distinction.

His name was Marvelous Marv. He came with the nickname. It didn't take much imagination to tag a "Marvelous" in front of the name Marvin. Perhaps he had picked it up as a high school football star in Tennessee, perhaps when he hit forty-two and forty homers in Denver in 1956–57, perhaps when he came up with the New York Yankees. For, despite his initials, Marvin Eugene Throneberry was—in his heart of hearts—a Yankee.

When he had come up to the Yankees, Throneberry was a well-regarded first baseman-outfielder, the latest in the string of Skowrons and Sieberns and Kubeks. In pregame practice he used to stand alongside Mickey Mantle in center field and the two of them would spit tobacco juice on the grass and laugh together.

When he played, Throneberry seemed to imitate certain mannerisms of Mantle—except that the ball did not soar into the bleachers as often, and occasionally he would fumble the ball in the field. Yankee fans did not find this funny at all, and neither did the kindly old manager named Stengel. Marv played 141 assorted games for the Yankees from 1955 to 1959, and he even batted once in the World Series of 1958. In 1960, he was dispatched on the underground railroad to Kansas City, the elephant boneyard of the Yankee farm system. Later he washed up in Baltimore.

But the Mets had big plans for Throneberry when they purchased him in early May. With Hodges playing on weak, thirty-eight-year-old legs, and Ed Bouchee and Jim Marshall ticketed for the great unknown, there was room for a solid, dependable left-handed first baseman. After all, Throneberry was only twenty-eight years old and had never been given a chance to play regularly, and he had been an unusual slugger in the light air of Denver. Unfortunately, the National League was closer to sea level and Marv's drives did not soar quite so far.

Met fans took a close look at the new first baseman with No. 2 on his back. He was average-sized, balding on the top, but affecting reddish-brown sideburns long before sideburns became camp.

The first instinct of the fans was that Marv was just another of the bums trying to play Hodges out of the lineup.

And Marv did not contribute to the relationship, not at first. He had a disdainful way of dropping his bat when he struck out, like W. C. Fields suffering a temporary setback at the gaming tables but letting the winning players know that he was really above playing for such low stakes. It could almost be said that Marv was snobbish. After all, he had played in Yankee Stadium. He had stood in the outfield grass and spat tobacco juice with the great Mantle. What was a nice Yankee like him doing in a place like this?

Thus Marv's first month was marked by a mutual indifference. Then it was June 17—time for Marv to begin his legend. There were approximately 13,000 fans on that pleasant Sunday afternoon. They had come to see the last-place Mets take on their nearest rivals, the run-down Chicago Cubs. They were about to see an epic defensive-offensive performance by Throneberry that would live in history. In fact, there are probably 200,000 people who claim to have been in the Polo Grounds that afternoon. This happens very often with historic contests.

In the very first inning, Don Landrum walked and Ken Hubbs struck out. Then Landrum broke for second on a hit-and-run play but was hung up between bases when Billy Williams missed on his swing.

Catcher Sammy Taylor threw to second baseman Charlie Neal, who began the seemingly inevitable rundown. But there was one hitch. The man on the other end of the rundown was none other than Marvelous.

Neal threw to Marv. Marv caught the ball. Marv threw to Neal. Neal caught the ball. So far, so good. But Landrum was edging toward first base, and he noticed that Marv was standing directly in his way—without the ball. This is not allowed. Landrum had no chance to reach first base because catcher Taylor and pitcher Alvin Jackson were now guarding that sector. So Landrum did the smartest thing of all—he ran into Marvelous Marv. Umpire Dusty Boggess observed the contact and ruled that Marv had "interfered" with the runner by standing in the base line, even though Landrum had sought the contact. So Landrum was awarded second base.

Now instead of having two outs, the Mets had only one. Marv did catch a throw for the second out. That left one out to go. But Ernie Banks walked, Ron Santo tripled, and Lou Brock hit a homer into the right-field bleachers, where no man had ever hit a ball before. The Cubs led, 4–0, as a direct result of Marv's interference. So much for the defense.

The Mets, for all their faults, did have some respectable hitting in 1962. In the bottom of the first, Ashburn bunted for a single, Chacon was out bunting, the elderly Gene Woodling—acquired the day before—walked, and Frank Thomas singled to make it 4–1.

The next hitter was Throneberry, who liked to say of himself: "I am a sweet hitter. Not really a great hitter. Just a sweet hitter."

Marv's sweet swing produced a smash off the wall near the Howard Clothes sign and into the right-field grass. By the time the Cubs tracked the ball down, two runs had scored and Marv was standing on third with a triple. Well, not exactly a triple. Gentle Ernie Banks politely called for the ball and stepped on first base. Yes, Boggess indicated, Marv had missed first base. Marv was out.

Out of the dugout roared the Old Man, eager to protest this injustice. But as he approached the umpire, Casey was met by his first-base coach, the implacable Cookie Lavagetto.

"It won't do any good, Casey," Lavagetto said. "He missed second base, too."

Stengel gave Boggess a brief, face-saving argument but quickly gave up. Back in the dugout, with Marv now keeping him company, Stengel saw Neal swat a homer over the left-field roof.

The Mets could have used Marv's lost run. They were trailing, 8–7, in the ninth inning with two outs and a runner on base. "Let's go Mets," the fans shouted. The batter was Marv. He struck out.

This day guaranteed Marv his place in Met history. The fans booed him harshly as he trudged to the clubhouse. But there was something brewing beneath the boos, and Stan Isaacs, the patron saint of underdogs, began to detect a love affair between the Met fans and their marvelous first baseman.

"The love affair is in the stage where the lovers snap at each other," Isaacs wrote in *Newsday*. "They already suspect they might be liking each other and that intensifies the bickering— until the whole thing flowers into true love."

The first sign of this love affair was the chant "cranberry, strawberry, we love Throneberry." Clearly, Marv was becoming a special hero to certain hip fans. Some of the reporters decided to ask Throneberry about his new role with the fans. The reporters found his locker beneath the sign "Marvelous Marv." All other players had the prosaic number and last name (17-Coleman) but Marvelous had his nickname.

Marv wasn't in his locker at the moment. The first thing he did after each game was brush his teeth, as if to take the bad taste of losing out of his mouth.

"What's the matter, boys?" Richie Ashburn cawed from the next locker in his Nebraska crow accent. "You waiting on Marvelous Marv?"

Soon Marv appeared from the bathroom, carrying his toothbrush. "Hey, Marv," Ashburn began, "tell them about your fans. Tell them how your fans love you." And Marv mumbled something like: "Aw, shucks."

But Ashburn did not give up. The right-wing right fielder was hitting around .300 and enjoying this twilight season. He had put in a good career already, and this joyride in New York was a fitting climax.

"Tell them how you're going to throw a party for your fans," Ashburn continued, "in a telephone booth."

Marv just muttered softly to himself at first, but in the days to come he began smiling at the reporters. Ashburn's needling was forcing Marv to come out of his shell. It was almost the way Casey and Joe Garagiola had created Yogi Berra's image a decade before with the help of some gullible columnists. Instead of a testy, suspicious competitor, Yogi became a witty, jolly elf, even if Garagiola and Casey made up most of his stories. Ashburn had more to work with in Throneberry, who had a dry country wit beneath his diffident manner.

"Marvelous, tell them what you told me on the bench," Ashburn said one day.

"You mean how I missed that throw intentionally because I wanted to hit that loudmouth in the box seats?"

But if Ashburn was striving to create a folk hero, there wasn't much he could do for Marv on the field. Marv just did what came naturally.

Marv was particularly weak on run-down plays. There was a game in St. Louis in late July when the Mets had Ken Boyer strung up between first and second. The elderly Stan Musial was edging off third base, hoping he would not have to do anything foolish like dash for home. However, Marv decided to engage Boyer in a footrace to second base, spotting Boyer a good ten feet. Musial could not resist sneaking home while Marv unsuccessfully chased Boyer to second. The run put the Cardinals ahead, and the Mets soon had their seventy-fifth loss.

"Hey," Marv announced to reporters before an ensuing double-header. "I've got good news for you. I'm only playing in one of those games today."

Then there was the day when Frank Thomas tried to play third base while Throneberry played first. There were very few fans in the box seats behind first base. Thomas started the inning by fumbling a grounder, putting the runner on first base. But he was not satisfied, so he heaved the ball a few yards past Throneberry, as the runner raced all the way to third.

"What are you trying to do, take my fans away from me?" Marv asked Thomas after the game.

"Don't worry, Marvelous, you'll get them back," Ashburn predicted.

By this time, nobody could steal Marv's fans. The only way he could lose them would be if they were ejected from the stadium, which happened one manic night. Five young men appeared in the Polo Grounds wearing T-shirts with M-A-R-V written on four shirts and an exclamation mark, naturally, on the fifth.

The young men become intoxicated with the marvelousness of the night, and they began dancing in a conga line on the roof of the dugout, which is not allowed because it is dangerous and also because the fans cannot keep up with the errors in the field. So the ever-present stadium police hustled the five young men out onto Eighth Avenue. It was too early to go home, however, so the young men turned their shirts inside out and paid their way back into the stadium.

Despite all this frivolity, Marv did not like the idea of losing and laughing. One night when Frank Thomas hit a meaningless three-run homer late in a 10–3 slaughter, the Big Donkey cavorted joyously in the clubhouse until Marv grumbled: "Some people think losing is funny. You'd never hear anybody laugh on the Yankees."

Marv's competitive instincts never deserted him, so it seemed only fair that he have an occasional good day.

Perhaps his sweetest moment came in August when somebody else was starting at first base. The inflammable coach, Solly Hemus, was thrown out of the game by the umpires, and old Gene Woodling was sent out to coach first base. But in the ninth inning, with the Mets trailing by three runs, Woodling was called out of the coaching box to pinch-hit.

"Marv, get out there and coach," Ashburn snarled at his friend. A great roar went up as the familiar No. 2 took an authoritative stance so close to his beloved first base and began flashing signals to all concerned.

The new coach didn't do much until Woodling got on base and the Pirates' lead was cut to two runs. Then the Pirates brought in the right-handed ElRoy Face and Casey looked around for a powerful left-handed hitter. The best one was standing near first base. The Old Man popped up from the dugout and pointed his finger at Throneberry, as thousands cheered.

The "sweet hitter" strolled into the Met dugout and rubbed his favorite pine-tar rag over the handle of his favorite bat as the excitement mounted in the stands. The fans roared as Marv strode deliberately toward home plate, taking a few practice swishes.

Then he belted a three-run homer into the right-field stands to win the game, 5–4, and touch off perhaps the longest, noisiest demonstration of the season. The fans would not soon forget Marv's finest moment.

"There is beginning to be the suspicion that the love for Marvelous Marv has oozed out of the press box into the hearts of the customers," Stan Isaacs wrote a few days later. "Walking through the stands, a fan club member in charge of measuring the public pulse begins to hear the appellation 'Marvelous Marv' ring out, not with scorn but with a tone that might be called exasperated affection. . . . Not that there aren't people still booing Marv. The day they stop booing Marv, the . . . fan club will disband."

In the long run, Marv came to appreciate the attention of the reporters and the fans. Even the boos didn't bother him any more. "They're not going to run me out of New York the way they did Norm Siebern," he said. "Do I look like I'm not hustling? These are just my natural movements. If I were to start dashing about like little Elio Chacon, just to look as if I were hustling, it would be phony.

"So long as they pay me, they can say what they want."

They paid him—and Marv earned every dollar. In 1962 he was one of the most productive Mets, batting .244 with sixteen homers and forty-nine runs batted in for 116 games, his best season in the major leagues.

And remember the Howard Clothes contest, the $7000 power boat for the man who most often hit the advertisements in the left- and right-field corners? Marv won that contest, and on the last day of the season was awarded the deed to the boat.

But there was a marvelous ending to that story. Ashburn also won a boat on that final day, in a contest for the most popular Met. In the winter, the tax people ruled that Ashburn did not have to pay income taxes on the boat because it was a gift. But Marv—poor Marv—was a different case. He won his boat in a competition of skill. He had to pay taxes on his boat. It was the ultimate bittersweet ending to a truly marvelous season for Marv Throneberry.

10

YOU MAKE YOUR
OWN LUCK

◆

In Los Angeles in 1962, a man racked his brains for a gimmick for a bar he was opening. Finally he had an idea—"The Losers." There are lots of losers, and he would honor a different one each week.

There were plenty of candidates in 1962. Eddie Fisher lost Elizabeth Taylor and the bar displayed pictures of both of them for a week. Brinks lost $1,551,279 in a holdup in Plymouth, Massachusetts, the largest holdup in United States history. A politician named Richard Nixon lost an election for governor of California and crankily announced there would be "no more Nixon" in public life—so he was a loser too. But the most frequent losers in the bar's weekly contest were the amazing New York Mets. They were losers all the time.

Sandy Koufax pitched a no-hitter against them. The opposition scored ten or more runs against them in twenty-three different games. Lou Brock hit a homer into the right-field bleachers of the Polo Grounds, the first time man had ever reached that sector. Then a few days later, Henry Aaron hit a homer into the left-field side of the bleachers, where only Joe Adcock had ever hit before. They lost on errors. They lost on bases on balls. They lost on bad bounces. They lost and lost and lost.

People were laughing at the Mets all over the country, but in New York they were staying up late to laugh at them on television. In the morning, red-eyed fans would nod to each other in easy recognition. "Did you see them last night?" one would ask. "Unbelievable," the other would reply.

Marv Throneberry was the symbol of the wretchedness, of course, but all the players contributed and all were branded. The pitchers suffered the most because the losses were tacked on their record and they were judged accordingly. And the pitchers who suffered and lost the most were, by the nature of the game, the best pitchers on the team. They were good enough to keep pitching—and keep losing.

Roger Craig lost the most games, twenty-four, but he also won the most, ten. He was a mature competitor who specialized in picking runners off base. He was also, if such a thing is possible, a stabilizing force on the team because of his gentle humor.

Alvin Jackson (8–20) had never been given a full chance to pitch in the majors. A good athlete, he would occasionally pitch a masterful low-run game when he managed to keep his pitches low. When his pitches were high, they took off into outer space.

Jay Hook (8–19) still managed to infuriate the Old Man, despite the Stengels' personal fondness for him and his family. For all his speed, Hook did not seem to pitch tight enough to the batters. It was said that he had once hit a batter in the head, sending him to the hospital, and he made up his mind never to hurt anybody again. And for all his skill in aerodynamics, the engineering graduate could not make his curve ball break sharply enough.

Craig Anderson (3–17) was another college man (Lehigh) with a pretty wife, and was another favorite of Edna Stengel. A tall, burly man, he won three of his first four decisions but then dropped sixteen straight. His gentle, educated manner drove Stengel up the nearest clubhouse wall, particularly after Stengel learned that Anderson had a generous annuity plan.

"He's got an-noo-i-tees," Casey would enunciate, "but he won't knock the batter on his butt."

The Mets did have one winning pitcher, Kenneth Purvis Mac-Kenzie, a left-hander with a degree from Yale. A look-alike of "Mr. Peepers," MacKenzie made the team almost by default because there were hardly any left-handers. In one of the early games, Casey allegedly handed MacKenzie the ball and snapped: "Make like you're pitching against Harvard." It was also Mac-Kenzie who once noted: "I have taken a survey and I find that I am the lowest paid alumnus in the entire Yale Class of 1956."

An alumnus of the School of Life was Sherman "Roadblock" Jones, a well-traveled right-hander, who knew fascinating facts that nobody else seemed to know. If a fastball pitcher was going against the Mets on a cloudy day, Roadblock would insist that the pitcher was blind in one eye. The Mets found themselves saying "Aw, come on, Road" to him. Jones might have been a classic Met but he lost his first four decisions and was soon gone.

Another brief Met was Wilmer "Vinegar Bend" Mizell, who had lost his fastball long before he got to New York. He lost two decisions and was dropped. The next the Mets heard of him was in 1968 when he won a congressional election in North Carolina, the first Met to serve in Congress.

One of the gloomiest pitchers was Bob Moorhead, a right-hander who couldn't gain a decision for half a season. When he finally lost a game, he seemed almost relieved to have a record of some sort. In September, after another bad game, he was sent to the clubhouse where his anger finally welled to the top. He punched a metal locker with his right hand, breaking his knuckles, and was through for the season.

Then there were the two Bob Millers. Robert Gerald Miller quit baseball when the Mets acquired him from Cincinnati in the spring and tried to farm him out. The Mets talked him out of the automobile business and back into the minors in the summer and finally called him up. But he did not pitch for a week, and he began to grumble that he wanted his chance to work. Finally they sent him into a game in Milwaukee, a tie in the bottom of the twelfth inning. Miller's first pitch was to Del Crandall, and it soared over the fence to end the game.

The Mets already had another Bob Miller, Robert Lane Miller, a young fastball pitcher from the Cardinals. Lou Niss, the road secretary of the Mets, solved the surplus problem by rooming the two Bob Millers together. "That way, if somebody calls for Bob Miller, he's bound to get the right one," Niss reasoned.

Robert Lane Miller was immature and often made mistakes on the mound, which was why he lost his first twelve decisions. No pitcher had ever lost twelve games in a season without winning at least one. He did not want to go down in the record books for his 0–12 record. So on the last Saturday of the season, he went out and beat the Cubs, 2–1, to escape the awful distinction. Having given so many unhappy interviews all season, he waited in front of his locker to tell the New York reporters how it felt to win a game finally. But all the New York press had jumped to the Dodger-Giant finale on the West Coast, so Bob Miller never got to tell a happy story that season.

All the other positions had their problems, too. Catcher Hobie Landrith, the first man drafted by the Mets, was expected to help the club defensively. But ten of the first eleven runners who tried were successful in stealing second base, and Landrith was a doomed man. A few days after Throneberry came over from Baltimore, Landrith was sent to the Orioles as payment.

Landrith was upset because he had brought his son with him on a road trip and he wasn't sure how the boy would take it. Hesitantly, Landrith broke the news.

"Oh, I knew that three days ago, Dad," the boy replied.

"How could you know that?" the father asked.

"I heard Mr. Niss talking on the clubhouse phone. He said you were traded."

"Why didn't you tell me?"

"You always told me not to repeat what I heard in the clubhouse."

Catchers often seemed to figure in these bizarre shufflings. A burly catcher named Harry Chiti was picked up from Cleveland for the familiar "player to be named later." Chiti had one game where he failed twice to bat runners home from third base. A few days later he was gone—back to the Cleveland farm system. Harry Chiti had been traded for himself. It was hard to tell who got the better of the deal.

One of the fans' favorite catchers was wiry little Choo Choo Coleman, who scrambled around in the dirt behind home plate. The pitchers claimed he was a hard target because he moved so much. When Coleman played for the Phillies, somebody had asked pitcher Chuck Churn who was the toughest man in the league to pitch to. Churn quickly answered: "Coleman"—his own catcher.

But Stengel defended Coleman by saying: "He can handle a low-ball pitcher because he crawls on his belly like a snake." Indeed, Stengel usually let Choo Choo catch when Alvin Jackson was pitching, and Alvin had some of his best games with Choo Choo behind the plate.

Choo Choo was not a very loquacious person, usually confining himself to "Hey, bub" as a greeting. So Ralph Kiner, the announcer, was a little dubious about interviewing Choo Choo. However, Kiner opened with what he thought was a safe question:

"Choo Choo, how did you get your nickname?"

And Choo Choo replied: "Dunno."

Kiner tried again. "Well, what's your wife's name—and what's she like?"

"Her name is Mrs. Coleman—and she likes me."

Some of the white players were a little hesitant about teasing the quiet Negro from Florida, until they realized that the black players also had their fun with Choo Choo. Charlie Neal, the sardonic ex-Dodger, claimed he had once bet Choo Choo that he didn't know his (Neal's) name.

"You Numbah Foah," Choo Choo replied.

Choo Choo's unique style soon made him famous throughout the land. When the Mets played in Dodger Stadium late in the season, some UCLA students hung a banner that said: FLASH— KENNEDY DISCUSSES THE RAILROAD STRIKE WITH CHOO CHOO COLE-MAN.

First base was more or less protected with Throneberry. Hodges suffered a kidneystone attack midway through the season and was out for the season after an operation. Second base belonged to Neal, the star of the Dodgers' 1959 championship. He had gone downhill quickly after that year, but the Mets were hoping that a change of scene would help him. It didn't. At thirty-one, Neal batted only .260 and was inconsistent in the field.

The shortstop was often Elio Chacon, the son of a famous Venezuelan athlete, Pelayo. Elio had beautiful brown skin and soft brown eyes, and he asked Lou Niss for tickets at every ball park in the league—"for my cousin."

"Elio has the biggest family in the Western Hemisphere," Niss commented.

At third base was Felix Mantilla, a slender Puerto Rican with a lusty good humor, who also liked to read books in a corner of the clubhouse before a game. Stengel seemed to have less patience with Mantilla than with any other player, once benching him after he made four hits in a game.

Mantilla hit .275, drilling line drives in every direction, but his fielding was a problem. Met fans liked to imitate him, crouching forward, then rocking back on their heels, waving their left hands casually at the imagined baseball. That was Mantilla playing a hard grounder.

But Mantilla would always remember the anarchy of the first season, like Coach Hemus making him and Rod Kanehl catch pop-ups during infield practice to determine who would start in the game. Casey's lack of confidence in him hurt Mantilla's pride.

Perhaps the best attitude on the team belonged to Richie Ashburn, the thirty-five-year-old outfielder. He wore bermuda shorts to the musty old Polo Grounds but there was nothing casual about him when he pulled on his uniform.

Around mid-season, Ashburn got the feeling that the umpires were deciding against the Mets on every close play. Ashburn's face became redder and redder with each close call. Finally he blew his stack and was thrown out of the game by the umpire. Afterward, Casey asked the umpire: "What did you say to my quiet right fielder to make him so mad?"

The umpire gasped. "Me? Casey, you should have heard what he said."

After Ashburn had been thrown out of two games within a week, Casey told him there was no point in fighting the umpires any more. The Old Man also gave Ashburn a day off so he could visit his family in Nebraska.

"He'll probably fight with his wife," Casey muttered.

Ashburn gave up running into umpires, but he forgot about running into brick walls. In Pittsburgh one evening he crashed into the right-field wall while chasing a fly ball. He argued that the ball was foul, and he stayed in the game. Afterward, Ashburn sat in front of his locker and complained about the call.

"The ball was foul, damn it," Ashburn said. "I'm just a little dizzy from hitting the wall."

"It's tough to lose a game like that," somebody suggested.

"You mean we lost the game?" Ashburn blurted. "We didn't win? What was the score? How did we lose it? We didn't lose it!"

The doctor was summoned and he sent Ashburn to the hospital for X-rays. "From the fifth inning on, this man has been playing on nothing but reflex," the doctor said. Ashburn did not want to go to the hospital.

"I'm good enough to play," he shouted. "I can play the next game. I just can't remember, that's all."

The injury was not serious, even though Ashburn never did recall the last four innings. A good case of amnesia wasn't such a bad thing that season.

Another outfielder was Frank Thomas, the bumptious steward-in-the-sky. Thomas hit thirty-four homers and drove in ninety-four runs, but he finished in the second division for the eleventh time in fifteen years.

Gus Bell, the third veteran outfielder who opened the season, was dropped early in the year, giving Jim Hickman and Joe Christopher more of a chance to play. Hickman was a powerful country boy with a habit of taking third strikes. Casey used to chant a little ditty at Hickman—"Oh, you can't improve your average with your bat upon your shoulder." Christopher was a moody Virgin Islander given to melancholy monologues on the power of positive thinking.

Finally, there was a separate category for Rod Kanehl, the utility man and Casey's pet player. Kanehl had been a farmhand in the Yankee system when Stengel was manager there. Wherever he looked, there were quality players like Bobby Richardson and Tony Kubek ahead of him, so he realized he would have to make it by a different kind of hustling. In an intrasquad game one day, he chased a long fly ball until it flew over a fence. But that didn't stop the former college decathlon star. He vaulted the fence and finally chased down the ball, with Stengel beaming approval.

The handsome Missourian made a lot of stops in the minor leagues but was never forgotten by Stengel. The Old Man made sure Kanehl was in the first Met camp, even though on a minor-league roster. This was Kanehl's biggest chance, and he did not fail. He sat up in front in all club meetings, blurting out the answers before Stengel could finish the questions.

Stengel fought to keep Kanehl, and Weiss had to relent. Kanehl immediately made himself valuable at all infield and outfield positions. He batted only .248 and his fielding was unsure at any position but he had speed and he wasn't afraid. He collected fifty dollars from Stengel for getting hit by a pitch with the bases loaded.

While most of the players stared blankly when Stengel talked, Kanehl seemed to dig the language. Perhaps Kanehl saw himself as a junior version of Stengel, for he had a comment after every game. The players might have resented this eagerness to please the manager and the press, but Kanehl was much too charming to be disliked. The players called him "Barracuda" because he would snap at anybody who tried to take away his turn during batting practice.

Also like a young Stengel, Kanehl investigated life in the big city. He brought his wife, "Big Red," and his four children to New York and took them sight-seeing while other players were watching daytime soap operas. Kanehl became fascinated with the subway system and toured the IRT, the BMT, and the IND until he knew all the routes by heart. The Mets learned of this particular fetish and changed his nickname from "Barracuda" to "The Mole."

On their way to last place, the Mets at least managed to lead the league in coaches. Their batting instructor was Rogers Hornsby, who had once batted .424 in a season and still believed that movies were bad for a hitter's eyes. Two other coaches were Red Kress, a friendly chap who sat with Casey in the dugout, and Red Ruffing, the former star pitcher for the Yankees.

The first-base coach was Harry "Cookie" Lavagetto, the Dodger who had broken up Bill Bevens' no-hitter in the 1947 World Series, while at third base was the ever-popular Solomon Joseph Hemus.

Solly was the live wire of the coaching staff, a former Cardinal shortstop who had later managed in St. Louis. He still had ambitions to manage and he was the only coach who tried to cajole the players into doing better.

Hemus was also the coach who would fight the umpires when he felt they were wrong, which was often. He and Ashburn had developed a theory that the umpires "screw us because we're horseshit." This theory got him excused early from several games.

Casey himself did not promote this theory. Casey was a positive thinker who proclaimed: "You make your own luck—some people have bad luck all their lives."

Stengel was trying to change the Mets' luck with the help of "The Youth of America," his vast mythical army of youngsters who were on their way to Met-land. There were precious few youngsters in this first year as Grant and Weiss tried to build a following with old, familiar faces.

But in the middle of the 1962 season, the Mets brought around a seventeen-year-old boy who had broken all of Hank Greenberg's home-run records at Monroe High School in the Bronx. The youngster was tall and slouchy and as colorful as concrete, even at seventeen. Yet Ed Kranepool had a good swing and the Mets were eager to sign him for a big bonus.

"Hey, kid," Frank Thomas shouted as the youngster took batting practice with the Mets. "How much money they giving you? Don't sign for less than a million." Kranepool just stared back out of his sleepy eyes, perhaps taking notes who his friends were.

Edward Emil Kranepool never knew his father, who was killed at the Battle of the Bulge just before his son was born. Mrs. Kranepool had worked hard to let her son play ball when he was young and the boy grew into a six-foot, three-inch basketball star with scholarship offers from many colleges. But after graduation Kranepool wanted to repay his mother so he gave up four years of his youth, forsaking college and basketball, and he took an $80,000 bonus from the Mets. He was the first Youth of America.

He shuttled around in his first season, finally arriving to the Mets late in September. He played three games, and on the last day of the season he whacked his first major-league hit, a double.

The Mets closed out the season in Chicago. On the last day they had a very good chance to win until one of their newest catchers, a former Dodger named Joe Pignatano, hit into a triple play. It was a fitting way to end the season. The Mets lost, 5–1, for their 120th loss against forty victories. No club in the history of baseball had ever lost more games in one season.

They also lost fifty-eight of their eighty home games, which was another record. But they drew 922,530 fans into the ancient ball park, far more than might have been expected.

There was considerable discussion whether the Mets had to be as bad as they were. Some people, like the announcer Howard Cosell, tended to take the simplistic approach and blame the manager. The players tended to blame their leaders for little things—an occasional forgetfulness, an insult, a lack of confidence. But the players knew there was no talent on the club and they knew they finished exactly where they belonged—sixty and a half games out of first place.

But also, of course, well on their way to a legend.

11

WE'RE STILL A FRAUD

◆

LOOIE KLEPPEL STOOD OUTSIDE Al Lang Field in St. Petersburg, surrounded by gaping tourists. The portly oracle of the bleachers had just seen Jay Hook beat Kansas City for the Mets' thirteenth victory in twenty-two exhibitions in the spring of 1963, and Looie was downright encouraged.

"They're gonna give the rest of the league 'Hail Columbia,'" he announced, brandishing his cane, his eyes flashing.

"I sat through seventy of their games last year. It got so bad some of the players looked like they were apologizing for living. This year it's different. This year we have some ball players.

"That Throneberry is listening to Hodges about first base and maybe he won't run up such a dental bill again. And our pitchers are coming into their own.

"The players have drank from the bitter waters of Marah—that's from the Bible—and now they're ready to win."

This was the gospel according to Looie, and such beliefs are possible under the Florida sun. The Mets had made many changes since the end of 1962 and the new faces encouraged the illusion of improvement.

Since the last gloomy out in 1962, Ashburn had retired to become a broadcaster in Philadelphia, but the Mets had also traded Mantilla to Boston for Tracy Stallard, a pitcher who gave up Roger Maris' sixty-first homer in 1961, and Al Moran, a minor-league shortstop.

There was also a trade with the Dodgers over the winter. Robert Lane Miller—the young right-handed Miller—went for Tim Harkness, a first baseman, and Larry Burright, a second baseman. Both had been substitutes on the near-championship team of 1962 and the Mets could only assume that they had some ability. Later Stengel would suggest, in his most paranoid moments, that good old Buzzie Bavasi had kept these two players all of 1962 just to set them up for a trade with the Mets.

After living with Harkness and Burright for a few weeks, the Mets were in no mood for further dealings with Bavasi. However, a curious chain of events again put the Mets in touch with the Dodger general manager.

The sequence started with, of all things, a newspaper strike in New York. Most of the New York writers were out of work during spring training but they managed, nevertheless, to get to Florida—without enough work to keep them busy. Thus they had plenty of time to chat with their old friend, Buzzie.

Bavasi is one of the most popular of all general managers. He will lend money to players, lend cars to visiting reporters, do favors for anybody, and never ask anything in return.

In the spring of 1963, Buzzie wanted to do a favor for Duke Snider, the aging hero of Bedford Avenue. The "Dook" had not been playing much in recent years and Bavasi felt he deserved the chance to finish his career as a regular—preferably in front of his old New York fans.

The New York reporters agreed with good old Buzzie and they began pressuring George Weiss about Snider. "It seems to me you're making a big fuss over an old ball player," Weiss said.

But late in spring training the Mets spent around $40,000 for the services of the thirty-six-year-old gray-haired idol of Flatbush, hoping he would transmit some old Dodger Class to the Mets. What Snider brought were his golf clubs, so he and Larry Burright could shoot a round after practice.

The Mets also picked up a pitcher, Carlton Willey, from Milwaukee near the end of training. Willey had not been used much by the Braves and he was eager for a chance to pitch.

Casey kept talking about his "Youth of America," and in truth there were a few young faces. Ed Kranepool, now eighteen, hit the ball well enough to make Casey bring him north.

"Who says you can't make it when you're eighteen?" Stengel snapped. "Ott made it when he was eighteen."

Another young prospect was Larry Bearnarth, twenty-two, a pitcher from St. John's University in New York. Handsome and articulate, Bearnarth made many friends in his first few weeks in camp. In later years, when the Tom Seavers and Jerry Koosmans began arriving, the highest praise you could pay them was to compare them, in personality, to the young Larry Bearnarth of 1963, who seemed to have a chance to be an early Met hero.

A third young Met was Ron Hunt, an infielder who had been conditionally purchased from the Milwaukee farm system. Nobody was counting on Hunt to help much until an intrasquad game at Huggins Field when Joe Christopher heaved a relay far over Hunt's head. Hunt cursed mightily at Christopher for overthrowing to him as old ladies cringed in the stands. But Stengel's elephant ears picked up the vibrations, and soon Casey was chortling about this cocky kid from Missouri who was going to fight his way onto the team.

There was trouble in paradise when Weiss tried to cut Marvelous Marv's salary. "Marv got the writer's good-guy award mixed up with the Most Valuable Player Award," Weiss sniffed.

Gene Woodling, now a player-coach, took Marv's side of the argument and was fired for interfering. Then Johnny Murphy, the assistant to Weiss, began negotiating with Marv. "People come to the park to holler at me, just like Mantle and Maris," Marv told Murphy. "I drew people to the games."

"You drove some away too," Murphy said.

"I took a lot of abuse," Marv said.

"You brought most of it on yourself," Murphy said.

Marv finally signed but he was under a cloud as the Mets prepared to go north.

Then they were back at the same old stand for opening day, with 25,849 fans in the Polo Grounds waiting to see if the Mets could possibly be as bad again. Looie Kleppel was there. Mother of the Mets was there. Marv Throneberry was there. So were

Casey Stengel, Duke Snider, and Ron Hunt. And the swinging roller—it was there too.

Shortly after 2 P.M., umpire Frank Secory tossed a baseball to Roger Craig. Wiry little Curt Flood of the Cardinals dug his spikes into the dirt. Craig threw a perfect pitch, down low, where Flood could only tick a piece of it.

The ball squirted down the third-base line. Charlie Neal darted in, scooped up the ball, and threw underhanded in one motion. The ball flew into right field, Flood went to second base, and 25,849 fans threw their arms into the air.

"Same old Mets," went the cry, bouncing off Coogan's Bluff and echoing across the river.

Before the inning was over, the Cardinals had two runs. The Mets managed two hits all game, and when Throneberry pinch-hit in the eighth inning, he struck out. The final score was 7–0.

"We're still a fraud," Stengel sighed after the game. "The attendance got trimmed again."

The attendance continued to get trimmed as the days passed. This peculiar combination of old Sniders and young Kranepools lost the first eight games, just one loss shy of the opening streak of 1962. But on April 19, with Milwaukee leading, 4–3, in the ninth, Ron Hunt slapped a two-run double for the first victory of the year.

Mrs. Payson was so delighted at being ahead of the 1962 pace that she ordered a bouquet of roses to the apartment of Ron and Jackie Hunt, just the way she would do if she had a winner in a big stakes race at Belmont. There was only one problem. Hunt suffered from a number of allergies, including hay fever, and he had to throw the roses out of the apartment before he could sleep that night.

The Mets swept the Braves four straight that weekend, prompting manager Bobby Bragan to grumble that the Polo Grounds was "a chamber of horrors." Most of the time, though, the horrors were reserved for the Mets. With Stallard and Hook giving up some frightening homers, with nobody hitting, with Burright and Moran making errors, it was time for a change.

The first change came on the sunny morning of May 9, when Marv Throneberry was told he was being farmed out to Buffalo.

Marv had been in trouble ever since his lengthy salary negotiations. He hadn't helped himself one rainy night when Stengel started him in right field, and he turned a single into a two-run error.

After that game Marv had groaned: "I'm gone, I can tell." He was right. The reporters gravitated to his locker when they heard the sad news and Marv smoked his last sad cigarette.

"I ain't gave up yet," Marv announced. "I'm going to leave my name up there above my locker."

The reporters shook his hand and said they'd see him soon. Then everybody left the clubhouse and Marv pulled off his uniform with the famous No. 2 on the back. After dressing, he packed his gear and headed for the door. He turned the doorknob to the left, and nothing happened. He turned the doorknob to the right, and nothing happened. He kicked the door and he began banging and screaming. It was half an hour before anybody returned to let Marv out—giving him a most unwelcome but somehow characteristic last thirty minutes as a Met.

On May 22 another familiar Met was gone. The Washington Senators, after firing manager Mickey Vernon, asked the Mets for permission to sign Gil Hodges, who was on the injured list again. The Mets released the aging first baseman so he could begin his new career as a manager. The Senators were so appreciative, they sent the eccentric outfielder Jimmy Piersall to New York.

When he was one of the most skilled outfielders in the American League, Piersall had always begged Stengel to acquire him for the Yankees because two kindred spirits would make a great team. Now they were united for the first time, but Stengel soon noticed that Piersall could no longer play regularly in the outfield.

Piersall did provide one thrill when he hit his one-hundredth career homer and jogged around the bases with his back first.

"I hit my four-hundredth homer and all I got was the ball," Duke Snider said admiringly. "You hit your one-hundredth and go coast-to-coast."

The Mets didn't mind Piersall's antics until it became apparent that his average was staying at .194.

"There's only room for one clown on this team," Casey said after the Mets dropped Piersall on July 22.

Other player changes came rapidly as the Mets sank into last place again. Charlie Neal was shipped to Cincinnati for Jesse Gonder, a catcher with a frightening reputation for dropping low pop-ups. And on July 11, Ed Kranepool was farmed out to Buffalo to work on his hitting.

The eighteen-year-old had been victimized by the experienced pitchers in the league, obviously over his head. When Snider had offered to help, Kranepool snapped: "You ain't going so good yourself." So it was decided to let the young man regain his confidence in an easier league.

Nobody characterized the Mets' suffering in this second season more than Roger Craig, the tall pitcher who wore cowboy boots and ran a riding academy outside Los Angeles. His losing outstripped even the Mets.

Craig's losing streak began on May 4 when he lost to the Giants, and it kept growing and growing. Craig rarely pitched badly, just badly enough to lose, and he was too good to be taken from the rotation. Twice he lost to the Phillies when Roy Sievers hit the same kind of pitch into the same section of the grandstand, just to disprove the old adage about lightning never striking twice. On August 4 Craig's streak reached eighteen losses, one away from the major-league record set by John Nabors of the Athletics back in 1916. It didn't console Craig when somebody discovered that the Mets had made exactly twenty-nine runs while he was pitching in his eighteen losses.

The friendly pitcher began getting mail from all over the country containing advice and prayers and good-luck charms. But the suggestion Craig heeded was about his number. He had been wearing No. 38 since joining the Mets, and it obviously hadn't done much for him. Now it was suggested that he try changing his luck with that luckiest of all numbers, 13. Well, why not?

On August 9 Craig drove in from Long Island with Norm Sherry and Larry Bearnarth. But their car was halted by a drawbridge. "Just my luck," Craig told his friends. "Maybe I'd be better off if it stays up all night."

The bridge was lowered and the three Mets drove to the ball park where Craig's new No. 13 was waiting for him. After posing for photographers, he called a clubhouse meeting to take care of a few bits of business as their player representative to management. Then he made a rather unusual comment for a professional athlete:

"Boys, I'd really like to win this one tonight," he said. The players were silent. What could they say?

On this night they gave him unusual batting support, giving him a 3–3 tie going into the last of the ninth. With two outs, it seemed likely that the game would go into extra innings. But the weak-hitting Moran doubled, sending a runner to third, and Craig knew he wasn't going to get a chance to bat.

"I wouldn't give a damn if he was my uncle," Stengel said later. "He was out of the game."

Tim Harkness batted for Craig and walked, loading the bases. Then the batter was Jim Hickman, the Tennessee boy whom Craig often called "Hilly-Billy," an easygoing, unemotional player. Hickman batted against Lindy McDaniel, the Cubs' best reliever.

Hickman didn't hit the ball very far—just a dinky fly ball to left field. Billy Williams drifted back, expecting an easy catch, but the ball ticked against the overhanging upper deck and plopped onto the field. The alert umpires signaled a grand-slam homer for Hilly-Billy, while Roger Craig raced toward home to make sure that everybody—all four runs—touched the plate in proper order. He wanted everything perfect.

"I've won World Series games and big games," Craig said as many of the 11,566 fans cheered below the clubhouse. "But this is one of the top two or three. I felt the pressure. It was almost like a World Series game."

In his own office, Casey then revealed how he had given McDaniel the famous "whommy" in the ninth inning, crossing his fingers and shouting "whommy, whommy" at the pitcher. It was an incantation that Casey saved only for crucial moments.

There were a few other thrills late in the season. The Mets

visited Yankee Stadium for the resumption of the old Mayor's
Trophy Game, which used to involve the Dodgers and Giants.
Around 50,000 fans—most of them Met fans—screamed and threw
firecrackers and displayed anti-Yankee banners as Casey threw
two of his best pitchers, Hook and Willey, at the relaxed Yankees and took a 6–2 victory.

After the mob had left the stadium, Yankee manager Ralph
Houk lit up a cigar and said with a giggle: "It wasn't as bad as
the Battle of the Bulge."

In another bright moment, a rookie named Grover Powell (who
claimed his middle name was Demetrius) broke in with a shutout over the Phillies. While the reporters were getting Powell's
life story in the clubhouse (it seems he had been kicked off the
University of Pennsylvania team for missing a bus), Casey
sneaked into the bunch of reporters and pretended to take notes.
As the reporters ran out of questions, Casey had a probing question of his own: "Wuz you born in Poland?"

Grover Powell soon developed a sore arm and never did much
for the Mets afterward. But on his symbolic tombstone in the
graveyard of promising failures, Powell is remembered with the
epitaph: "Wuz you born in Poland?"

The season bumbled into its final weeks with the Mets still
behind everybody, including their fellow expansion team, Houston. The Colts had beaten the Mets out of the starting gate and
seemed to have an advantage in good young players.

The Mets had Hunt, who was leading the team with .272, and
they also had Kranepool, sort of. When recalled from Buffalo,
Kranepool refused to rush to catch the team plane to St. Louis,
insisting on going home to change his clothes. Stengel began to
lose his patience with the young man.

"He ain't my kingdom," the Old Man snapped.

In the closing days, the Mets did bring up one of Casey's
heralded "Youth of America." He was quite a young man with a
deep scar down the right side of his face.

Cleon Jones had batted .360 at Auburn and .305 at Raleigh in
his first professional season, and now he was in the last days of
the Polo Grounds, speaking quietly when approached by the press.

He was a native of Mobile, Alabama, the same city that had

given Henry Aaron to the Milwaukee Braves. He had gotten the scar when he was seventeen, sitting in a friend's car parked in a quiet street. A young man driving angrily barreled into the parked car, sending Jones flying through the front window. The doctors gave him transfusions and later they sewed his face together, performing delicate work around the eye, but there wasn't much they could do about the scar. In later years Jones would appear shy, and people would be hesitant about inquiring about the scar.

He had signed with the Mets after a year of college and had reported to their instructional school in Florida in the fall of 1962. There he became friendly with another promising young outfielder named Paul Blair, who was later drafted by the Baltimore Orioles.

"Cleon was shy, real introverted," recalled Ed Kranepool, who had also played in the instructional games. "I don't think Cleon ever said much to anybody. He and Blair were pretty friendly and I think they were both hurt when the Mets let Blair go."

In later years, Blair would become a star sooner than Jones, and Weiss would be criticized for not protecting Blair while keeping Jones. But stocking a roster is a complex job. Perhaps it is fair to Weiss to note that he signed both Blair and Jones and kept one of them.

Now Jones was with the Mets, thinking, "What the hell am I doing up here?" He batted 2–for–15 in the Polo Grounds and then the wreckers moved in. The Harlem period was over.

The Mets finished up the 1963 season with an attendance of 1,080,108 fans in the Polo Grounds, an improvement over 1962. But artistically, there was still a long way to go, as they won 51 and lost 111 and finished last again.

Snider batted only .243 with fourteen homers and Kranepool hit only .209 with two homers. Thomas slumped from his productive 1962 season while Moran, Harkness, and Burright didn't hit at all.

The best pitching record belonged to Carlton Willey, the softspoken hardware-store owner from Cherryfield, Maine, who had a 9–14 record with an earned-run average of 3.10. And young Larry Bearnarth, the hope of the future, was 3–8 as the star of the bullpen.

But the rest of the starting pitchers lost too often. Craig was 5–22. Galen Cisco, a former linebacker from Ohio State, was 7–15. Hook was 4–14 and Stallard was 6–17. Even Craig Anderson came back from Buffalo late in the season to lose two more games, running his losing streak to eighteen. He was still five games away from the major-league record for consecutive losses but he had a good chance to break it—if he could make the team in 1964.

It wasn't much, but it was the kind of thing a Met fan could look forward to as they approached the brave new world of 1964.

12

MOSES AND THE PROMISED LAND

◆

NOT MANY PEOPLE ever see monuments named after them during their lifetime but William A. Shea had that rare thrill in 1964. The city of New York named its new municipal stadium in Flushing after the man who had prodded organized baseball into moving back to New York, whether or not President Warren Giles thought his National League needed a franchise there.

Somebody jokingly asked Bill Shea how long he thought the new stadium would continue to keep his name. "Oh, until about five minutes after I'm dead," Shea said with a laugh. But he was too modest. Even though he was not connected with the Mets in any way, and had gone back to a full-time law practice, Shea was vitally connected with New York baseball and deserving of being immortalized in the new stadium.

The next question was whether Shea Stadium would be ready for the opening of the 1964 season. It had been promised for 1963 but the unions and the weather had both delayed the construction interminably. While the Mets were down in spring training, workmen were still fixing the field and installing seats and connecting ramps to the different levels. The morning of the opener they were still painting and drilling and wiring, but the

seats were in place and the field was marked with limestone—
what else was necessary?

Queens County, the home of Shea Stadium, is the easternmost
of the five boroughs in New York, a bedroom community which
had grown up in the 1940s and 1950s, a combination of quiet
residential neighborhoods, high-rise apartments, some businesses,
some flourishing slums.

In 1964 it also had the controversial World's Fair, which Robert
Moses had been planning and dreaming about ever since the
1939 World's Fair—with its Trylon and Perisphere—had closed
down. The new fair and the new stadium backed into each other
at the foot of Flushing Bay, a mile south of LaGuardia Airport,
wrapped in a maze of parkways and expressways. The new fair
would often be criticized as an artistic and financial wasteland,
but what about the stadium?

From the outside, there was very little beauty in the $25,500,-
000 stadium. Its alternating blue and orange steel plates glittered
in the sun but they did not hide the asymmetrical ugliness of the
outside. The stadium had been built from the inside out, with no
solid façade. The exterior was really its interior, with steel beams
and juts of concrete and cables soaring at odd angles. With a
breeze blowing off the bay, you might have been standing outside a Siberian power station.

Inside, the stadium was somewhat more appealing, with its
pastel seats, its circular tiers, and the absence of any obstructing
poles and beams.

But the open feeling was also a weakness since the seats sloped
back from the field at sharp angles. The $1.50 seats in the top of
the upper deck might as well have been in Connecticut or New
Jersey because nobody up there would ever see the twinkle in
Casey's eye. In the Polo Grounds, the overhanging grandstands
had produced an intimacy between player and fan. The round-
ness of Shea Stadium discouraged that intimacy, which was not
all bad, as far as the players were concerned.

Also, there were no bleachers in Shea Stadium, no traditional
75-cent haven for the tired, the hungry, and the poor. Even
Yankee Stadium still had its 75-cent bleachers where fans could
drink a beer and take a nap in the sun. Where bleachers should

have been, Shea Stadium had bullpens and a barren strip of weeds, then parking lots and junkyards, then the tidal bay. In the background was the skyline of downtown Flushing and the ever-famous Serval Zipper sign. But a whole era of Jim Hickmans and Don Bosches would perform without proper appreciation from bleacherites.

In a classic example of letting its patrons eat cake, Shea Stadium did have the plush Diamond Club for its season ticket holders, a restaurant in the upper right-field section where fans could eat, drink, and watch the game through the cigar haze, win or lose.

Before the 1964 season began, there was still some question whether people would support the Mets on the fringe of the suburbs. In the Polo Grounds the Mets had been an obsessive diversion. You rode the subway and paid $1.50 and turned on with the freak action.

But the Mets were up against a different crowd now—theoretically. They were appealing to a suburban, success-oriented crowd. Would a father with a high-paying job pack up his 2.3 children and drive his station wagon all the way in from Split Level Land to watch a team that could not win? If these fans did not support the Mets, then Shea Stadium might eventually become the world's biggest outdoor bowling alley.

The first game in Shea Stadium was scheduled for April 17, in the face of a threatened massive traffic tie-up by civil-rights demonstrators, who were concerned about job opportunities at the World's Fair. But the only traffic jam was from Met fans who poured out of Queens, out of suburban Nassau and Suffolk, from New England and New Jersey and the rest of the city. They took the elevated subway's new cars, created for the Fair and named "The State of Missouri," "State of Maine," and so on. The Transit Authority said it carried 34,000 fans to Shea on that first afternoon. But the paid attendance was 50,312 and there seemed to be almost that many cars on the approach roads. Traffic Commissioner Henry Barnes had to fly over in a helicopter after the game to unsnarl the jam.

Inside, the atmosphere seemed just about the same as in the

Polo Grounds. In the upper reaches of the grandstand, the banners were flapping in the breeze:

SPEONK LOVES THE METS

HARTSDALE SAYS WHERE'S MARV?

MIDWOOD HIGH SCHOOL ELECTS CHOO CHOO VALEDICTORIAN

The fans cheered as the players sloshed through practice on the muddy field, then they cheered as a new Met pitcher, Jack Fisher, threw a called strike on the first pitch to Ducky Schofield of the Pittsburgh Pirates. But things went downhill after that. Willie Stargell hit a homer and the Mets finally lost, 4–3, on a late-inning run off Ed Bauta, a Cuban relief pitcher.

It was not the last loss for the Mets in their new home. The next loss came the next day. Soon things were back in the same routine as in the Polo Grounds: the club was losing but the fans kept coming.

The makeup of the fans seemed to change a little. Looie Kleppel and Mother of the Mets stopped coming because there was no forum for their lectures, no bleachers where they could express their freedom of speech. There seemed to be somewhat fewer black and Latin fans now that the club had moved from uptown. But if the Met fan turned a lighter shade of pale in 1964, his noise level remained constant—hysterical and zonked out.

There were more new faces in the stands than in the dugout in 1964. One of the most prominent new fans was an advertising designer from Glen Oaks named Karl Ehrhardt, who carried a neat, bright placard that said: WELCOME TO GRANT'S TOMB.

M. Donald Grant's ushers dutifully confiscated that bit of subversive literature but Ehrhardt was soon back with several dozen signs for each occasion. If a Met hit a homer, Ehrhardt would rummage through his signs and produce one that said: BEAUTIFUL. If a manager visited the pitching mound, a sign would appear saying: IS THIS TRIP NECESSARY? If a batter was hit by a pitch, the sign would say: OUCH! Ehrhardt would occasionally criticize his least favorite ball player, nineteen-year-old Ed Kranepool, calling him: SUPERSTIFF. The artist soon became a landmark at Shea Stadium, a literary barometer of the highs and lows of Met fortunes.

Another creative soul asked the question one day: IS ED KRANEPOOL OVER THE HILL?—a hard question for a nineteen-year-old to field.

There were also group trends in the new ball park, trading in individuality for togetherness. One group frequented the loge boxes, just below the press box, as many as twenty men all wearing yellow rain slickers and white pith helmets. They chanted football-type slogans like "hey-hey, ho-ho, Mets-Mets, let's go." They weren't witty but, on the other hand, they were loud. They blew on party horns, they twirled clackers, they acted like middle-aged men at a New Year's Eve party.

"Where were these guys when Marvelous Marv was booting the old gonfalon around?" sneered some of the purists in the press box.

Eventually somebody did a story on the husky leader of the group and found out. The man was a doctor. Soon Dr. Dominic Principato, a radiologist from a Flushing hospital, and his friends began showing up in Houston or Philadelphia, wearing their yellow slickers, shooting cap pistols at umpires or opposing players.

Another new trend at Shea was the bevy of pretty girls who worked as hostesses in the stands and in the Diamond Club. The press began interviewing these newsworthy creatures almost every day, but the best interview was done by Marv Albert, a young bachelor from radio station WHN. He married one of the prettiest of the hostesses and lived happily ever after.

In a short time it was obvious that all the good feelings of the Polo Grounds had been transferred out to Shea. For whatever irrational reason, the Mets still attracted a broad base. It also helped that a new wave of enthusiastic reporters was now covering the Mets. The men who were most in touch with the scene were: Leonard Koppett, who had switched from the *Post* to the *Times;* Steve Jacobson and Joe Donnelly of *Newsday;* Bob Sales of the *Tribune;* Phil Pepe and Larry Fox of the *Telegram;* and Maury Allen and Vic Ziegel of the *Post.* They were all attuned to the old and the new aspects of Casey's amazing club.

Meanwhile, down on the field, things remained mostly the

same. The Mets had never been known for their good starts. Certainly 1964 was no exception.

The bad luck had begun down in Florida when Carlton Willey, their best pitcher in 1963, had been hit in the jaw with a line drive. The slender Maine native had pitched twenty-one scoreless innings in exhibitions but the line drive (by Gates Brown of Detroit) put him in the hospital, unable to eat or play ball. He would never recover from the layoff and would never win another game for the Mets.

The most promising part of the 1964 spring training concerned two youngsters who were not even carried north. Casey had spotted a little shortstop named Derrel McKinley "Bud" Harrelson in the first week of camp and wondered if he had the nerve to keep the youngster, who had only one year of low minor-league ball. But Weiss intended to let the skinny young man work his way slowly through the system, and Stengel sadly dispatched him to the minor-league camp.

The other prospect was Ron Swoboda, a muscular outfielder who had been signed off the University of Maryland and had not yet played in a professional game. Swoboda had tremendous power and energy. The elderly Duke Snider giggled when he saw this young brute do push-ups after a strenuous practice. Casey again wondered if he dared to keep the brawny rookie, perhaps remembering how he had kept the young Mickey Mantle in 1951. But then somebody reminded Casey that Swoboda did not exactly resemble Mantle, particularly in the outfield, so Casey sadly shuffled Swoboda off to the Buffalo camp. The Youth of America was still in the future.

For 1964, Casey would have to content himself with some new players who were not particularly young. The new workhorse of the staff was Jack Fisher, a hefty right-hander who had been a promising Baltimore pitcher several years before. "Fat Jack" had distinguished himself by allowing Ted Williams' last homer in 1960 and Roger Maris' sixtieth homer in 1961. He was a willing worker who picked up where Roger Craig left off.

Craig had been traded to the Cardinals for George Altman, a tall outfielder who always seemed to terrorize the Mets. Altman was a soft-spoken man with a college education and he figured to give the Mets some needed polish. But he pulled a muscle early in the spring and would never really be able to help the club, no matter how hard he tried.

Just before the season opened, the Mets unloaded the former Duke of Flatbush, sending Snider to the Giants, where he could pinch-hit and grow old gracefully.

The Mets then demonstrated they were vastly improved by taking only five games to post their first victory, as Alvin Jackson shut out the Pirates. Then they went into a little slump. When Bill Wakefield, a rookie, lost to Cincinnati in the first night game at Shea, the Mets' record was 3–16. It was time for some kind of change.

The biggest weakness seemed to be at shortstop, where Al Moran and Amado Samuel couldn't hit or field. So George Weiss made one of the best deals in Met history, sending Jay Hook— by now a thoroughly shell-shocked pitcher—to the Milwaukee Braves for Roy McMillan, a spindly old shortstop with scars all over him.

McMillan was not a big name in New York, where fans had idolized Phil Rizzuto and Pee Wee Reese and Alvin Dark. The new shortstop had played his entire big-league career in Cincinnati and Milwaukee, where the communications media had never quite noticed his brilliance.

"Guys from other clubs used to ask me how come Mac made those great plays against only them," chuckled Ted Kluszewski, the old Cincinnati slugger. "I told them, 'Hell, he makes those plays against everybody.'"

When McMillan arrived, he was almost thirty-four and he looked ten years older. He had suffered numerous arm and back injuries, leaving him with an odd sidearm delivery. He looked as if he were pushing the ball, but it always arrived at first base in time. "He can thow," Casey pronounced, omitting the "R" as he usually did.

McMillan seemed to be compensating for the stereotyped gabby Texan, because he didn't talk much at all. When reporters made jokes about the hapless Mets, McMillan blinked from behind his thick glasses. He would not rebuke anybody for laughing, but he would not join the laughter, either. The only thing he knew in baseball was competence, and he transmitted this feeling to some of the other Mets.

In 1964, McMillan would bat only .211 with twenty-five runs-batted-in and one homer, but he was clearly the most valuable player on the team. He sacrificed runners to second, he chopped grounders to the right side to advance runners to third, he held the infield together, he saved runs for the pitchers. At isolated moments, for a few brief seconds, he pulled the Mets up to respectability. His old admirers like Kluszewski said, "You should have seen Mac when he was young." But the old McMillan was better than anything the Mets had known.

This new season in Shea seemed destined for many wild days and nights, but one of the earliest highlights came in Chicago, where the Mets had always known some slight success. On May 26, the Mets took advantage of friendly breezes, bright sun, and the soft Cub pitching staff to defeat the Cubs, 19–1. The Mets made twenty-three hits that day.

That evening, a newspaper in Waterbury, Connecticut, received a telephone call from a fan. "Hey, I hear the Mets scored nineteen runs today," the fan said.

"That's right," the operator replied.

"But did they win?"

They could have used some of those runs a few days later on May 31, when they played a Sunday doubleheader against the Giants. This day also marked the return of Ed Kranepool, who had been farmed out to Buffalo once again to regain his batting stroke. Kranepool played in a doubleheader in Buffalo on Saturday night, making six hits. Then he flew to New York in the morning, stopping only for a roll and coffee. There were 57,037 fans in Shea as Kranepool walked out to first base.

The Mets lost the first game, 5–3, and fell behind in the second game. But Joe Christopher tied it with a homer in the seventh, and the Mets and Giants struggled on into extra innings. After the first few extra innings, a spirit of adventure developed in the ball park as most of the fans tried to stick it out until the end.

In the evening, John Daly began the television program *What's My Line?* by saying: "I've just been watching the most incredible ball game. The Mets and Giants are in the twentieth inning." The next sound his producers heard was the click-click-click of people switching to the marathon Met game.

The players were rooting for the game to last twenty-seven innings so they could say they played the equivalent of four games in one day. The major-league record was twenty-six innings for one game. But in the twenty-third inning, Galen Cisco gave up a triple to Jim Davenport, an intentional walk, and run-scoring singles to Del Crandall and Jesus Alou.

In the bottom of the twenty-third, the seventy-three-year-old manager was still delivering his "whommy" to the Giants, but it was no use. The Mets lost the second game, 8–6, but it took seven hours and twenty-three minutes, the longest game in history. When the doubleheader ended at 11:20 P.M., the players had been working for nine hours and fifty-two minutes. But Ed Kranepool was disappointed.

"I wish it had gone longer," Kranepool sighed. "I always wanted to play in a game that started in May and ended in June."

There were some surprises in June, too. On Father's Day, June 21, Jim Bunning of the Philadelphia Phillies brought his wife and oldest daughter to town for a tour of the World's Fair after he pitched the first game of a doubleheader at Shea. Bunning had some magic ability to turn himself on whenever he pitched, and this day he was snorting more fire than ever.

"Boys, watch Jim Bunning today," manager Gene Mauch said, as he observed his ace during warm-ups. "He's going to pitch a special game today."

Mauch was so right. Bunning pitched a perfect game against the Mets, only the eighth perfect game in history. Even the 32,026 fans in Shea were rooting for Bunning near the end, as he threw a strike past young John Stephenson. Then Bunning began the really strenuous part of his day—answering questions, giving interviews, rushing into New York to appear on the *Ed Sullivan Show*. His wife and daughter didn't get to see the World's Fair with him that day.

The next honor belonged to Ron Hunt, the tough second baseman, who had shouted and fought his way onto the Mets in 1963. This year Hunt was voted by the players as the All-Star second

baseman, giving him a chance to start in the All-Star game at
Shea. The National League won when John Callison of the
Phillies hit a homer, but the Met fans were more thrilled at seeing a Met in the starting lineup. Hunt was the first young star
the Mets ever had, and he earned every honor that came to him.

He was the product of a broken home, and he had been raised
mostly by his grandparents, alternating between the streets of
St. Louis and the farmlands of Missouri. He picked up the
resourcefulness of both a country boy and a city boy, playing
rough and knowing how to protect himself, but beneath the gruff
exterior there was a warm and grateful young man.

"I just hope I can hang around here until we get into the
World Series," he said one day. "Look at the way these fans are
now. Can you imagine what it would be like if we ever won the
pennant? They wouldn't let us go home. It would be wild."

Of all the Mets who passed through in those first few years,
Hunt seemed closest to the ideal of a World Series ball player.
He couldn't know it at the time, but it would take a series of
trades, beginning with him, to build the Mets to the fantasy level
of contenders.

Hunt batted .303 in 1964 and was the most popular player
on the Mets. But not even Hunt and McMillan could keep the
Mets from their eventual destiny.

"We're gonna finish thirtieth," Casey moaned, meaning tenth
for the third straight season.

Old faces came and went. Frank Thomas was peddled to the
Phillies. Frank Lary was purchased from the Tigers, pitched
thirteen games and was shipped to the Braves. Craig Anderson
came back, lost another game to make it nineteen straight, then
was dispatched forever. Burright, Harkness, Moran, Samuel,
Hook—all were weighed in the balance and found wanting.

Other new faces appeared—Hawk Taylor, a catcher with some
power; Charlie Smith, a streaky third baseman who hit twenty
homers; Fisher with his 10–17 durability; Wakefield, the bright
Stanford boy who replaced Bearnarth as the ace of the bullpen.

Even two of Casey's familiar "frauds" had good seasons. Chris
Cannizzaro, a catcher who had been shuttling around for two
seasons, batted .311 in sixty games before hurting a leg. Joe
Christopher took extensive instruction from coach Sheriff Robin-

son and finished the season with a .300 average. Kranepool raised his average to .257 after the tearful two-week banishment to Buffalo.

The attendance at Shea was 1,732,597 as the Mets finished their last game there. Then they went on the road for the final weekend with fifty-one victories, their total of 1963. Their last three games were in St. Louis, and the Cardinals were fighting for a pennant. If the Mets should lose all three, it could be said they had not improved at all in 1964.

On a dark, strange Friday night in St. Louis, the Mets picked up their fifty-second victory as Alvin Jackson shut out Bob Gibson, 1–0, on a base hit by Kranepool. The Cardinals rushed home to worry about that loss, but they only had a few hours. They were due back in old Busch Stadium early in the morning. The Saturday game was to be played at noon because of the annual parade of the Veiled Prophet, one of the major events in St. Louis, which would take place later in the afternoon.

Blinking in the strange noon sunshine, the Cardinals seemed to have the staggers. Altman, Christopher, Bobby Klaus, Kranepool, and Smith all hit homers—tying the Met record for one game—and Tommy Parson relieved Fisher for a 15–5 victory.

One more victory and perhaps the Mets could knock the Cardinals out of a pennant, but on the last Sunday Gibson came back with one day of rest to help beat the Mets, 11–5, and win the pennant.

"The Mets let me down," moaned Chico Ruiz of the also-ran Cincinnati Reds. "They only beat the Cardinals two out of three." The pixie Ruiz had expected the Mets to sweep all three.

The two victories did put the Mets ahead of their 1963 pace, however, and thirteen ahead of their 1962 pace. But they finished tenth again, behind Houston for the third straight season, and a few voices of criticism were heard.

There was no point in criticizing the players, who obviously had their own problems, and few fans cared to blame the National League owners for stacking the deck against the Mets, or blame Weiss for concentrating on old players. No, anybody who was dissatisfied with the Mets' progress found one easily identifiable target to aim at. It was the Slickest Manager in Baseball.

13

TRAVELS WITH CASEY

◆

WHEN THE SECOND GUESSING STARTED in 1964, Casey was still not booed extensively at the ball park. Met fans were still too deep in their euphoria to become nasty, as Jet fans and football Giant fans often became.

But privately, in living rooms and offices and taverns, when people talked about the Mets they looked for a scapegoat, and most often the scapegoat was Casey.

"Casey's too old," they said. "The parade's passed him by. He sleeps in the dugout. He doesn't know his players' names. He's more interested in funny remarks than in winning. He likes old players. He won't give kids a chance. He thinks he's still managing the Yankees the way he shuffles men around. He never was a good manager back in Brooklyn and Boston."

The critical fans got their ammunition from several sources. Few reporters could find anything to pin on Casey, but one rugged opponent was the talented broadcaster for the American Broadcasting Company, Howard Cosell.

A highly intelligent former lawyer, Cosell repeatedly attacked Casey as a selfish man who cared only about making jokes, a master salesman who survived because he mesmerized the press by doling out funny lines, making their jobs easier. Cosell frequently called for Casey's ouster, but his campaign could be seen as something other than enlightened comment. Sometimes the best way to make a reputation is to criticize the biggest target in town.

Another frequent critic was Jackie Robinson, another intelligent and highly opinionated man who would occasionally get headlines by accusing Casey of "sleeping on the bench" and making fun of his players. Evidently, Robinson had been stung by Casey when he was a Dodger and his resentments stayed with him. Casey laughed off Robinson's comments by snapping: "Tell Robi'son he's Chock Full of Nuts." (A reference to Robinson's one-time employer.)

From time to time there would be sniping at Casey in his own clubhouse, like when Frank Thomas carried on a whispering campaign that Casey was not using the right men or the right strategy. But clubhouse lawyers are everywhere, and the criticisms often seemed to conflict:

Casey wouldn't give young players a chance; Casey would not pick a lineup of experienced players and stick with them; Casey did not know his players; Casey played personalities.

And yet—considering the depths the Mets plumbed for those first three years, there was very little open criticism of Casey. No player ever directly confronted Casey, as happens on other teams. No Met player ever made a direct statement of "play me or trade me," partially because nobody was having enough success to consider such a blast. But a truly antagonistic manager who finished thirtieth would have touched off all sorts of wars of liberation.

In recent years, Dick Williams and Carl Yastrzemski could not get along in Boston; the Pittsburgh Pirates held clubhouse meetings without manager Harry Walker; Billy Martin and Dave Boswell of Minnesota fought in the street in the middle of the night. By contrast, Casey ran a happy ship.

One reason why the players did not revolt was that Casey had changed his approach after leaving the Yankees. He had openly sniped at most of his players on the Yankees when he felt they weren't producing. But he realized that the Mets were merely living up—or down—to their potential and he was much too sensitive to whip them. Occasionally he would try to prod a quiet underachiever like Jim Hickman or try to goad Ed Kranepool into instant maturity. But most of the time Casey was gentle and considerate. When pressed for a reason for the Mets' failure, he blamed the other owners who had rigged the expansion draft.

"When I get into the World Series, I am going to give my share to the other owners," he said. "I will make sure that Mr. Niss gets them good tickets at the World Series because they were so wonderful to us."

No matter what Weiss and Stengel tried, it did not work. Casey constantly threatened to "back up the moving van," and the Mets led the league in player changes. But young or old, they just didn't produce. If the Mets came up with a Snider or an Altman, he would inevitably show his age or hurt himself, and Casey would grumble (along with his critics) that he probably should have been going with his younger players.

So he would experiment with a youngster like Kranepool, only to see the first big bonus player victimized by older pitchers, fall into slumps, begin to sulk, fail to hustle. Then Casey would grumble (along with his critics) that he probably should have been going with older players.

If anything, Casey's instincts drew him toward the Youth of America. He dared to start the eighteen-year-old Kranepool in right field on opening day in 1963. He sadly farmed out young Bud Harrelson in 1964 and later insisted that McMillan was basically a splendid caretaker at shortstop "until Harrelson is ready." It was Casey who heard Ron Hunt screaming for the relay throw in an intrasquad game. It was Casey who got two good years out of personable "Big Ben," Larry Bearnarth. It was Casey who dared to dream of Jerry Hinsley and Bill Wakefield, Ronnie Locke and Grover Powell, the strong young arms in the Youth of America.

The trouble was, the Youth of America could not be purchased overnight. Weiss had been against spending big bonuses with the Yankees, but now Mrs. Payson and M. Donald Grant assured him that it was all right. They were even willing to spend $500,000 for a Willie Davis or a Joe Torre—maybe even a million dollars for Willie Mays if the Giants dared—but money alone could not purchase good major-league players. The only way was to sign young prospects and wait for them to develop, and time was not on the side of Casey Stengel.

But if he might not be managing when the Youth of America finally arrived, at least Casey could build something durable. He could make the New York Mets into a popular national institution. And this he started in the spring of 1962 by signing autographs with the legend "Join the Mets." He carried on the crusade in his twenty waking hours a day, chatting with people, making them overlook the current dreadful record.

Even as his critics began harpooning him in 1964, Casey was the heart and soul of the franchise. Without him, the fans would still have come, the sponsor would still have put the club on television, the players would have been no better or no worse, the writers would still have stayed on the beat. But with him, the entire Met scene was a joyful, optimistic happening. For some people, it might have been the best years of their working lives.

Things happened around Casey that did not happen on other teams. His wit and perception made them happen. Also through Casey, millions of people got inside baseball, got inside a strain of America that they never would have visited with all the prosaic managers. For Casey became more than a manager in his years with the Mets. He became a great novel personified, a picaresque wanderer, a Tom Jones, a Don Quixote, a Huckleberry Finn. I had the privilege of traveling with Casey in those early years. I wrote about one of those trips for *Newsday*:

"A couple of years ago, author John Steinbeck drove off in a panel truck to see America. He brought with him a dog named Charley with whom he claimed, as lovers of dumb beasts will, a mystical communion.

"The result was an earnest little travelogue concerning the faces and attitudes of the people. The book was called *Travels With Charley*, and it promoted Steinbeck the Nobel Prize he had earned some three decades before (for *The Grapes of Wrath*).

"Well, there are no Steinbecks traveling with the Mets, and the only dogs around the club are the rejects from other baseball teams. But the Met reporters have their own affable companion on their long trips through the land—a gay bowser of seventy-three named Charles Dillon Stengel.

"Casey is a seasoned traveler who thrives on the same hard-ships that wear down men fifty years younger. Each return to a city is a challenge to Casey. He collars the first cab driver or bell-boy he meets and asks what has been built, torn down, improved, or altered since his last trip. He displays a true tourist's curiosity toward restaurants, joints, hotels, parks, roads, and bridges. And he never forgets the faces of people he has met in his cities."

The trip went something like this: April 24—Casey is used to crowds but not the mobs in front of the Pittsburgh Hilton. He thinks this is truly an amazing reception for a team with a record of 1–5. But then somebody informs Casey that the crowds are for another veteran traveler named Lyndon Baines Johnson, who is making a flying visit to Appalachia to promote his twin crusades against poverty and the Republican Party.

Casey surveys the milling crowds. "He wanted to see poverty," Casey snorts. "So he came to see my team."

The players smile at this remark but inside the Hilton it is not so funny. The hotel has forgotten to make up the rooms, so they have to walk the lobby for an hour or two. The young players want to rest before the game, but the seventy-three-year-old manager is more interested in capturing the hearts and minds of the population.

"Yes, yes, I'd love to get you all tickets," he says, winking at a bellhop. "But I'm afraid it's a sellout. They always sell out when my Metsies come to town."

Forbes Field is not sold out this night, but 13,117 fans have bought the cut-rate tickets for Teen-Ager Night. The rock band turns the youngsters on, and they roam through the park singing and cheering. Some of them smash electric bulbs and there are a few muggings in the restrooms. The Mets peer nervously out of their dugout and go down placidly, 9–4, to the biggest neme-sis, Bob Friend. Casey seems thankful for surviving.

"They looked like they was never in this ball park before," he sighs. "We had to push a couple out of the dugout near the end."

April 25—This game is close but Fisher loses, 5–4, and Casey is mad. He bursts out of the clubhouse and stomps toward the team bus, through the concession area with its oily popcorn odor. His shiny suit picks up dirt as he brushes against the filthy walls.

"Casey, Casey, give us your autograph," three young men shout. "We're from Long Island. We made a banner out of our window shade at college."

Casey stops and looks at them. "Is that right?" he asks. "What college?"

"St. Francis of Loretto," says Mike Asselta of Farmingdale.

"Where's that?"

"Eighty miles away," says Tom Cooper of Northport.

"You came eighty miles away to see my Mets?" Casey blusters. "Well then I gotta sign your window shade."

He scribbles "Join the Mets, big bonus for everybody" and hands it to Tom McCloskey of Brentwood. Then he stomps into the bus and stares off into space, still mad about losing.

April 26—The Mets lose the opener, 4–3, as Larry Bearnarth fails in relief. But in the second game, Tracy Stallard takes a 3–0 lead into the ninth inning, and Casey knows he has a real chance to win a game.

But the Pirates score one quick run and dangerous left-handed Jerry Lynch is due to bat. Casey waves in twenty-two-year-old Ron Locke, a squeaky-voiced former shipyard worker from Rhode Island, who has never pitched in a major-league game.

The Pirates counter with another of their fine pinch hitters, right-handed Gene Freese. Casey must use Locke for at least one hitter, so he crosses his fingers and holds his breath.

Freese has been waiting to play for six hours today, so he swings at the first pitch, a fastball over the middle of the plate, and he slams a long fly to left field. Kanehl rubs his back against the 391-foot sign and catches the ball as a run scores. But now there are two outs and Casey comes running out of the dugout to bring in a right-handed pitcher for the final out. As he reaches the mound, Casey says to Locke: "Nice pitch."

Ed Bauta gets the last out and the Mets win, 3–2. On the plane to St. Louis, Casey takes a brief nap. But when they arrive at the Chase Hotel, Casey perks up again. St. Louis is a special city for him. It is downstate from Kansas City, his home town. He was married in Belleville, Illinois, just outside St. Louis. He has many friends in St. Louis, and tonight he is surrounded by twenty people in the lobby of the Chase Hotel.

"I knew your brother," a man says.

Casey is off and running. Lou Niss, twelve years younger than Casey, stands in a corner, reading a newspaper. The Mets' road secretary is exhausted.

"I like to stay up with him," Niss says, "but I just can't make it. Casey, I'll see you in the morning."

"Yass, yass," Casey jokes. "Mr. Niss has had a tough day. Mr. Niss flew our airplane from Pittsburgh. Did a fine job. He deserves the rest."

April 27—No game today, so the Mets organize a party for the press at Stan Musial's restaurant. Casey sits at the head of the table and monopolizes the conversation.

Musial, who had retired before this season, is visiting his restaurant tonight and he asks if everything is all right. Casey makes a face as if he had a bellyache, then pulls Musial into a chair next to him.

"I was managing in Boston," Stengel recalls, nodding at Musial, "I see this guy in batting practice and I know he can't hit the snake (the curve ball). I tell all my pitchers to throw him the snake, see? So this guy hits three doubles off my pitchers and I tell them, 'Forget about the snake.'"

Musial cackles his shy, modest laughter.

"You figured I had a chance to make it, huh, Case?"

Now the reporters tease Casey into doing his annual imitation of the shuffling penguin walk of Lou Niss, complete with holding his elbow to his waist, with a cigarette lighter sticking out at a forty-five-degree angle. Everybody laughs, including Niss.

The next stop is the Chase Club back at the hotel, where Robert Goulet is opening tonight. Casey blusters into the room and is greeted by a tall, well-built headwaiter.

"This guy used to pitch batting practice for me but I told him to get into another business," Casey says.

The headwaiter leads us to a table alongside the stage.

"Excuse me, excuse me," Casey says as we squeeze through

the crowd. "We're all reporters with the New York Mets. We're slick young reporters from New York."

Robert Goulet, dark and trim and bright-eyed, enters the stage from the other side. He is working his way around the stage, singing a romantic ballad in an act that has been designed for little old ladies in fur coats. But when he reaches our table he looks down and sees only men—one of them a wrinkled old man with elephant ears.

Goulet jumps back and holds his hands in the air. Can it be? he thinks. He peers back into the darkness. The old man with the elephant ears stares back at Goulet. The singer is trying to stay with the lyrics, but the band is winning the race.

Goulet grins like a little boy, bows down to one knee, a genuflecting reflex from his days in *Camelot*. He tries to remember the lyrics, but he is lost.

"Ladies and gentlemen," he says. "I know there's a lot of Cardinal fans in the room tonight but I'm a Met fan. I always have been. And in the room with me is the greatest Met of them all. I just know he's going to beat your Cardinals tomorrow night. Ladies and gentlemen, I love this man—Casey Stengel!"

The audience rustles and flutters and applauds. Casey is grinning now, as the spotlight encompasses him and Goulet. Then the crowd hushes because Casey seems ready to speak.

"Yass, thank you, thank you," he says, waving at Goulet. "He's just like me. He has ef-feminine appeal."

The people understand that Casey means the ladies love him just as they love Goulet. They laugh again, then Goulet resumes his act, avoiding our corner for fear of losing his concentration again.

After the show, Casey invites us to drink with him in the Carousel Lounge. Most of the reporters want to go to sleep, but Casey wants to talk about his team.

"Well, let me ask you something, why wouldn't you play Kranepool?" He begins in his Socratic questioning style. "Listen. He's only nineteen and he runs like he's thirty, but who else do I have? That's right. That's what I'm trying to tell you."

And on and on. All of it is interesting, but it is late.

April 28—Casey is up at 8 A.M. on five hours' sleep. He meets two of his young players, Jerry Hinsley and John Stephenson, in the lobby after breakfast. Hinsley is an apple-cheeked young- ster from Las Cruces, New Mexico, who throws as hard as a young Bob Feller. Casey has high hopes for him.

"I want to ask you a few questions," Casey begins. He invites them to his suite and keeps them for an hour and a half, talking baseball. Later they say they understand almost everything he said. That night the Mets lose, 8–0, but Hinsley pitches well in relief.

April 29—The unfortunate Bearnarth is whacked in the hip by a hard ground ball as the Mets lose again in the late innings. Casey has very little to say.

April 30—The Mets travel to Cincinnati on the day off and Casey disappears in the evening to watch the Reds-Phillies game on television in his room. This is part of his secret for staying up so late most nights. Some people are secret drinkers. Casey is a secret sleeper. Every so often he gets a good dinner and a good night's sleep. Then he is set for a week.

May 1—The Mets lose again, to make their record 2–11. There is not much gaiety and light around Casey tonight.

May 2—On a bright afternoon, Alvin Jackson beats the Reds with a two-hitter and Casey rides again. "Hey, Hinsley, you see that?" he shouts. "Very easy, wasn't it, Hinsley? That is called a win, Hinsley. A victory. Nothing to it."

At night the writers repay Stengel for his company in St. Louis with a dinner at a German restaurant. Five boisterous salesmen at the next table shout that they are Met fans. Casey lifts his beer stein and offers a toast to the Youth of America. Ve may finish tirtieth," he says. "But ve vill go down mitt honor."

May 3—The Mets lose a doubleheader, but Casey never loses his fans. A hundred people are waiting outside the clubhouse after the game. Casey signs a dozen autographs, then decides he has done enough. He breaks into a trot up the steep cement incline, dodging and feinting past youngsters, like Buddy Young giving the swivel hip to a tackler. One little boy falls to the ground while trying to keep up with Casey. Other children pat the old man on his solid back. Thump, thump.

Casey sleeps on the flight to Milwaukee. When we arrive, he

sits up front next to the driver of our chartered bus and learns that one of his favorite restaurants has been torn down to make room for an apartment house.

"Geez, whaddaya know," Casey mutters.

May 4—The Mets lose on the last play of the game when Ron Hunt tries to sneak home but is tagged out by burly Ed Bailey. The two men collide and Bailey takes a swing at Hunt. Both teams pour onto the field for one of those milling-about baseball fights.

Denis Menke, the Braves' shortstop, is trying to stay out of trouble when he feels a pair of strong arms clamp him from behind. Menke twists to get free. His assailant falls down and Menke looks to see who it was. There under a tangle of legs is the Slickest Manager in Baseball. Menke sees the headline in the newspaper: "Menke Kills Casey Stengel." He reaches down and helps the manager up. Stengel's face is red and he is ripping mad. Finally the "fight" is ended.

In the clubhouse, Casey denies being on the field but the players wink and confirm that the seventy-three-year-old man was right in the middle of the action.

"I laughed so hard when I saw Casey that I couldn't hit anybody," Tracy Stallard says.

Casey is defending Hunt for trying to race home on the grounder to short.

"Sure, he took a chance," Casey roars, so all his players can hear him. "Sure, he ran into the catcher. What did you want him to do, get tagged like a goddamn fairy? We got enough guys on the team who'll tippy-toe up to the catcher and say, 'Oooh, pardon me, I'm out.'"

We work late on our stories this night and get back to the hotel expecting the evening to be over. But there in the lobby is our friend, looking for somebody to talk to. We take him to the Casino, an old favorite joint down the street, where we replay the fight. Casey still denies being on the field.

Casey prefers to change the subject by reminiscing with the bartender about 1944 when he managed the minor-league Milwaukee Brewers.

"We had a tornado and it blew me across the street," Casey

tells us. He gets off his bar stool and imitates himself being caught in the wind. He looks like Peter Pan.

The bar closes and our party of eight repairs to a sleazy rib joint across the street. As it happens at closing time in every city, the dregs of humanity flush out of the bars and into the all-night restaurants. Tonight there are some hoods with shaggy hair (remember, this is before the gentle, long-haired hippie movement) and motorcycle jackets. They look like trouble. We eye them nervously. Then one of the hoods spots Casey Stengel.

The hood's girl friend, who looks to be sixteen years old, prods him into getting Stengel's autograph. We cringe when he comes close but he starts by saying: "Please, Mr. Stengel . . ."

Casey asks the girl's name, so he can write a personal message. The other hoods wander over. One of them says, "Hey, I hear you guys may make a trade with the Braves."

Casey regards the youths as if they were John McHale, the president of the Braves. "Now, you want to give me McMillan, who is thirty-three, and we don't know if he can throw. Then who do you want, Hook? Hook has won a lot of games for me and he has a lovely family. Edna says I can't trade him. Would you like to talk to Edna for me?"

The questioner gapes, surprised that Casey would give him a meaningful answer to a bold question. His friends nod with respect. They bid Casey good night. Then they retire to their section of the room. The reporters relax. They also remember Casey's answer about the proposed trade. So, there is some truth to it, after all. Finally, around 4 A.M., Casey and his friends return to the hotel. Casey buys a paper and disappears.

May 5—The players whisper that Casey is sore from being knocked down in the fight, but he puts up a good front. The Mets lose again, to make their record 3–15. It is a dreary way to start the season, but at least the Mets have their fans. A group of Marquette students has carried Met banners in the left-field bleachers all game. Afterward, they wait outside the Met clubhouse, cheering Casey and the former Brave, Hawk Taylor. They roar "Let's Go Mets" as the bus pulls away to the airport. The players seem to have forgotten their miseries for the moment as we head for home.

Without Casey, would it ever be possible to forget their miseries? Would the fans be able to love this team under a more grim administration? Would high school players be lured by the bonus money from a dismal team if they didn't know about Casey's "Youth of America?" At times it seems that Casey is playing it only for laughs. But some of us know what he is building, and we are proud to be here while he is building it. Nothing that will happen in the future—the far future, we assume—would be quite so meaningful if there had not been a Casey Stengel to create the Mets.

14

YOGI, SPAHNIE, AND A BROKEN HIP

◆

AFTER THREE YEARS of managing this awful team and finishing thirtieth, Casey had every right to retire and it is quite possible he was thinking about it. But two conditions held him back.

For one thing, Casey wanted to lead the Mets out of last place before he retired, so he could finish on the upswing. For another, there were rumors of managerial roulette going around in late 1964, and Casey wanted to beat the odds—and the sharpshooters. He was able to laugh off the occasional Howard Cosell or Jackie Robinson or the former player who accused him of "sleeping in the dugout." But when Casey heard the whispers about candidates to succeed him as manager, he may have decided to stick around another year, just for the fun of it.

Casey may have felt the chill breeze from San Francisco, where Alvin Dark had gotten himself in trouble with the owner, Horace Stoneham. Dark had gotten the Giants some uncomfortable publicity for indiscreetly voicing his rather bizarre socio-anthropological views of the mental capacities of his Negro and Latin players. But more important to Stoneham, Dark had refused to socialize with the gregarious owner of the Giants.

With the Giants about to finish fourth in 1964, Dark's admirers were looking for a soft spot for him to land.

M. Donald Grant and G. Herbert Walker of the Mets' Board may have been partial to the former Giants' shortstop. But when Casey decided to come back, there wasn't much they could do. Dan Topping had bungled the Yankees' image for a generation when he fired the Old Man in 1960, then handed him the microphone. The Mets could not afford to make the same mistake, and they did not do it. With a week left in the 1964 season, Casey let Weiss know he wanted to come back and he was rehired immediately.

"You'd think they was trying to put me in a museum," Casey snapped to the reporters about the rumors about his retirement. "But you don't see me going for no museums, do ya? And if you look it up, nobody else in here is getting younger while I'm the only one getting older."

If defiance of old age was to be the symbol of 1965, the Mets came up with some ancient playmates for the Old Man. First, Yogi Berra was mysteriously fired by the Yankees after merely managing them into the seventh game of the World Series. Weiss and Stengel eagerly snapped up their prize prodigy.

"Mr. Berra always knew the pitchers and he liked to talk to the batters, and besides which he got them into the World Series, so you'd have to say he ain't failed yet," Stengel said. "Besides, maybe he can still swing the bat for me."

A month later, the Mets obtained another elderly star, Warren Spahn of the Milwaukee Braves. The great left-hander was hired to be a pitcher and a pitching coach.

Yogi and Spahnie, the odd couple. Spring training of 1965 turned into a circus as Casey tried to squeeze one more season out of both of them, with exactly opposite reactions.

Yogi had not played in 1964 as he managed the Yankees, and he had clearly lost his great competitive desire. When Casey pressed him into some exhibitions, Yogi swung halfheartedly at bad pitches and tried to force his body into shape.

Spahn was just the opposite of Yogi. He was going on forty-four, he was balding and wrinkled, and his large hooked nose made him look like a pelican that has been swooping down on the sea since time began. Spahnie was one tough old bird. His body was still strong and his arm was still alive and his will to succeed was tremendous.

Few athletes have even been so caught up in their own achievements as Spahn. He stayed in the game not only for his love of money but also for his love of statistics. He was always chasing Christy Mathewson in one category or Grover Cleveland Alexander in another. He wanted to be first in every pitching statistic in the book—even if he had to pitch until he was sixty. And with his determination, that seemed quite likely.

In his last few years in Milwaukee, Spahn had begun to lose almost as many games as he won. Manager Bobby Bragan wanted to give his younger pitchers a chance but found it impossible with Spahn dominating the scene. That was why the Mets were able to acquire him rather easily.

In spring training, the new pitcher-coach gave himself the most favorable pitching assignments, letting the other pitchers fall into line behind him. One day the pitchers were scheduled to spend an hour practicing their sliding in a sand pit behind left field. Spahn appointed Gary Melvin Kroll, a hulking and religious youngster, who for some reason he persisted in calling "Hall," to supervise the drill while Spahn pitched batting practice.

When asked for the pitching rotation for the early exhibitions, Spahn fumbled through a notebook and grumbled, "Cisco . . . and Wakefield . . . and Hall . . . and, uh, hasn't Casey given all this to you? Maybe tomorrow I'll be Coach Spahn, but right now I'm Pitcher Spahn and I'm not helping anyone sitting around in my wet sweat shirt."

Spahn worked himself into keen pitching shape, far ahead of his other pitchers, but he had a positive affect on many players for a while. If this was how a great player was—haughty, insensitive, single-minded—the other players decided they would give it a try. They overlooked the fact that Spahn had a unique temperament and also a magnificent body and a great arm.

Just before the Mets headed north in 1965, history repeated itself like bad goulash, when Weiss reacquired Frank Lary, the old Detroit bulldog who had pitched for the Mets in 1964.

When reporters tried to figure this deal out, it became apparent that Lary had been loaned to Milwaukee for some sort of pennant drive but was now being returned. Or had Lary been traded for himself, like Harry Chiti back in 1962?

There were other changes in 1965. Hot Rod Kanehl had been released as a player and the Mets had not been able to find a suitable job in their organization for the personable handyman. He would have made an excellent coach or minor-league manager immediately, but they were too busy with their reclamation project on Spahn to keep Kanehl in the organization.

In two off-season deals, the Mets had traded George Altman to the Cubs for Billy Cowan, a young outfielder, and traded Tracy Stallard to the Cardinals for pitcher Gordon Richardson and outfielder Johnny Lewis.

There was also a new look in public relations men in 1965. Tom Meany, the old reporter, had handled the job for the first two seasons but he was in ill health. Then Herb Heft came over from the Minnesota Twins in 1964 before taking a job with the Baltimore Bullets basketball team in 1965. By a sad coincidence, both Meany and Heft died soon after moving on to other jobs.

The new publicist in 1965 was Harold Weissman, the former sports editor of the defunct New York *Mirror*. Harold had a million contacts in sports and was a twenty-four-hour man on his job. He also had a young assistant named Matt Winnick. One more step had been taken in the building of a dynasty.

Also in 1965, Ron Swoboda made his debut after a year in the minor leagues. The muscular young man obviously had trouble catching fly balls but Casey insisted on keeping him for his power. Swoboda hit a pinch-homer off Turk Farrell in his second at-bat, and Casey started using him regularly. Soon the fans at Shea had their biggest hero since Marvelous Marv.

RON SWOBODA IS STRONGER THAN DIRT, one banner proclaimed, making him sound like a miracle detergent. As a new, improved version of Marvelous Marv, the ex-rookie had his imperfections. One game he would never forget came in St. Louis on May 23 in alternating rain and sunshine.

The Mets somehow took a 7–2 lead into the ninth inning, when an error by McMillan set up two Cardinal runs. Then the champions loaded the bases as Bearnarth pitched to weak-hitting Dal Maxvill. Bearnarth got Maxvill to hit a soft fly to right field—toward Swoboda—and there was a problem. The rookie had forgotten to bring his sunglasses out with him after the last rain delay and now the sun was shining brightly, directly into his eyes. He groped under the ball, blinded by the sun. At the last moment he fell to his knees, the ball plopping only a few feet away, as three runs scored on the tainted "triple."

Swoboda was so disgusted when the inning was finally over that he stomped on a batting helmet, catching his spikes in the shattered plastic, and he hopped around the dugout like a one-legged rooster. Stengel snarled at him and ordered him out of the game. The Mets lost a few innings later in a ghastly afternoon for Swoboda.

However, Casey played him the next day and kept him in the lineup. The young man hit fifteen homers until the pitchers began throwing him curves and change-ups at mid-season. He finished the season with nineteen and Casey kept him in the lineup, poor fielding or not.

Other experiments went even less well. Berra played briefly but was delighted when they told him he could be a coach again. The only man who wasn't delighted was Wes Westrum, a former Giant player and coach, who felt he could steal the other team's signals if the Mets let him coach at first base. But Casey wanted to show off Berra, so he made Westrum sit in the dugout, a very good break for Westrum in the long run.

For a while, the Mets were almost respectable as Spahn had a 4–4 record, and the Mets were 20–29 almost one-third through the season. But then Spahn started to lose regularly, and people began wondering how many chances Coach Spahn was going to give Pitcher Spahn in his race to catch Kid Nichols, the tenth leading winner in pitching history.

"Don't go putting words in my mouth," Coach Spahn snapped as he flapped away from the reporters. And from the next locker came the soft Alabama drawl of Frank Lary, Spahn's buddy, who liked to conduct informal critiques of the press.

"That's a stupid question," Lary would comment.

These two hard-bitten old professionals had fallen upon bad

times, and they were setting an example for the impressionable young Mets. For the first time in history, the Met clubhouse became a series of cliques. If the players had effected khaki uniforms and beards, the clubhouse would have resembled Flagler Street in Miami a few days before the 1961 Bay of Pigs invasion when you could smell intrigue in every papaya juice stand.

Some people suspected that Spahn was setting himself up as a potential manager in case Stengel should retire at the end of 1965. It also seemed likely that Spahn would destroy the genial tradition of the Mets if he ever gained more authority. However, on July 8 Lary and his 1–3 record were sold to the White Sox and, on July 19, Spahn and his 4–12 record were given an unconditional release. Their arms had lost their ability, and there seemed no other reason to keep them around.

Spahn was released on a Monday. The following Saturday was Old-Timers Day at Shea Stadium, a particularly happy day for Casey because many of his friends were visiting from all over the country. He watched them cavort in the traditional old-timers game, then he partied with them late into the night.

In the early hours of July 25, with Edna back home in California, Casey decided not to go back to his hotel to sleep. Instead, he accepted an invitation from Joseph DeGregorio, the comptroller of the Mets, to sleep at DeGregorio's house, a few minutes from Shea Stadium.

While getting out of DeGregorio's car, Casey felt a "twinge" in his left hip. As he lay in bed, the pain grew worse. Soon Casey was in Roosevelt Hospital, where Dr. Peter LaMotte, the team physician, recognized a bad break in the neck of the thigh bone, near the ball of the hip joint.

Before the doctor operated, Casey picked Wes Westrum to run the club until he got back. Then the seventy-five-year-old manager was wheeled in for an operation that happens to many people his age. On August 13, Casey was released to his suite at the Essex House.

"There are no severe pains," he told reporters, "and you can say I'm very much on the go. I can stand and dress myself now. In fact, I can do almost everything. The only thing is, I'm still somewhat handicapped with my walking but there's nothing wrong with my feelings."

The Mets continued their dreary way under Westrum and the only suspense about 1965 seemed to be whether the Old Man would ever come back to manage the club.

Two weeks after his release from the hospital, Casey had a consultation with Dr. LaMotte, a trusted friend since the first days of the Mets. The steel ball the doctor had implanted in the hip socket was working perfectly, but Dr. LaMotte made no promises of how the hip would react in the future. By not promising 100 per cent mobility for the next 100 years, the young doctor may have been throwing a gentle hint at his friend that perhaps it was time to retire.

On August 25, Casey called up George Weiss and said, "George, you'd better count me out for next year."

Weiss was not surprised. He was always in the habit of thinking ahead. They waited a few days, just in case Casey wanted to reconsider, but with Edna at his side there was no reconsidering.

On Monday, August 30, the Mets called a press conference in the restaurant of the Essex House. There Casey announced that he was retiring to become a member of the Mets' board and also their West Coast scout. "I want it understood that nobody put pressure on me to resign. I couldn't strut out there to take out a pitcher. There's no time for me to run the club freely. I didn't want to delay the game."

Casey said he had no suggestions about the next manager. "I recommended Mr. Westrum for this year. They will pick a man for next year."

Then he reviewed his years with the Mets.

"I am disappointed in the ball club but I am not disappointed in the staff or the fans. They were wonderful. I'm proud to be connected with this club. When I started, you would have liked to finish higher. I wanted to leave behind eight or nine men who could last ten or twelve years. Well, there's Hunt and I know he's first-division. There's Swoboda, and nobody will laugh at him in a year. The shortstop (McMillan) was wonderful. Then there are some young ones."

And so, with his eye toward the future, the Old Man retired.

Mrs. Joan Payson (right), the majority owner of the Mets, attends the opening game of the World Series in Baltimore. Her tall companion with the sunglasses is New York Mayor John Lindsay.

George Weiss,
first president
of the Mets

M. Donald Grant,
chairman of
the board

John Murphy,
general manager,
1968–69

Bing Devine,
general manager,
1966–67

Wes Westrum,
manager,
1966–67

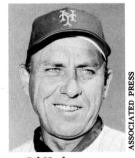

Gil Hodges,
manager
since 1968

Casey Stengel, as a thirty-two-year-old outfielder for the New York Giants in 1922, taking a practice swing in the Polo Grounds

Casey, forty years later, was back in the Polo Grounds trying to explain why his Amazing Mets had lost their first six games in history

The clubhouse before the Mets' first play-off game in Atlanta in 1969, as they calmly watched a few innings of the Baltimore-Minnesota game on television. Seated in the back are (left to right): coach Joe Pignatano; Tom Seaver; coach Yogi Berra; Jerry Koosman; and manager Gil Hodges. Bobby Pfeil has his hand on his face while Nolan Ryan, Tug McGraw, Jack DiLauro, and Jim McAndrew sprawl on the carpet.

Three straight victories over Atlanta and the Mets broke out the champagne. Jerry Grote and Rod Gaspar douse candidate-Mayor John Lindsay.

Jerry Koosman (No. 36) and Tom Seaver (No. 41) shown pitching during the World Series. Koosman is wearing the gray road uniform while winning the second game in Baltimore. Seaver is wearing the white, striped home uniform while winning the fourth game at home.

Tommie Agee makes a diving, skidding catch to save several runs in the third game of the Series. The quiet center fielder had made another spectacular catch earlier in the same game.

*The controversial play that ended the fourth game. Pete Richert's throw hit
J. C. Martin on the left hand as Rod Gaspar raced home from second base. The
photographs show Martin illegally running to the left of the base line.*

Jerry Grote and Jerry Koosman go into victory dance after the last out was made in fifth World Series game. Joining them is Ed Charles.

Perhaps the happiest person in the room was Edna, who had rushed back from California to keep him company as he recuperated. She sat back during his retirement party and said: "Whatever Casey does is all right with me." She knew her man, knew how important it had been for him to come back to the Mets. But now the decision had been made. Now she looked forward to teasing him into taking his therapeutic swims at their pool, to do his exercises, to stay home in his Japanese bedroom, and to help promote the Valley National Bank.

"I know it's going to be rough for Casey to take off the uniform," Edna said, gazing proudly at the tough old man, "but I never wore a uniform."

15

IT'S THAT
AIR-CONDITIONING

◆

WES WESTRUM DRANK HIS THIRD CUP of black coffee. In front of
him were the remains of a ham-and-egg breakfast splattered with
the ashes of his tenth cigarette. His eyes were red and it was
eight o'clock in the morning. The new manager of the Mets
rubbed his knuckles into the remaining strands of hair on his
head. "My hair is falling out."

When the manager spoke, his voice pitched and heaved from
side to side, as if he were talking around a great gas bubble somewhere inside of him. "I can't sleep," he said.

The night before, the Mets had kicked away another game in
the Astrodome in Houston. When we had questioned him right
after the loss, he had started to talk but turned away as a great
gasping sob escaped from him. Now in the morning in the coffee
shop, he seemed embarrassed. "I almost broke down last night,
didn't I? I really wanted to win that one. I would have bet my
wages we would. Then we lose another one.

"I sleep for an hour and then I'm awake again. I have a lousy
cold and I cough a lot. I think it's that air-conditioning."

He had come down for breakfast at 7 A.M. He would return

for lunch at eleven. "I burn up a lot of energy," he said. "More than I used to."

People had always wondered what would happen if a normal human being tried to manage the Mets and now they were finding out. Wesley Noreen Westrum had a fine background as a player and a coach, and no doubt he would have made somebody a fine manager. But there was only one man who could manage the Mets—at this stage of their history—and not have his hair fall out.

Westrum was no stranger to New York, having caught 919 games for the Giants in the Polo Grounds. He had been the regular catcher in the pennant years of 1951 and 1954, and his only bad memory was when Leo Durocher had forced him to play with numerous hand injuries. The bones had never healed correctly, and Westrum had been unable to hold a bat properly, so he blamed Durocher for his lowly career average of .217.

When the Giants moved out to San Francisco, Westrum went with them as a first-base coach who could pick off the opposing team's signals. With a series of whistles, Westrum could tip off the batter what pitch was coming. He felt his value was never appreciated by Alvin Dark, and the two men grew further apart. In 1963, it became apparent that Westrum would not be working for Dark in the future, so a unique trade was arranged with the Mets. Cookie Lavagetto, a native of the Bay Area, was allowed to move to the Giants while Westrum moved to the Mets, the first trade of coaches in baseball history.

Westrum coached first base for the Mets in 1964 and felt he contributed to the hitters with his sign-stealing. He was hurt when Casey installed Berra at first base in 1965, but the move worked in Westrum's favor, because he sat next to Casey in the dugout and helped him keep track of the lineups. When Spahn was dismissed, Westrum was named pitching coach. Then, six days later Casey broke his hip and said from his hospital bed: "Wes is the one."

The dumpy, round-shouldered man thought this was immense good luck for him, but now he was discovering that managing the Mets can do very bad things to a man's health. Undoubtedly, Westrum had always assumed that a little stronger discipline, a little more attention to details, would win an occasional game for the Mets. Any man who has never managed will assume he can sneak a victory here and there. But as soon as he had to press the buttons, Westrum found that the Mets' gears did not work as easily as he had hoped.

Furthermore, Westrum soon realized the immensity of replacing Stengel as a source of news and commentary to the New York press. When he was talking for the record after games, Westrum refused to acknowledge that anybody ever did anything bad. He called his players "Mr. Swoboda" or "Mr. Kranepool," and his comments after a game were limited to a general "Oh, my God, wasn't that awful?"

Once after a close game, Westrum muttered: "Well, that was a cliff-dweller." Of course, Casey had been known to throw a malaprop around too, but his usually were done intentionally.

As a coach, Westrum had often delighted some of the reporters by his great debates with the third-base coach, Don Heffner, a conservative chap who looked remarkably like Barry Goldwater and even thought like him. Heffner believed strongly in the return to the old values and felt that baseball—as well as life in general—had been going downhill rapidly since around 1932. Westrum enjoyed baiting the serious old-timer.

"Back in the good old days, every player could lay down a perfect bunt," Heffner might mutter.

"I don't see much wrong with Mr. Mays or Mr. Mantle," Westrum would retort, winking at his appreciative audience.

The two men had spent many long hours on airplanes and buses arguing the 1930s against the 1950s, but all that dialogue had faded when Westrum was named manager for the rest of the season. Now he was on his own. All the good-natured and meaningless chatter of coaches and reporters could not help Westrum now. He was managing the Mets. Nothing could help him.

The 1965 season was bleak, as the Mets slipped backward to a 50–112 record, worse than their second and third seasons. Berra, Spahn, and Lary had failed to have comebacks. Cannizzaro and Christopher slumped back to their levels. Billy Cowan struck out 45 times in 156 at-bats and was shipped away. Hickman fell short again. Hunt was injured and batted .240.

The pitching was equally dreary as Bearnarth lost the edge on his sinker ball at the age of twenty-five. Willey's final comeback failed, while Cisco, Jackson, and Fisher still lost. Huge, gentle Gary Kroll had a 6–6 record before George Weiss deposited him at Buffalo in some bookkeeping maneuver. Kroll was insulted and took the rest of the season off.

There was some comic relief as Chuck Hiller came over from the Giants to wear Marv's old No. 2. Hiller replaced the injured Hunt at second base and was soon nicknamed "Dr. No" because he had "no hands," as the ball players say. He fumbled so many ground balls that everybody in Shea Stadium began holding their breath when the ball rolled to him. Some said it was the uniform number but Hiller had always had this problem.

But in the middle of the weedpatch of the 1965 Mets, a few green plants sprouted that gave hope for the future. Frank "Tug" McGraw was a twenty-year-old California boy, cocky and inconsistent. Casey had kept him despite his inexperience, and occasionally McGraw's speed would get the batters out. One night he helped beat the Phillies and, in his excitement, he leaped off the mound and waved his hands after the final out. The Phillies cursed him from their dugout, calling him a "bush bastard," and McGraw smiled at them. He definitely violated the fraternity rules.

McGraw had another reason to leap on August 26 when he beat another left-hander named Koufax, the first time the Mets had beaten the Dodger star. After the game, McGraw bubbled and compared himself to the young gunslinger who came to town to challenge the old sheriff to a shoot-out. This young gunslinger was shot out of the saddle a few times himself, finishing with a 2–7 record, but his 3.31 earned-run average and his youthful speed and eagerness gave the club a lift. He was also very popular with his teammates because he had studied barbering and could give a fine haircut in the spare hours on the road.

Late in the season, McGraw was joined by the most encouraging squadron of Youth of America the Mets had ever assembled. They arrived on a Thursday morning, after finishing the International League season the night before in Rochester. They had barreled down the New York Thruway all night, eager to reach

Shea Stadium. By a coincidence, this was an afternoon when
Casey bid farewell to his players just before returning to California. So Casey could look around the clubhouse and see his legacy:

There were Kranepool and Swoboda and McGraw, who had
been there all season, and there were the weary boys from Buffalo
—Buddy Harrelson, the spindly shortstop Casey had discovered
two springs before; Cleon Jones, the promising outfielder with
the scar on his face; Dick Selma and Dennis Ribant, two hard-
throwing right-handers; Greg Goossen, a muscular catcher. Casey
looked at them and smiled. His vision was finally coming true.

The Mets managed to win nineteen and lose forty-eight under
Westrum in the last two months of 1965 to assure themselves of
their favorite last-place position. At first it was generally assumed
that he was merely watching the store for Stengel, but then the
front office began screening candidates for 1966. They probably
considered Eddie Stanky, Yogi Berra, Alvin Dark, and Bob Scheffing, but they could not agree. Finally on November 18 they
agreed that they needed a manager to represent them at the
winter meetings, so they gave the job to Westrum. He had been
with the club two years now, he had tasted authority, and he was,
after all, an old Giant.

In the winter between 1965 and 1966, Weiss made several
moves in an attempt to get out of last place. On October 19 he
acquired a former Houston bonus player, catcher Jerry Grote, who
had spent three years shuttling between the Astros and their farm
team. Grote had good ability but his temper and lack of concentration hurt him until the Astros decided to get rid of him.

He was a rugged San Antonio native who had been signed
off the Trinity College campus in Texas. As a teen-ager, he had
played in an All-Star game in New York, impressing his teammates by doing push-ups with another all-star on his back.

"He looked like he had spent a lot of time plowing the back
forty," recalled a young math major from Texas named Davey
Johnson, who would later sign as a second baseman with Baltimore.

Weiss also traded Alvin Jackson and Charlie Smith to the Cardinals for Ken Boyer, the shopworn third baseman. The departure
of Jackson made sleepy Jim Hickman the last surviving original

Met. Nobody was more amazed by this development than Hickman, who was beginning to like the big city. He was even talking of staying on as a coach, a put-on for everybody who knew the easygoing country boy.

The Mets also picked up pitcher Jack Hamilton and outfielder Al Luplow, and they traded Joe Christopher for Eddie Bressoud. But their most exciting move of all came just before spring training opened, when they acquired Dick Stuart, Dr. Strangeglove himself.

Big Stu had batted only .234 for the Phillies in 1965 and his fielding had been characteristically terrible. But the Mets wanted him to platoon with the lethargic Kranepool. Big Stu flamboyantly predicted great things for himself and even promoted a television program for himself in New York—the first Met to reach such status. Once again the Mets were trying to squeeze one more good year out of an old player, just as they had with Snider in 1963, Altman in 1964, Spahn in 1965.

This time the Mets won their second game of the season, getting closer all the time to that longed-for opening-day victory. They also won their third game, putting them over .500 for the first time in history. But then they lost five straight and things returned to normal.

But the front office was dedicated to getting out of last place in 1966, and they kept making moves to get help. On June 10 they went into the grab bag of old-timers and plucked out Bob Shaw, the curly-haired right-hander from San Francisco, who was noted for his pride in his good looks and the possible spitball he threw. Shaw had made himself unpopular in San Francisco by offering too much advice to the other Giants, and the grumpy manager of the Giants, Herman Franks, was glad to get rid of him. Shaw won his first four starts and Westrum chuckled to think he had taken Shaw away from the unpopular Herman.

But just when Shaw joined the club, Stuart was released. His batting average was .218, and his defensive ability was not quite enough to save his job.

The concentration on older players seemed to be paying off in the short run because the Mets stayed out of last place from the start of the season. When Shaw beat the Cubs on July 31, the

Mets had a 47–55 record, the closest they had ever been to mediocrity at this stage of a season.

Also, the Mets had some help in 1966. They had always been able to beat the Cubs more easily than any other team, and 1966 was no different. The Cubs were, in their own way, as fouled up as the Met organization. Owned by the chewing gum man, P. K. Wrigley, who paid very little attention to the team, the Cubs had staggered through the early 1960s with a bizarre system of revolving "head coaches." They even had a former navy officer act as "athletic director" one season, provoking all kinds of jokes about the Cubbies trying to join the Big Ten.

The "head coach" system was a system worse than anarchy. One head coach would snarl at his players and refuse to let them shave after a game. But the players would growl and endure this treatment because they knew that next week this head coach might be at Wenatchee and next week's head coach would even let them shave during a game or take champagne baths—who knew?

Finally the Cubs tried Bob Kennedy as a permanent head coach but he was fired after 1965 and replaced by Leo Durocher, the former Dodger and Giant manager, who had more recently been coaching the Dodgers and living the good life in Hollywood. Durocher had not lost any of his charm over the years. He let everybody know that the old system of head coaches was vanished. Leo was the boss—period. He also surveyed the Cubs, who had finished eighth in 1965, and made the proclamation: "The Cubs are not an eighth-place ball club."

How right Leo was. He patiently used his best young players and was a model of good manners in 1966, learning all about his new team. And the man who once said "nice guys finish last" completely validated his own theory by acting like a sweetheart in 1966—and finishing last. The Mets won sixty-six, lost ninety-five, and finished ninth, seven and a half games ahead of kindly old Leo. They beat the Cubs in ten of eighteen games, and they also beat the Astros in eleven of eighteen.

One of the big reasons why the Mets moved up was Cleon Jones, who batted .275 in 139 games. For several years it had seemed he might never make it. One spring he had a chance to stay with the club until he brought his wife down from Alabama on her spring vacation from high school. Then he stopped hitting and was shuffled off to Buffalo. In 1965 he had argued about batting with his manager at Buffalo.

The Jones of 1966 was a contrast to the Jones of 1963. The Mets had sent him to a good dentist to get his teeth fixed, and one teammate was sure that made a big difference.

"Cleon never used to open his mouth because he was ashamed of his teeth, all full of holes," the teammate said. "But after the dental work, he really relaxed and became a very funny guy."

Late in the season, the Mets brought up a young fastball pitcher named Nolan Ryan. He pitched twice and was nervous and wild, but everybody agreed he just might be the next Bob Feller within a couple of years.

The other young players had mixed seasons. Hunt batted .288 but played in only 132 games and managed to annoy Westrum because of his frequent aches and pains. Harrelson filled in when McMillan was hurt. Grote batted only .237 in 120 games. Swoboda slumped to .222 and Kranepool hit .254.

But Westrum backed up the youngsters with older players like Boyer, who hit .266, and pinch hitters like Bressoud, Hiller, and Luplow. The manager got the most out of older pitchers like Shaw, Hamilton, and Bob Friend, the former Pirate star. Dennis Ribant had the first winning season by a Met starter, 11–9, while Fisher had a good 11–14 mark.

The front office recognized that the unglamorous Westrum had contributed to the improvement in 1966. Near the end of the season, they gave him a raise and another one-year contract for 1967.

16

MAN WITHOUT A COUNTRY

◆

ON NOVEMBER 14, 1966, the Mets called a major news conference at their Diamond Club to announce that George Weiss was retiring as president of the Mets—and would be succeeded by Vaughan Palmore "Bing" Devine.

Weiss was his old inscrutable self at this final conference, as he blinked and stared off into space. The Mets had finished ninth in 1966, and they were fully established as the most popular team in the city. Weiss had already been eulogized once for his role with the Mets when M. Donald Grant regarded a packed Shea Stadium and told Weiss in a strong voice: "This is a tribute to you, George." And now the tributes came again. But Weiss had always thought of himself as the molder of dynasties and perhaps he was uncomfortable at the freakish success of the Mets.

"This culminates a lifetime of the happiest kind of work I could ever indulge in," he said without changing his blank expression. "This time I go out with the right kind of taste in my mouth."

If this was a criticism of the way the Yankees had let him go, it was the first time he ever indicated any bitterness. In his heart of hearts—like Marvelous Marv—he had always remained a Yankee.

"I would have to say that the thing I am most proud of was hiring Casey Stengel twice," Weiss continued, as the reporters nodded amen. He had also hired Bing Devine once.

Devine had come to the Mets late in the 1964 season after being fired by Gussie Busch, the beer baron who owns the St. Louis Cardinals. While Devine had been learning the first names of the people in the Met organization, the team he had built in St. Louis had roared past the staggering Phillies to win the pennant and the World Series.

In the Cardinal clubhouse after the last game of the Series, the players had put their arms around the new executive of the New York Mets and reassured him that the championship truly belonged to him. After this bittersweet moment, Devine returned to his office in Shea Stadium and resumed his career-in-exile, far from the city that he loved.

Devine had worked all his life to become the general manager of the St. Louis Cardinals. He had played ball in the sandlots and worshipped the old Gashouse Gang. As a youngster he had driven around the National League with his parents during summer vacation, following the Cardinals from city to city. When he applied for a summer publicity job, he was already a familiar figure to the Cardinal family. He worked for the Cardinals while attending Washington University in St. Louis. Then at the age of 24, he became the business manager in Johnson City, Tennessee, in the Class D Appalachian League.

Two things happened to him in Johnson City. One, the regular second baseman got spiked, so Devine signed himself to a contract and played a few games with no success at all. Two, he met and married Mary Anderson, a pretty Johnson City girl.

Then Devine made all the stops in the Cardinal system until 1957, when he replaced Frank "Trader" Lane as Cardinal general manager. But St. Louis had traded one trader for another, as Devine soon acquired Curt Flood, Julian Javier, Dick Groat, and Bill White. Early in 1964 he traded for a young left fielder named Lou Brock, who would play them into a pennant in September.

But the surge by Brock and his teammates was not enough to save Devine's job. Like any wealthy and powerful man, Busch had a legion of advisors who would tell him anything he wanted to hear. Some of these advisors whispered that the Cardinals should be doing better than they were. So on August 17, with the Cardinals nine games out of first place, Bing Devine was suddenly out of a job.

Busch tried to tell people that Devine had resigned. "I was asked to leave," said the honest Devine.

In one of their most imaginative moves, Grant and Weiss immediately scooped up Devine and put him in a front-office job. The only assumption anybody could make was that Devine had been hired to replace Weiss eventually.

But while Devine moved into the New York organization, his heart was back in the suburb of Ladue, Missouri, where his three daughters went to school and where his wife led the Pinch-Hitters, a group of St. Louis baseball wives who involved themselves in many community functions. The Devine ladies came to New York for summer vacation and enjoyed sight-seeing, but their roots were in St. Louis.

Thus, for most of the year, Devine would race to LaGuardia Airport on Friday afternoons and catch a jet home for the weekend. On Monday morning he would fly back to New York. He kept a room in the Americana Hotel, and his idea of a big night in New York was to stroll down Broadway and buy himself one of those ice-cream floats at the corner stand known as Orange Julius.

His tastes in food were extremely simple, running to steak and soda. He did not drink coffee or alcohol. He did not put mustard on his ball-park hot dog. Exotic foods seemed to frighten him, like the night he threw a party at Mike Fish's Italian Restaurant in Chicago. I don't think he will ever get over sitting near me and my heaping bowl of squid and linguini in white wine sauce.

However, Devine's imagination came alive for baseball. He was willing to consider any trade, any strategy, any rules' change. He loved innovations. He utilized an electronic recording system, so his far-flung scouts could make nightly reports by telephone without him having to monitor the calls. As an executive, he was a pinball wizard with all lights flashing.

It took Devine only nine days to shuffle three players off the roster. Five days after that, he drafted two players at the winter meetings. Then he got down to work.

On November 29, Devine traded Ron Hunt and Jim Hickman to the Dodgers for Tommy Davis, the Brooklyn boy who was trying to regain his skills after severely breaking his leg. With Hunt's departure, the Mets lost their first homegrown hero. Injuries had plagued the scrappy infielder in his four years in New York, and he had fallen from his 1964 All-Star form. Also, Westrum had decided that Hunt was not giving everything he had, and Westrum began sniping at Hunt in his late-hour diatribes. Hunt was not unhappy over being separated from Westrum, although he said he was very sorry to leave New York and the people who had adored him so openly.

Met fans were tempted to grumble over the loss of their first young star. (They were not as sentimental over losing the last original Met, Hilly-Billy Hickman.) But the fans were excited over gaining Davis, a former Boys High athlete who had been talked into signing with the Dodgers just before they sneaked out of Brooklyn. "T.D." had batted .346 and driven in 153 runs in 1962 but had broken his leg early in 1965 and never regained a place in the Dodger lineup or in the affections of manager Walter Alston. Once again, Met fans grew excited over somebody else's unwanted star.

Devine was not finished dealing, however. On December 6 he unloaded Dennis Ribant, the squeaky-voiced little right-hander whose 11–9 record in 1966 made him the first winning starter in Met history.

Westrum had always seemed surprised when "Nervous-Nervous" won a game and Devine undoubtedly agreed. He followed the old Branch Rickey theory that it is better to trade a man a year too early than a year too late.

In return for Ribant, the Mets received Don Cardwell, a grizzled right-hander, and Don Bosch, an outfielder from the minor leagues. Cardwell was a strong six-foot, four-inch, 220-pounder who had won 80 games and lost 103 in Philadelphia, Chicago, and Pittsburgh. He was a good hitter and a good fielder but hardly a winner. He would be thirty-one years old when the 1967

season started and he was not—the Mets stressed—the key man
in the trade. The key man was Don Bosch.

Bosch had been the terror of the International League, batting
.283 and playing center field as well as Willie Mays, in the ex-
pansive words of Bing Devine and Pirate officials. Met reporters
snickered, but politely. They would remember to watch Don
Bosch very carefully on the first day of spring training.

Spring training began with Devine and Westrum sitting on the
pink and red benches where Stengel and Weiss had once sat.
The familiar cast of reporters rubbed suntan lotion on their heads
and rushed out for a look at Don Bosch. They looked around at
all the normal-sized players. Then, in the middle of the outfield,
they spied a diminutive new Met.

"Who is that?"

"He's wearing No. 17."

"My God, it's Don Bosch."

The reporters skimmed through the press guide to read more
about the man who could cover as much ground as any outfielder
in captivity. Bosch was listed at five feet, ten inches, weighing 160
pounds. Both of these figures seemed hyperbolic.

Later the reporters noticed that Don Bosch, at twenty-four
years of age, had streaks of gray in his hair. And they soon made
Bosch the butt of the spring-training humor. Considering the
buildup the Mets had given Bosch, it was important for the reporters to examine him carefully. However, each unkind story
seemed to make Bosch try harder, and the harder he tried the
less he produced.

Tommy Davis, an extremely sensitive and moody athlete, felt
sure that the press was responsible for the bad start by the new
man. Davis also felt that Bosch had real ability, enough to play
center field for the Mets. In truth, Bosch was a lovely man with a
good sense of humor, even about himself. His teammates called
him "Socrates" because of his flippant wisdom. But he was under
severe pressure in New York and would fail several trials with
the Mets.

True to their tradition, the Mets lost their opening game in 1967
with Cardwell the losing pitcher. By mid-season they were 31–47.
Davis was not hitting; Cleon Jones was backsliding and Westrum

was lamenting his "mental mistakes"; Ken Boyer and Bob Shaw were shot; Jerry Grote was on his way to a .195 season. The fans began to get a little restless.

There were, however, a few new Mets who provided some talent and stability. In May, Devine purchased a thirty-four-year-old third baseman named Ed Charles from Kansas City. Charles was a Negro from the South who had known trouble in his childhood but later acquired a discipline and humility that is rarely seen in a clubhouse. He began attending college in his late twenties and wrote inspirational poetry, paying for the printing and mailing it to young fans who asked for autographs. Charles soon made Ken Boyer obsolete, and he drew the Met players closer together with his warmth and maturity.

Also, Divine found a former Cardinal pitcher named Ron Taylor, suffering from a bad back in the Houston organization. A twenty-nine-year-old Toronto native with a degree in electrical engineering, Taylor had been urged by his relatives to give up playing games and begin his adult life. But he resisted. Where else could he wear his cap sideways, roll his eyes like Sylvester Pussycat, and claim "I just found out what's driving me crazy— it's baseball." Taylor's back was improved and he soon became the Mets' best relief pitcher.

Even with Harrelson replacing McMillan at shortstop and Swoboda playing competently, the Mets would have been a complete drag in 1967—except for one man. By the middle of the season it was obvious that the Mets finally had a blue-chip athlete. His name was George Thomas Seaver and he was twenty-two years old.

17

WHO IS THIS KID?

◆

THE SUN WAS GOING DOWN in California, disappearing behind the grandstand at Anaheim Stadium, and 43,000 fans began to gather sweaters around them. The National League and the American League All-Stars were tied going into the fifteenth inning, and the game gave every indication of lasting forever.

But in the top of the fifteenth, Tony Perez of Cincinnati lofted a homer to give the Nationals a 2–1 lead. Since Perez had batted for Don Drysdale, the Nationals would have to come up with a new pitcher in the bottom of the inning.

In right field, the bullpen door swung open and a young man strode onto the grass, a blue warm-up jacket wrapped around his arm. The uniform said "New York" on the front and had No. 41 on the back. The fans thumbed through their programs.

"No. 41 . . . Tom Seaver . . . New York Mets," they told each other. "Hoo-boy, the National League is down to using Mets. They're really in trouble now."

Tom Seaver, in his second professional season, passed by the cocky Pete Rose at second base. Seaver smiled.

"Hey, Pete, why don't you pitch and I'll play second base," Seaver suggested.

"Naw, you do it," the Cincinnati star replied. Rose did not look at all worried about having a Met protect his lead.

Seaver reached the mound and prepared to pitch to the best hitters in the American League. The first batter was Tony Conigliaro and he flied to right. The next batter was Carl Yastrzemski, who was on his way to winning every major batting title. Seaver pitched carefully to the powerful left-hander and walked him. But Bill Freehan flied to center and Ken Berry struck out, and the 43,000 fans and the national television audience of 60,000,000 saw familiar heroes like Ernie Banks and Orlando Cepeda race out to the mound to congratulate the young star.

The fans didn't know it, but when Seaver had reported to the clubhouse earlier in the day, he had been mistaken for the bat boy. Lou Brock saw Seaver in his street clothes and said: "Hey, son, would you get me a beer?" When Brock found out who Seaver was, he broke into his high, infectious horselaugh. "Does your guardian know you're out so late?" Brock asked.

Nobody was mistaking Seaver for the bat boy after the game. Drysdale offered Seaver the "game ball," the final ball used in the game, but Seaver handed it back. "You won the game, you get the ball," Seaver told the winning pitcher. "I've got the memories."

Everybody agreed that Seaver would soon have more memories. He was on his way to being everything to the Mets that Drysdale had been to the Dodgers. Drysdale's own manager, Walter Alston, had chosen Seaver for the All-Star team because of his six victories, five losses, and 2.68 earned-run average in his first three months in the major leagues.

Now, as the fans filed out of Anaheim Stadium, they were discussing the trim, eager youngster who had wrapped up the game for the National League. Then, when they checked their programs, they discovered that Seaver was a California boy from the grape valleys of Fresno.

George Thomas Seaver was born on November 17, 1944, in Fresno, the son of a former Walker Cup amateur golfer and a vice-president in a raisin company. The boy grew up in middle-class suburbia, playing ball and learning to compete. When he was graduated from Fresno High, he weighed only 160 pounds, and he took a job lifting crates of raisins for $2.05 an hour.

"I thought I wanted to be a ball player but I wasn't sure," he said later. "I thought I might want to be a dentist but I wasn't sure about that. I was trying to find myself. I knew I didn't want to lift crates at $2.05 an hour for the rest of my life."

Like so many other young men who are confused about what to do, he then joined the Marines to get a six-month service hitch out of the way. He came out twenty pounds heavier and several years older in outlook.

"I realized how fortunate I was. It opened my eyes to see how so many people were messed up. People go through life thinking the world owes them a living. The world owes them nothing. They owe the world something."

Seaver entered Fresno City College and discovered that his extra twenty pounds had given him a fastball. He also discovered a pretty blonde named Nancy McIntyre. On the last day of the semester he introduced himself to her and asked her to go for a ride.

In the fall, Tom transferred to the University of Southern California and began attracting major-league scouts. The Dodgers drafted him the following spring, but they panicked when he talked about a $70,000 bonus. So he was still an amateur the following January when the Atlanta Braves came along. The Braves signed him for $50,000 but they overlooked one little thing —Seaver had already pitched two exhibitions for U.S.C., which starts its baseball program early.

Under baseball rules, no player may be signed after his college season has begun. Somebody pointed out this fact to William Dole Eckert, the Air Force supply general who had mysteriously been recruited to be Commissioner of Baseball a few months before. Eckert's three-year regime would be marked by inexperience and indecision, but this time there were clear guidelines. Eckert ruled that the Braves had forfeited all rights to the young pitcher.

But then the National Collegiate Athletic Association stepped in and declared he could no longer play amateur ball, and U.S.C. rescinded his scholarship. So Seaver was left without any team, amateur or professional.

When the Seavers tried to clarify Tom's position, they were put in touch with Lee MacPhail, a warm and wise man who was working as the commissioner's right-hand man between terms as general manager for Baltimore and the Yankees. MacPhail arranged for Seaver to be signed by any club—except Atlanta—that offered to match the $50,000 bonus.

Three clubs agreed to pay that price. One was Philadelphia, one was Cleveland, and the third was George Weiss and the New York Mets. The commissioner held a drawing and the Mets, for the first time in their miserable lives, got lucky.

Seaver took his bonus and bought a new car, an engagement ring for Nancy McIntyre, and he put the rest of the money in the bank. Then he reported to the Mets' top farm team in Jacksonville, Florida.

In his first professional game on April 25, he pitched 8⅔ innings and beat Rochester, 4–2. "Fun is fun," wrote one Rochester reporter. "But, really, who is this kid?"

In Seaver's next start, he shut out Buffalo, 2–0, on two hits. "This kid didn't beat a bunch of rookies," said Red Davis, the Buffalo manager. "He beat a veteran club. From what I saw tonight, he could be a great one."

Five days later, Seaver beat Buffalo again, 12–1. "Well, we won't see him again," sighed Clay Dennis, the general manager at Buffalo. "He'll join the Mets by mid-June."

However, the front office did not rush Seaver up to the varsity. He was allowed to pitch a whole season in the top minor league, where he pitched thirty-four times, won twelve, lost twelve, and married Nancy McIntyre. He was 21;—it was a very good year.

In the spring of 1967, Seaver came to Met camp hoping to stick around for a few weeks. But he struck out Harmon Killebrew, the great blue ox of the Minnesota Twins, in the first inning of the first game—and that gave him ideas. He won a starting job with the Mets and beat the Cubs, 6–1, in his first major-league decision in April.

By early June, Seaver was literally a household word in New York. His brother Charles, working for the Welfare Department, visited a client one day and saw Tom's picture pasted on a wall. "The fellow knew a lot more about him than I did," Charles Seaver said.

The Mets were learning about their young ace too. Ron Swoboda, now known as "Rocky" for his earnest, stumbling approach to fly balls and other challenges, was quick to praise the rookie pitcher. "He's very mature for a twenty-two-year-old," Swoboda said. "Tom knows how to handle himself. He doesn't do cartwheels when he wins and he doesn't tear up a clubhouse when he loses. He inspires confidence when you play behind him. You know he won't give up one of those long potatoes and take you out of a game in a hurry. With him in there, we have a chance to win every time."

"There was an aura of defeatism and I refused to accept it," Seaver would say a year later. "Maybe some of the others started to feel how I felt because I noticed that the team started to play better behind me than it did for any other pitcher."

The reporters also came to appreciate Seaver, who was majoring in public relations at U.S.C. and was always co-operative. He could discuss books like *Death of a President* and *Catch-22* and was usually aware of current events. It must also be confessed that some of us reporters enjoyed watching Nancy Seaver, in miniskirt or pants suit, rooting so fervently for her husband. Nancy had a lot to cheer about in 1967. Tom finished the season with sixteen victories, thirteen losses, and a splendid 2.76 earned-run average in 251 innings. He finished about six miles ahead of the Mets.

Except for Seaver, the Mets seemed to stand still in 1967. The talent was starting to arrive but there were days and nights when it seemed that Westrum would never put it together.

One of the manager's biggest problems was the catching. As a former catcher himself, Westrum was particularly critical of Grote, and he usually had good reason. The catcher had youth and speed and a strong arm, but his mind often seemed to be wandering, or he would be too harsh when talking to his own pitchers.

There was one game in particular that caused the two men to become estranged. In late July, Westrum used two other catchers before sending Grote into the seventh inning of a night game in Los Angeles. Grote immediately began grumbling to the umpires about their calls, another bad habit he had developed.

When Grote reached the dugout in the eighth inning, somebody heaved a towel on the field, which is grounds for dismissal. Home-plate umpire Bill Jackowski didn't see it, but Harry Wendelstedt came bounding all the way from third base, raising one finger on one hand and five on his other hand, signifying that No. 15 had thrown the towel. No. 15 was Grote. He was out of the game—and the Mets had no catchers, unless Westrum could find some way of activating himself in a hurry. Instead, Westrum asked Tommie Reynolds, a young substitute outfielder, to strap on the "tools of ignorance" for the first time in his life.

Reynolds did the best he could as the Mets and Dodgers battled into the eleventh inning. But then a pitch got past him and the winning run trotted home from third base. The Mets argued that the batter had tipped the ball but Jackowski raced off the field, blurting to reporters: "Hey, boys, gimme a break, I've had a tough day."

It was the old Solly Hemus theory of "They screw us because we're horseshit," but Westrum did not blame Jackowski or Reynolds.

The next morning the manager fined his catcher $100 for not having enough sense to stay in the game. The manager also announced the fine to the reporters, which managers do not usually do. The $100 did not bother Grote much but the public revelation probably did. After that, as Walter Winchell might have written, one did not invite Jerry Grote and Wes Westrum to the same party. They were, as Winch put it, *pffft*.

Westrum could also not cope with Cleon Jones, the outfielder who had seemed so promising ever since he slipped shyly into the old Polo Grounds in 1963. Jones had come out of his shell and batted .275 for the Mets in 1966, but then he slumped again in 1967, and Westrum began alternating him with left-handed hitters who were obviously not of the same calibre as Jones.

The two men hardly talked to each other, although they had plenty to say in private. Westrum felt that Jones made "too many mental errors," while Jones felt that "the man just won't give me a chance." It got so bad that Jones developed a phobia about going to the ball park. If he read that a right-hander was starting for the other team, he knew he would not be in the lineup. There were days when he moped around his apartment until his wife had to push him out the door to go to work.

After mid-season, however, Westrum announced that Jones would play every day "because I can't have him sitting around." It is quite possible that Westrum was ordered by the front office to play this valuable piece of merchandise so the Mets could either build with him or trade him away. But Westrum made it sound like a man driving his second car around the block once a week, just to keep the tires from losing their shape and the battery from running down.

"I'm gonna send Wes a telegram thanking him," Jones said, only slightly sarcastically, when he heard he was going to play every day. Then his roommate, Tommy Davis, talked him into a more positive attitude and Jones began hitting again. He finished the season with a .246 average, which was better than Westrum did. Westrum did not finish the season at all.

18

THE FORDHAM FIREMAN

◆

THE METS SANK INTO TENTH PLACE again on August 20 and were about to clinch their favorite position a month later when Westrum announced his resignation. He had been waiting for his contract to be renewed, and the longer he waited the more he realized that it was not going to be.

"Primarily and honestly, I came to the conclusion that the strain of waiting, in addition to the physical and mental strain of managing, had become increasingly severe, and that maybe the whole thing had developed into a blessing in disguise," Westrum said as he beat the Mets to the punch.

Devine offered Westrum a job in the organization, but the paternal Giants soon brought him home to coach first base and steal signals for lovable Herman Franks.

Salty Parker, a coach, handled the Mets in their last eleven games and they finished with a 61–101 record, the second best in Met history, five and a half games behind their 1966 pace. The Cubs moved up to third place as Leo Durocher decided "this time, no Mr. Nice Guy," and the Astros finished their usual ninth. Thus the Mets finished behind their fellow expansion team for the sixth time in six years. And now the "search" began for a manager who could somehow, anyhow, at least catch the Houston Astros.

The early speculation centered on three men the Mets had stockpiled within the system—Yogi Berra; Bob Scheffing, the former manager in Detroit who was now the minor-league co-ordinator; and Whitey Herzog, an energetic and popular coach under Westrum who was now a prime scout for the Mets.

There was another candidate named Gil Hodges, but he already had a contract as manager of the Washington Senators. Since leaving the Mets in 1963, the strong and quiet man had forced the Senators upward every season, from tenth in 1963 to a tie for sixth in 1967. They had also won more games every year—from 62 to 70 to 71 to 76. Despite lethargic management, weak personnel, and low attendance, Hodges had personally energized the Senators—sometimes with rules, sometimes with instruction, sometimes with encouragement, sometimes with downright force.

Some of the Senator players had found him to be strong-willed and dogmatic, but a Washington reporter said "there are a lot of losers on this club and they don't like being pushed." It seemed clear that Hodges was a manager who knew the application of power.

Hodges still maintained his home on Bedford Avenue in Brooklyn, not far from the site of old Ebbets Field. He flew home to Brooklyn whenever the Senators had a day off. Unlike Walter O'Malley, Hodges' roots really were in Brooklyn. The New York fans had hardly forgotten Hodges, because whenever the Yankees played the Senators, reporters would persistently tease Hodges about coming back to the Mets. And Hodges would say in his low, patient way:

"I have a contract with the Washington ball club. I am happy in Washington. Nobody has approached me from New York and I do not expect anybody to approach me. I am happy here. But you are very kind to be thinking about me, gentlemen." Then he would give them one of his inscrutable, muscular smiles.

While the reporters were recruiting Hodges over the years, the Met hierarchy had not forgotten him either. Devine would say in later months: "There was a strong feeling for Gil long before I had anything to do with policy-making on this club." Now that Devine was running the club and looking for a manager, he suddenly learned that his prime candidate was the manager of the Washington Senators.

Technically, one club is not supposed to recruit a manager from another club. But there are ways for gentlemen to circumnavigate the rules. The way the Mets did it was for Johnny Murphy, the number two man in the front office, to approach his old Yankee teammate, George "Twinkletoes" Selkirk, now the Washington general manager. Selkirk realized that his old friend was serious about wanting Hodges, and he gave his permission for Murphy to negotiate.

Devine began talking with Hodges in a car on the way to the airport during the World Series in St. Louis. The talk must have gone well because the Mets called a news conference two days later to announce that Washington had released Hodges from his obligation, and the Mets had signed him to a three-year contract for $65,000 a year.

When anybody raised the question of whether the Mets were within the law to raid Washington for a manager, General Eckert, the owners' commissioner, popped up to say: "Everything was quite proper, quite in order, under the baseball rules for Gil to come back to New York."

As payment for Hodges, the Mets sent Washington perhaps $100,000 and later sent Bill Denehy, a promising young pitcher.

The Mets also received a bonus because Hodges was able to bring three of his trusted coaches over from Washington—Eddie Yost, the old third baseman who used to lead the league in walks; Joe Pignatano, the Brooklyn boy who later played for the Dodgers and even hit into a triple play in a brief trial with the Mets; and Rube Walker, the jolly, round catcher behind Roy Campanella in the 1950s, now a jolly, round pitching coach with strong authority under Hodges. Gil also announced that his old World Series rival, Yogi Berra, would remain to coach first base.

There was some criticism of the deal in the Washington newspapers, because the fans and reporters did not like to see a successful manager spirited away. There was also the rumor that Devine was not delighted to be playing these politics, but the decision was out of his hands. Besides, as an exile himself, he

could understand how important it was for Hodges to come home
again to New York.

Devine had never lost the aura of the man without a country,
as he commuted between his home in Ladue and his desk in
Flushing. Ever since Gussie Busch fired him in 1964, Devine
had reason to believe that he would never have a baseball job
in St. Louis again. It was baseball or St. Louis—but not both.

When Devine accompanied the Mets on a trip to St. Louis, he
was treated in Busch Stadium like a long-deposed prince. Head-
waiters bowed to Devine in the Redbird Roost, the dining room
in the new stadium. Reporters bustled around him. Fans waved
to him. Cardinal players put their arms around him. Club officials
whispered with him. There were times when it seemed that
the whole damn ball park would break down and cry at the
stupidity of his banishment.

Even though Devine now earned his living 875 miles away
from Busch Stadium, Gussie Busch had not been able to forget
the deposed prince. In December, 1964, Joanne Devine, Bing's
oldest daughter, had written a long letter to Busch concerning
the firing of her dad.

"I think I realize how badly you wanted to bring a pennant to
St. Louis," Joanne wrote. "But you lost faith in your own organization . . . and there was a man with a dream. . . .

"It does seem unjust that other men—however fine they may
be—are reaping the benefits of a situation which my father tried
hard to build.

"Of course, I didn't write this for any reaction . . . A man in
your position could never retract any commitments or admit a
wrong, if one has been done. . . . Very sincerely, Joanne Devine."

Wonders of all wonders, Busch answered her letter, ending
with the following statement:

"The fact that my decision did not reflect upon Bing's character certainly is indicated by the high esteem that all his friends
have expressed upon many occasions since that time."

The reminders must have been frequent in the unusually
familial and sports-minded city, but the beer baron could ignore
the sentiments so long as Bob Howsam was general manager.

Then, when Howsam flew the coop to Cincinnati, Busch appointed popular Stan Musial general manager for 1967. But Musial cut out after one year, and Busch needed a general manager again. He wanted somebody who knew baseball and he wanted somebody who knew St. Louis. What, some brave soul whispered, what about Vaughan Palmore Devine?

Who said that Gussie Busch could not retract a commitment? Gussie Busch could do anything he pleased. On December 5 he appointed Bing Devine as his once-and-future general manager.

The Mets, needless to say, did not stand in Devine's way. Having recently recruited somebody else's manager, perhaps against Devine's better judgment, they could not very well object to Devine going home again to St. Louis.

A few weeks later, M. Donald Grant edged up to Johnny Murphy at the Mets' office Christmas party and whispered that Murphy was the new general manager of the Mets. For Murphy, who was as much a New Yorker as Devine was a St. Louisan, the appointment was a culmination of a lifetime in baseball.

John J. Murphy was born in New York and attended Fordham University in the Bronx. His father retired as chief clerk in the Department of Water Supply, and his older brother, Thomas F. Murphy, was once police commissioner of New York and later appointed a federal judge by President Truman.

Johnny Murphy served in flannel uniforms going directly from Fordham to the minor leagues to the New York Yankees in 1932. There he became one of the first great relief pitchers, known as "The Fordham Fireman."

Murphy was also one of the early player representatives, fighting for a pension plan and better working conditions. He was so conscientious that the Yankees called him "Grandma."

In World War II, Murphy left the Yankees to serve as director of Employee Services in Oak Ridge, Tennessee. He started with nine employees and wound up housing and feeding 14,000. "People wondered what was going on," he later recalled. "Four companies and 65,000 people eventually flocked there. All kinds of materials poured in and nothing went out—until 1945."

What finally went out was the atomic bomb. In later years Marv Throneberry also went out of Tennessee.

Back in baseball after the war, Murphy finished up with the Boston Red Sox in 1947 and joined their front office in 1948. He was farm director in Boston in 1961, when his old boss from the Yankees, George Weiss, brought him home to New York.

Murphy worked quietly for the Mets, often traveling with the club, occasionally scouting other teams. He sought no allies in the press. When Devine was brought in as the heir-apparent to Weiss, nobody suggested that Murphy had been given a bad deal. If Gussie Busch had not been able to swallow his pride, Murphy would probably have finished up his career as a No. 2 man. But now at nearly sixty years of age, he was finally No. 1.

There was one noticeable change in administrations. Murphy had a love for French cooking, and the bartender in the press room, a gracious ex-fighter named Lou Napoli, always stocked a bottle of Murphy's favorite wine. But at the press conference for Murphy's new job, everybody was served the finest Beaujolais, a luxury that the hot dog and soda man, Bing Devine, would not have deemed necessary.

Trader Bing had done something more important than order wine, however. He had negotiated a deal with the Chicago White Sox which Grant and Murphy soon completed. In the biggest trade in their history, the Mets sent Tommy Davis, Jack Fisher, and a young pitcher named Billy Wynne in return for a quiet infielder named Al Weis and a quiet center fielder named Tommie Agee.

Agee had been Rookie of the Year in the American League in 1966, when he batted .273 with 86 runs-batted-in. But he slipped to .234 in 1967, and Eddie Stanky, the manager, hired a private detective to follow Agee on his nocturnal wanderings. Whether or not that step was necessary, the White Sox decided to unload the twenty-five-year-old athlete.

Hodges had seen Agee for two years in the American League and was delighted to obtain him. Cleon Jones was also happy, since he and Agee had been best friends growing up near Mobile, Alabama. Jones predicted that Tommie Agee would be a very important player for the New York Mets.

After concluding the deal that Devine had begun, the Mets cut down on their shuffling. Murphy and Hodges seemed intent on building a serene, secure administration. For instance, in all other Met spring training camps, the players had been so numerous that more attention was paid to cutting the squad than to teaching and improvement. But Hodges wanted to drill only his forty best players in the spring of 1968, showing them how to handle pick-off plays and cut-off plays and run-down plays, things the Mets had been botching up since Adam and Eve and Marvelous Marv. And so a new, patient, and determined Met administration prepared for what would hopefully be a new era, beginning in 1968.

19

A MATTER OF RESPECT

◆

TOMMIE AGEE PICKED UP HIS BAT and walked to home plate as forty Mets and ten reporters leaned forward to watch his first at-bat in a New York uniform.

The scene was St. Petersburg, Florida, in the first exhibition game of 1968 between the Cardinals and the Mets. Pitching for the Cardinals was their fastball hero of the 1967 World Series, Bob Gibson.

Gibson's first pitch was a fastball. The ball soared at Tommie Agee's head, and there was no time for him to react. In this quiet ball park of senior citizens, the noise echoed like a gunshot.

Agee went down, and for a long time he did not get up. The trainer and the players hovered over him, to see if he was alive or dead. But the batting helmet, dreamed up by Branch Rickey twenty years before, had saved his life. Finally, Agee stirred himself and wobbled off the field as the senior citizens patted their hands politely. At the hospital, X-rays said there was no concussion. After a few days' rest, Tommie Agee could play ball again.

And that was how the new era began for Agee and the New York Mets—with a fastball in the head. It seemed so typical of the Mets. It was like Grover Powell pitching a shutout and then hurting his arm in 1963. It was like George Altman pulling a muscle in the spring of 1964. It was like trading for Don Bosch

and finding gray streaks in his hair at the age of twenty-four. It
was like getting caught in the elevator in St. Louis before the
first game in 1962. *Same old Mets.* Cross this year off the calen-
dar, boys.

But while Agee waited for his head to clear, other Mets discovered a new sense of discipline in the training camp.

"There's no lollygagging," said Cleon Jones. "We used to chase
fly balls in bunches of sixes and sevens. Now we have one coach
hitting fungoes to two guys. Nobody stands around waiting for
something to do."

"The past is gone," Johnny Murphy said. "I never did believe
that people came to see us because we were colorful stumble-
bums. We'll draw ten times as many people by winning. We may
be cool and businesslike this year and still be tenth in the league
—but it'll pay off some day."

Two new Mets were particularly cool and businesslike. Al
Weis was under careful inspection in this spring. The previous
summer, while still with the White Sox, he had been knocked
down at second base by Frank Robinson of the Orioles, who was
trying to break up a double play. Robinson suffered from a concussion and double vision, while Weis was out for the season with
a torn knee. Hodges had seen him frolicking around in the fall Instructional League and asked to have him included in the Davis-
Agee deal. The manager knew that Bud Harrelson would be
absent on occasion because of army reserve duty, and Hodges
wanted Weis, a native Long Islander, as his backup infielder.

Only five feet, ten inches tall and 165 pounds, Weis was color-
less and quiet. The same could be said for tall, handsome J. C.
Martin, a catcher who had come from the White Sox in a separate deal. Martin (the initials stood for Joseph Clifton) was a
solid catcher but only a .223 hitter. The Virginian talked as little
as Weis, but both of them were mature and hardworking, and
Hodges had a place for both of them.

Maturity was still a distant goal for Tug McGraw, the lefty
who had beaten Sandy Koufax in 1965 and leaped high off the
mound in joy. Now almost twenty-four, McGraw had spent his
last year between the minor leagues and the U.S. Marines. ("I
am now a paid killer," he announced to the Mets.) McGraw was

competing with Alvin Jackson, who had been brought back from St. Louis, and McGraw probably lost all chance when he brought his dog to camp, and his dog did his thing outside Coach Joe Pignatano's motel room. Soon McGraw was back in Jacksonville, searching for control—on the mound and off.

Agee returned to the lineup a few days after being hit by Gibson, and he moped through the exhibitions. But maybe things would change when the season opened.

The Mets opened their season in San Francisco and amazingly took a 4-0 lead, seemingly on their way to their first opening-day victory. But the Giants made it 4-2, then scored three straight times in the ninth for a 5-4 victory. Once again, the Mets were 0-1 to start the season.

After four games, they were 2-2, and Agee had made five hits in sixteen at-bats. Maybe he was going to be all right, after all.

Then the club played a night game in the Houston Astrodome on April 15. That is, the game began on April 15. When it ended, it was April 16—and Houston won it, 1-0, in the twenty-fourth inning on an error by the new Met, Al Weis. The loss took six hours and six minutes, the longest night game in history, and in that time Tommie Agee went hitless in ten at-bats. His good start was now wiped out.

Agee's luck soon got worse, after he returned to New York. His car was stolen on his first excursion into the city, and he had neglected to provide insurance. This discouraged him about the big city and he claimed he spent the rest of the season firmly encamped in his motel room near Shea Stadium. Eddie Stanky's gumshoes would have had an easy time trailing him in Flushing.

After that marathon in Houston, Agee went hitless in four straight games before Hodges gave him a rest. The replacement was Don Bosch, now relaxed and humorous, telling reporters "Hey, I'm gonna play today" like a latter-day Marvelous Marv. But the unfortunate young man still had trouble hitting, and Agee was soon back in the lineup, not that he did any better.

Could this really be happening? Was Tommie Agee destined to be the ultimate Met fraud? A few fans, violating the Met tradition, began booing him, while the players stood on the dugout steps and cheered as Agee trudged to home plate. The Mets believed in Agee. They believed because Cleon Jones told them to believe.

Cleon Jones and Tommie Agee had been friends ever since County Training High School back in Mobile, when Cleon was the halfback who threw the option pass to Agee for five touchdowns. Jones was five days older but Agee was always a year ahead in school. "That's because I was smarter," Agee told Jones.

From the early days back in the neighborhood in Plateau, Jones seemed to have a deep respect for his quiet, serious friend, calling him "Number One." Tommie and Cleon started college at Grambling, but Tommie later took a $65,000 bonus to sign a baseball contract, and Cleon transferred to Alabama A. & M., where he scored seventeen touchdowns in two seasons before signing with the Mets for hardly any bonus at all.

It was only by coincidence that they wound up side-by-side in the Met outfield in 1968, but it was a good break for Agee. The talkative Jones kept reminding people to "wait until Tommie starts hitting. He's a great ball player."

The Mets waited, and waited, and waited. At one point Agee tied Don Zimmer's Met record by going hitless in thirty-four straight times at bat. He did not drive in a run until May 10, when he homered off Phil Regan of the Dodgers.

On May 16 he won a game by dribbling a grounder between first and second bases for a single in the bottom of the ninth. Tom Seaver jumped out of the dugout and applauded as Agee came off the field, but the new man remained funereal, and his slump continued.

Still, Hodges continued to play him, even when Agee was bogged down at .150 by May 24. Agee publicly thanked Hodges for his faith and promised to "do something to help that man." But there wasn't much he could do.

The Mets were tied for last until early June, when they won three straight from their old friends, the Cubs. Then their attention was jolted out of the arena of fun and games.

Late on the night of June 4, Senator Robert F. Kennedy of New York was murdered in Los Angeles. The Met players were as shocked as most private citizens were. But then something happened that took the Mets into the spotlight of this tragic event.

The senator's funeral was scheduled for Saturday, June 8. Baseball's commissioner, the cautious General Eckert, did not seem to understand that some official response was expected from his office. Eckert had been hired by the owners to do their bidding. When the owners, for their own blind or selfish reasons, could not agree on the way to honor the dead senator, the matter fell into Eckert's hands.

Eckert made a strange compromise. The games in New York and Washington were to be postponed, since those two cities were involved in the funeral ceremonies. But all other clubs could begin their games as soon as the burial was completed. The club owners, unwilling to sacrifice the income from a Saturday in June, eagerly scheduled their games for the evening.

This compromise was not good enough for the Met players, however. Few of them were politically minded or from New York or unusually loyal to the Kennedy family. But they voted unanimously not to play their game on Saturday in San Francisco.

"We're from New York," said Ed Kranepool, the Mets' player representative. "It's a matter of respect for us not to play."

The club officials immediately accepted the players' decision and informed the Giants they would not take the field that Saturday, whether it be a day game or a night game. This upset the Giant management, for it had scheduled "Bat Day" for Saturday and expected a paying crowd of 30,000 for the popular giveaway. The Giants were not drawing good crowds, and the minor officials feared calling off the game without consulting Horace Stoneham, the owner of the club, wherever he might be.

Stoneham was known to isolate himself for hours or days at a time, and this was one of those times. His wife said she did not know where he was. His nephew, Chub Feeney, who was the general manager of the Giants, said he did not know where Horace was.

Finally, sometime Friday morning, they found Horace and they patiently explained to him about the senator and the New York Mets and Bat Day. When Horace was ready to make a decision, the Giants produced a masterpiece of a statement that ended:

"The Giants sincerely regret the disappointment of thousands of young fans who had intended to attend the Bat Day game tomorrow and are compelled now to rearrange their plans . . ."

The Mets were furious over the wording of this statement. They cursed the Giant management for its obtuseness and they criticized the commissioner for his lack of comprehension.

"The same thing happened when Martin Luther King was killed," Kranepool noted. "He was a great American and the commissioner left it up to the clubs. It should have been the same rule for everybody."

Never had the Mets been so united. They were proud of each other for the unanimous vote and they were proud of Hodges, Murphy, and Grant for backing them up.

All over on that sad Saturday, anarchy reigned because of the avarice of the owners. In Cincinnati, several idealistic players refused to take the field, causing arguments among the Reds. In Pittsburgh, Maury Wills of the Pirates refused to play and was fined a day's pay by Joe E. Brown, the general manager. And when Rusty Staub and Bobby Aspromonte refused to play that day for the Houston Astros, they were docked a day's pay by Judge Roy Hofheinz, the Texas politician who was a close friend of Lyndon Johnson.

But in San Francisco, the New York Mets did not play baseball. Hodges suggested that he would probably go to church that morning. He also suggested that the players might avoid carousing in public places that day, having gone on record with their brave and respectful stand. The manager reinforced their feelings that they had made a meaningful gesture; there was a closeness between the Mets that had never been present before.

Perhaps it was just a coincidence, but after their strong stand, the Mets went on another winning streak and moved close to a .500 record, never quite making it but giving promise for future months and seasons.

The biggest star in early 1968 was a big red-cheeked left-hander named Jerry Koosman, who had learned to throw a baseball in the family hayloft in northern Minnesota. Koosman had not played high school ball because he was too busy helping on the 600-acre farm, but he had out-pitched grown men in the summer beer leagues.

In the Army Koosman had run into John Luchese whose father was an usher at Shea Stadium. Luchese Jr. wrote Luchese Sr. about this hard-throwing lefty, and the father alerted the Mets, who had heard of Koosman from another source. Soon scout Red Murff was bargaining with Koosman over a pitcher of beer. With each glass, Murff threatened to lower the bonus. Finally Koosman signed for $1200 before he wound up paying for the beer.

Koosman had a reputation as a goof-off in the lower minor leagues but by 1967, his third season, he pitched nine games for the Mets. In 1968 he was ready. He won his first four decisions and helped keep the Mets close to that long-anticipated .500 mark.

The pitchers had a new, improved Jerry Grote to pitch to. Perhaps Grote was intimidated by all the former catchers on the Met staff (Yogi Berra, Rube Walker, Joe Pignatano, and even Hodges). They requested him to mix his calls better while catching, and they requested that he speak nicely to his pitchers, since they were, after all, on the same team. They also requested that he cut down on his swing and try to meet the ball. All of a sudden, Grote began punching base hits into the corners (the Mets joked that he was "unconscious"), and the pitchers began enjoying him more.

Another new Met was Ken Boswell, a young bachelor from Austin, Texas, who may have had the worst set of hands of any second baseman since Chuck "Dr. No" Hiller. But Boswell also had a quick left-handed swing, and Hodges kept working him into the lineup.

Maybe the most heartwarming development in 1968 was the rejuvenation of Ed Charles. The wise old poet had been lopped off the roster after 1967 to make room for younger players. But in his last fling at baseball, he tried out for the Mets again in the spring of 1968 and succeeded.

Charles was thirty-five but had been in the major leagues only six seasons, having run into a quota system for Negro players.

The Milwaukee Braves tried a dozen all-white second basemen while he was batting near .300 in the minor leagues. "Baby," Charles sighed in his later years, "that was a hurtin' thing."

Charles finally got himself traded to the Kansas City Athletics, where the quota was a little higher, and he batted .288 as a rookie. The eccentric owner, Charles O. Finley, tried to cut his salary but the athlete was becoming used to the ways of baseball's various Mr. Charlies. He hopefully settled down in Kansas City, began studying poetry in college, married, and had a son. But even here he knew heartbreak, as he soon learned that his son suffered from cerebral palsy and would need special care throughout childhood. But through all his troubles, Charles' message was hopeful instead of bitter.

A religious person might say that Charles had endured all these sufferings for a purpose, and that purpose might have been the welding of a ball club in New York in 1968. Charles soon became the most popular man in the Met clubhouse. The Mets had always been a basically white team, as opposed to teams like St. Louis and Pittsburgh where many of the leading players are blacks, but Charles seemed to raise all twenty-five players beyond race. Everybody liked to call him "old man" or variations on that theme. They roared when Nick Torman, the swinging clubhouse man, left various souvenirs in Charles' locker. They laughed when Charles threw towels, wet towels, in Torman's face. When players would tease him, Charles would feign disappointment and say: "All right, if you want to be that way." Then everybody would break out laughing. By mid-season, Charles was playing regularly and batting over .300 and the whole team rejoiced with him.

Another reason why the Mets were a harmonious ball club—while other clubs knew racial tensions—was Rocky Swoboda. He got along very well with Charles, Alvin Jackson, Agee, and Jones, the four black players on the team. Once it was written that Swoboda had invited the four to his home for a Maryland crab dinner. Rocky got a few hate letters for it, but he also helped set an example in the clubhouse, making less idealistic white players reach out with just a little bit of themselves.

By mid-season, the Mets had a 39–43 record, and for the first time in their history they placed three men on the All-Star squad.

Jerry Grote was voted to start for the National League, and he batted twice before leaving the game. Seaver pitched the seventh and eighth innings, giving up two hits but striking out five men—Carl Yastrzemski, Joe Azcue, Boog Powell, Mickey Mantle, and Rick Monday.

With the National League leading, 1–0, in the ninth inning, Koosman came in to face the left-handed Yastrzemski and struck him out to end the game. The Mets had gone from a stage when they were included on the All-Star team as a formality to a point where they contributed to the victories.

However, they began to slump after the All-Star game. Dick Selma, the strong-willed pitcher who had once paid for his own operation, hit a losing streak, Harrelson's knee needed an operation, and Boswell and Ryan were frequently away on military reserve duty.

Ryan was still the next Bob Feller or the next Sandy Koufax, but it was always next—never now. He suffered from blisters on his fingers, and the only thing that toughened the skin was a pickle brine that trainer Gus Mauch purchased in a supermarket near Yankee Stadium.

The young right-hander was still inconsistent. He could strike out eleven men in seven innings but then grow tired and lose the game. Just when he seemed to be getting in a groove, he would be called away to reserve meetings in Texas. When he returned, his rhythm would be gone again. But Walker and Hodges were patient with him because they knew what he could become.

To bolster their pitching staff, the Mets called up James Clement McAndrew from Jacksonville in July. The slender right-hander from Lost Nation, Iowa, had a degree in psychology from the University of Iowa and had also taught in the Job Corps. He felt as if he had joined the Poverty Corps, because he lost his first four starts as the Mets failed to score a single run for him. He finally found how to win, as he shut out the Cardinals.

More pitching help came from Calvin Lee Koonce, a cool and fair-haired righty from Hope Mills, N.C. A former bonus boy with the Cubs, Koonce had come over to the Mets late in 1967 and credited a good performance to his spitball.

Pitchers do not usually go around admitting they throw a spitball, and Koonce claimed he "gave up" the illegal pitch after Hodges arrived. He must have been throwing something good because he helped as a starter and reliever in 1968. A stockbroker in the off-season, he also had ambitions to play professional golf in the future.

There were still several gaps on the squad, particularly in the power department. But every time the old Mets would have fallen into a deadly eight-game losing streak, Seaver or Koosman would shut somebody out. There were other games when it almost seemed the Mets were afraid to lose, for fear of getting an icy stare from the manager.

Going into the last week of the season, they had a record of 71–86, only five victories more than Westrum's 1966 record. And they still had to hold off the Astros for ninth place, so each game was going to be important. Hodges must have felt they were important. He was smoking three packs of cigarettes a day and he was starting to feel pains in his chest.

20

HEART ATTACK

◆

It was the last Tuesday night of the 1968 season. The Mets were opening a series in Atlanta and Gil Hodges, as usual, pitched ten minutes of batting practice, throwing overhand with an easy motion. Then he swatted some fungoes to the outfield. Sometimes Hodges even jumped into the batting cage to hit a few solid-sounding fly balls. But he was not feeling well this night, so he headed for the dugout.

In the second inning, Hodges felt pains running across his chest. He had felt uncomfortable on the previous weekend in Philadelphia but he had put it down as a cold perhaps, or maybe the result of too many cigarettes. He was up to three packs a day now, which wasn't helping his chest pains at all.

Hodges could not sit comfortably in the dugout, so he whispered to Rube Walker that he was going to lie down in the clubhouse for a while. He deputized his trusty pitching coach, who was kind of a Friar Tuck to his Robin Hood, to run the club in his absence.

The manager lay on a rubbing table in the trainer's room for an hour. Then Gus Mauch, who had suffered a heart attack in 1960, became worried and called for the Braves' team physician. Before long, Hodges was in Crawford W. Long Hospital, under the care of Dr. Linton Bishop, who had once treated a heart patient named Lyndon B. Johnson.

The first electrocardiogram showed no heart attack but it did indicate certain "changes" taking place in Hodges' heart. In effect, the doctors could foresee that Hodges was about to suffer a heart attack.

By this time the game was over, and the Mets realized their manager was hospitalized with chest pains. The reporters asked where Hodges was but the loyal Walker and Pignatano refused to say anything. They did not want Joan Hodges to learn anything back home in Brooklyn until there was something definite to tell her.

At 12:30 A.M., Dr. Bishop called Mrs. Hodges and said her husband would be hospitalized for several days. She and a friend, Mrs. Vivian Gold, caught a 3:30 A.M. flight to Atlanta and were met at the airport by Walker and Pignatano. In the morning Hodges greeted his wife and enjoyed a breakfast of juice, cereal, and scrambled eggs. He also visited with Rube Walker, discussing plans for the last four games.

That afternoon, a second electrocardiogram showed that Hodges, since his first test, had suffered a "small coronary thrombosis but that his condition is good," according to Dr. Bishop. "There is no doubt in my mind," the doctor continued, "that he will be able to resume his full duties in the future."

Hodges said: "I realize I need a rest, and that's what I'm going to do." His wife took a hotel room in Atlanta and visited him as he rested, dieted, and began the fight against smoking.

The Met management insisted right from the start that Hodges was the manager for 1969 and that there were no doubts about his resuming full duties. The club had finished at 73–89, the best record in its history, and much of the credit could be given to Hodges.

With young players finally arriving on the squad, the manager had given them a stable and secure environment. He was in the first of a three-year contract, so he had the security to build. He also knew he had the affection of the New York fans. And there was the new serenity of the John Murphy front office.

Hodges' staff had a part in the success too. Walker was in

charge of the pitchers. If he told them to run, it was the same as if Hodges had told them. He also laid out the pitching rotation and Hodges approved it. Pignatano was kind of a straw boss, jollying with the players, letting them know that he knew all the angles and had probably exploited a few of them in his own time. But he could also be very direct when he felt somebody was testing him. Eddie Yost and Yogi Berra coached on the baselines and offered quiet and sound advice.

His quartet of coaches had enabled Hodges to remain aloof from most of the problems. He could joke with the players or take a few swings in batting practice without disrupting the routine. The players all realized that behind that bland façade was a tough man who could—in Casey's immortal words— "squeeze your ear-brows off."

When Hodges did have something to say, the message usually came across. There was the time in spring training when Rocky Swoboda pulled the old Sammy Drake trick of disappearing to the bathroom when he was due at bat. When Rocky returned, he found somebody else in the on-deck circle and was told he was out of the game. The sensitive young slugger realized that details were a little more precise in the new administration.

Hodges was able to make a ruling without much conversation. There was the trip when several younger players purchased cowboy hats and wore them on the team plane.

"Enjoy the hats," Hodges said cheerily, "because tomorrow you won't be wearing them." The next day, the hats were no longer to be seen.

Hodges also enforced training and curfew rules more strictly than Stengel or Westrum. A home-loving man who liked to play cards with his wife in the evening, Hodges naturally assumed that all players should enjoy peaceful evenings at their respective quarters. Occasionally he would force himself to stay up until midnight around the hotel to see which players were sneaking in past curfew.

One morning Hodges called the squad together in Florida and said he knew four of them had broken training the night before. He wanted them to turn in their $50 fines privately, or else he would embarrass them by naming names.

A few hours later, Piggy whispered to Hodges: "Hey, Gilly, you're going good. You've got nine checks already."

The discipline had its positive side because the players knew what they were expected to do. Hodges didn't give them pep talks or exhort them to "do or die." If anything, he was uncommunicative and tended to hold his anger inside him. But the Mets became emboldened by his firm leadership and they began playing the game harder than Mets had ever played.

In the old days, the Mets had been dumped on their collective rear ends by the good, hustling players like Willie Mays and Frank Robinson. But now it was Cleon Jones and Tommie Agee who were getting the reputation for hard slides. The Houston Astros were nursing several grievances against certain hard-sliding Mets and even started a fight in the Astrodome one night.

There was no doubt that the Mets were a different team under Hodges. The groundwork of Weiss and Devine, of Stengel and Westrum, was finally paying off in response to the leadership of one special man. But now that special man lay in a hospital in Atlanta, with the biggest challenge of his life in front of him.

Baseball had really put few demands on Gil Hodges. He was naturally disciplined, so he did not have to force himself to be. His magnificent reflexes, his size and strength, had made him an All-Star slugger and fielder. A more fiery disposition might have ruined his placid skill.

Before this, the biggest challenge of Hodges' career had come when the Dodgers switched from Brooklyn to Los Angeles. He slumped from a .299 average with 98 runs-batted-in in 1957 to .259 with 64 RBIs in 1958, a predictable slump for a thirty-four-year-old player, but one obviously complicated by his homesickness for the comfortable life back home in Brooklyn.

Later with the Mets, Hodges had been thirty-eight years old and bothered by a bad knee. In the spring of 1963, Casey had waited for Hodges to push himself into condition. Finally Casey could stand it no longer and penciled Hodges' name into the starting lineup. Hodges began to sweat when he saw his name, and he began absentmindedly tapping one fist into the palm of his other hand.

"He's never had to push himself before," said one of his old friends from Brooklyn. "I've never seen Gilly look scared."

As it turned out, the knee was too far gone for him to help the Mets in 1963, and he soon moved on to manage the Senators. As a manager, he demonstrated inner strength and intelligence that might have seemed out of place in this bland Hoosier. Yet now, recuperating in the hospital, he was being asked to push himself back from this murky accident that had happened deep inside his forty-four-year-old heart.

Just as he had done in that spring of 1963, Hodges began to work himself back slowly. He padded around his hospital room and he watched the World Series on television. "The only game that excites me is a Met game," he told the doctors. He played gin rummy with his wife and smiled when he lost. Then he checked out of the hospital and resumed his recuperation in an Atlanta hotel. On October 23, Joan and Gil Hodges flew to St. Petersburg, where he loafed around and watched an occasional Instructional League game.

The doctors had estimated that in four or five weeks Hodges would be walking and exercising. But when he returned to Brooklyn in November, Hodges had admittedly done very little exercising.

Reporters heard about this and began speculating whether Hodges would be able to come back and manage. They pointed out that Lyndon Johnson had come back from a serious heart attack in his fifties to manage an entire country but apparently motivation was the key to any recovery.

Hodges spent December in Brooklyn. He was supposed to take long walks, but when the Mets held a telephone press conference for him one day, he said:

"I haven't walked for five days now because it's just been too cold," he said. "That's why I'm going back to Florida. They want me to walk twenty blocks. I don't think I ever walked twenty blocks in my business."

He did say that he expected to resume full authority when spring camp opened in February.

"If the doctor gave me a bad diagnosis, I'd change doctors, that's all," Hodges said with his characteristic droll delivery.

He finally gave up smoking, fought off his wife's fine Italian cooking, and dropped to 201 pounds from the 225 he had been carrying in September. Then he went south and started exercising. In February he was cleared for full-time duty and reported to spring training. It had taken a little longer than expected, but now Hodges seemed ready for the rigorous days ahead.

There was an immediate problem in spring training as the Players Association conducted a boycott of the camps to back up its negotiations with the owners. Any player with major-league experience was asked by the Players Association to stay out of camp. Some clubs had almost 100 per cent absenteeism among their veteran players. The Yankees, now under the enlightened leadership of Michael Burke of the Columbia Broadcasting System and Lee MacPhail—Tom Seaver's benefactor—told their players they would not be persecuted for sticking together during the negotiations.

But M. Donald Grant chose to negotiate with his players, pressuring the less secure players into signing contracts, and the Mets had a divided camp in February.

Ryan, McGraw, Koonce, and Grote were among the handful who showed up for the first workouts, while Seaver, Koosman, Jackson, Taylor, and Harrelson played catch in their "minicamp" in a park in St. Petersburg. Working out in tennis sneakers and bermuda shorts, the five Mets were served lunches daily by Nancy Seaver. But they indicated they would not strike for long.

"I believe baseball remains one of the few things that reward individual effort in our country," Seaver said, "and I want it to remain that way. I don't want to become unionized. . . .

"I feel a certain loyalty to the club, which has treated me royally. . . . I feel a certain loyalty to my family and to myself. . . . On the other hand, I believe in what the Association is trying to do and I have a certain feeling for my fellow players."

A few players, like their representative, Ed Kranepool, vowed to stay away from camp until the strike was settled. When the owners and the Association finally agreed to terms on February 24, the players began to report to camp. But there was the possibility that the Mets would be split for months to come because some had honored the strike and others hadn't.

Some faces were missing when the squad finally assembled. Dick Selma and Larry Stahl had been selected by San Diego while Don Shaw had gone to Montreal as the National League expanded to twelve teams. Three promising youngsters, Jerry Morales, Ernie McAnally, and John Glass, had also been swiped by expansion. Don Bosch had been sold to the Expos while Jerry Buchek, Billy Short, and Phil Linz had all been dropped since the end of 1968.

The most important new face seemed to be Amos Otis, a light-skinned Negro who had grown up near Jones and Agee in Mobile. Otis had batted .286 as Jacksonville won the International League play-offs in 1968. The Mets were convinced that Otis was going to play third base or the outfield for them in 1969.

Other clubs expected great things of Otis, too, because they kept asking for him in a trade. The Mets were finally in a position where they had talent that every other club wanted. The Mets were not against a trade, either. The Philadelphia Phillies were offering their unpredictable slugger, Richie Allen, if the price was right. In the Mets' case, the price was Seaver or Koosman. The Mets turned that one down. Allen might be the next Babe Ruth if he could show up on time for the games. But the Mets didn't dare give up a Seaver or a Koosman for Allen, so they countered with Ryan or McAndrew. When the Phillies said, "And Amos Otis," the deal fell through.

Another club came even closer to the big deal. The acerbic general manager of the Atlanta Braves, Paul Richards, had managed to alienate one of his stars, the husky Joe Torre. They had been feuding in 1968 and the players' strike made bitter enemies of them. Now Torre was sulking at his home in Manhasset, Long Island, only twenty minutes from Shea Stadium. The Braves would be glad to let Torre play in his hometown. All it would take was Ryan, Grote, and that young fellow, Amos Somebody-or-Other. The next sound you heard was the hollow "thunk" of the Atlanta-New York deal falling through the trap door and into oblivion.

"Otis is one of our untouchables," Murphy said on March 17, also naming Seaver, Koosman, Swoboda, Grote, Jones, and Harrelson. (But not Agee.)

"I never knew the Mets had so many untouchables," groused Richards. "I'm surprised they didn't win the pennant."

It was a remark that Murphy and Grant would have cause to savor in the months to come.

So the Mets did not make any deals in the spring of 1969. Instead they added young Gary Gentry to their pitching staff, groomed Otis to open the season at third base, held their breath on Tommie Agee, and inspected Bud Harrelson's repaired knee.

Hodges had a calm, healthy spring except for the morning he tripped on his walk and suffered contusions of the ankle. He went fishing in the evening, chasing the players from his favorite spot on the pier, helping his wife pull in a twenty-nine-pound drumfish off the Intracoastal Waterway. The manager took all the draggy bus rides to Orlando and Sarasota; he made all the decisions in the dugout; he never needed a minute off.

When asked how his team would do, Hodges estimated that it should win eighty-five games in 1969. That would be good enough for third place, maybe even enough to challenge the Cubs for second place. Nobody expected the Mets to challenge the Cardinals. You don't go about overthrowing a dynasty with rookies named Wayne Garrett and Rod Gaspar.

And so the Mets headed north to open the season with an outpatient for a manager. Hodges had come through fine in spring training, but that is a casual and enjoyable period for most baseball people. The real test would come when the Mets started throwing the ball away in some chilly ball park in the first month of the season. When the losses started to count, how would Gil Hodges' personal electrocardiogram respond?

21

THE MANAGER
GETS MAD

◆

THE SEASON STARTED as all other Met seasons had started—with a loss. The Montreal Expos, the new expansion team playing its first game, beat the Mets, 11–10, on a raw, windy day at Shea. And to rub it in, the winning pitcher was Don Shaw, the left-hander drafted from the Mets in the fall, and one of the Expo outfielders was Don Bosch.

The 44,541 fans laughed at the antics, which included a homer by a rookie relief pitcher named Dan McGinn, three errors by the heavy-handed Ken Boswell, and five sloppy innings by Tom Seaver. "Same old Mets," laughed the multitudes.

The same old Mets even lost seven of their first ten games. In other years, it would have been a signal to call off the season. But the Mets had too much pitching to fall into any deep slumps. Seaver, Ryan, and Koosman won within four days, and the Mets made their move toward what seemed their ultimate goal—mediocrity.

The Cubs came to New York in April and won three out of four games. In one of the losses, Seaver was mad at himself for letting Ferguson Jenkins, a pitcher, and Don Kessinger and Ron

Santo hit home runs off him. He vowed he would not let them dig into the batter's box the next time he faced the Cubs.

The Mets visited Chicago in early May and lost the first two games. Then it was Seaver's turn on Sunday. The first time Santo came to bat, Seaver knocked him down with a fastball over his head. The Cubs did not care for this, so Billy Hands hit Seaver in the forearm when Seaver came to bat. Seaver did not care for that, so he hit Hands in the leg when he came to bat.

By this time, the umpires figured out what was happening and they warned Seaver about throwing beanballs, a warning carrying an automatic $50 fine. Seaver did not seem to mind the money.

"Santo was hitting me well," Seaver told Larry Merchant of the *Post*. "Possibly he's taking the bread out of my mouth. I had to make sure he respects me. You can't let a hitter dominate you or intimidate you. There has to be respect. I had to let Santo know I knew what he was doing to me."

Seaver beat the Cubs in that game, making the fine a little easier to take. In the second game, the new, mature Tug McGraw also beat the Cubs. The brash left-hander, who had compared himself to a tough young gunslinger when he beat Sandy Koufax in 1965, was now an old married man of twenty-four. During the winter he had organized a youth program in his hometown of Vallejo, California, encouraging youngsters to stay in school, to investigate the problems of drugs, to seek good vocational training. Then he came to spring training and advanced his own vocation, making the team with a good showing.

A week after the double victory, the Mets dipped down to their new Tidewater, Virginia, farm team and recalled Art Shamsky. The tall, dark first baseman-outfielder had come over from Cincinnati in 1968. He had good power potential, having once hit three homers in a game for the Reds after coming in as a late-inning replacement. He was well-received in New York, which is always delighted to find a Jewish ball player. The New York *Post* even had him write a clubhouse gossip column in 1968, ghosted by Maury Allen. Shamsky was in a good position to hear the gossip. Since he batted only .238 and was weak defensively, he was not on the field very often.

But 1969 started even worse for Shamsky. He injured his back in spring training and was afraid he might need an operation. Rest cured the back, however, and Shamsky was ready to begin training. When Johnny Murphy sent him to Tidewater to let him play himself into condition, Shamsky balked. The Mets finally promised they would consider recalling him as soon as the minimum twenty-one-day period was ended. He played well in Tidewater and was back in New York after twenty-one days.

In his first game back, Shamsky drove in a run with a pinch hit—but the *Post* did not ask him to resume the column.

By May 15, the Mets were still floundering a few games below .500 and some of his friends thought Hodges was holding in his anger, never a healthy sign for a heart patient. The people told Hodges to let his emotions go, not to hold himself in check.

On May 15, Don Cardwell made a throwing error on a sure double play in the second inning. The Atlanta Braves followed with two hits for three runs. The Mets made another error later, plus several sloppy nonerrors, and lost the game, 6–5, when Felix Millan made a leaping catch of Cleon Jones' bases-loaded line drive in the ninth. True, the Mets could say they had almost pulled a victory from defeat. But Hodges had a different point of view.

When the players trooped back to the clubhouse, Hodges had the door locked while the reporters waited outside. Outside the heavy door, the reporters could hear nothing. But inside, the players could hear plenty.

The men sat on the stools in their cubicles while the manager stood in the center of the clubhouse. Without raising his voice, Hodges reminded them that they were currently in a major-league clubhouse, which required a major-league effort from all of them. There was no dialogue, because Hodges did not run a democracy. When he stopped talking, the meeting was over.

When the door opened, the reporters were cautious about asking Hodges about the meeting. Nobody wanted to be the one to cause a second heart attack. But on the other hand, Hodges seemed rather healthy and secure as he stared down his friends from the press—in a friendly way, of course.

"Well, couldn't you give us an idea?" one of the reporters asked.

"We had a meeting. It's a clubhouse thing. It pertained to the game," Hodges said casually.

The players were not eager to discuss the meeting but eventually it was learned that Hodges had chewed them out. One player described the manager as "heatedly exasperated."

"He didn't single out any players by name," said Tug McGraw. "The players who were yelled at knew they were the ones being yelled at. If the shoe fits, wear it."

"We needed it," Seaver said. "I expect it to help us. We're mature. We are supposed to be able to take it. The man is on our side. He's a perfectionist. That's fabulous. I strive for that myself."

The perfection came quicker than expected. The Mets won two straight in Cincinnati. Then Seaver pitched a three-hit shutout in Atlanta to pull the Mets' record to 18–18, the first time they had ever hit .500 this late in the season.

Reporters burst into the clubhouse expecting a wild champagne party. Instead they found athletes sitting around sipping on beers and sodas, just like always.

"Tom, Tom," Jack Lang said to Seaver, who was normally so reponsive to whatever was blowing in the wind. "You're a .500 ball club. Aren't you going to celebrate?"

Seaver surveyed the delegation of reporters. "What's so good about .500?" the pitcher asked. "That's only mediocre. We didn't come into this season to play .500 ball. I'm tired of the jokes about the old Mets. Let Rod Kanehl and Marvelous Marv laugh about the Mets. We're out here to win. You know when we'll have champagne? When we win the pennant."

"Great," muttered Maury Allen. "But I'll be too old to enjoy it."

The press had a great time laughing about the players' refusal to celebrate their own mediocrity. Then it seemed only fitting that the Mets lost their next five straight. Perhaps they would break out the champagne if they ever reached .500 again.

There was a sad note at this time when Alvin Jackson was sold to Cincinnati. The little lefty, still the leading all-time Met winner, had dug his roots in the Long Island suburbs, and his vivacious wife, Nadine, and his two boys were familiar sights at

Shea Stadium. But sentiment didn't help Little Alvin, and he
moved on to Cincinnati.

Jackson had been made expendable by another left-hander,
twenty-six-year-old Jack DiLauro, a refugee from the Detroit system. DiLauro was purchased from Tidewater when Nolan Ryan
suffered a pulled groin muscle. The new man worked so well
to left-handed hitters that he won Jackson's job when Ryan came
back. The Mets soon discovered that DiLauro could do a fine
imitation of Ed Sullivan, and he helped enliven some of the long
plane rides and hours in the bullpen.

The most encouraging new man was Gary Gentry, a poker-
faced right-hander who was being called "The Next Tom Seaver."
He was only twenty-two years old, and he had two years of minor-
league ball, but he looked as if he had been a professional for
a decade. He was dark-eyed and slender, not the extrovert that
Seaver was, but he had the same secure background in family
and sports.

When he was graduated from high school, Gentry had been
pursued by several clubs but his father insisted he go to college.
Ed Gentry had been a pilot in World War II and the Korean
War, and then, in his thirties, had studied to become an elemen-
tary schoolteacher. The father stressed education to the son, and
the son listened.

"My father said that I couldn't sign. He said he would make
the decisions then and in two years I could make my own."

So Gary spurned the drafts of the Orioles, Astros, and Giants
and went to Phoenix Junior College for two years. Then, in his
first season at Arizona State, he had a 17–1 record and won two
games in the College World Series. His ratio of 229 strikeouts
in 174 innings was one of the best in college history. This time
the bonus offer was from the Mets, and it was a good one, so Ed
and Gary Gentry agreed it was time to sign.

Gentry pitched at Williamsburg and Jacksonville, and then he
came to St. Petersburg in 1969 with his pretty blond wife, Janet,
his small son, Christopher, and his large St. Bernard dog. They
all made the team.

Gentry denied that he was "another Seaver" when people
praised him for his maturity and drive. "When I look at Tom, I

just hope I can pitch like him some day," Gentry said. "Tom always knows what he's doing."

Things were getting better all the time. The Mets now had a twenty-two-year-old pitcher emulating a twenty-four-year-old veteran.

Two other young players made the club in 1969. One was Wayne "Rusty" Garrett, a freckle-faced redhead with the Tom Sawyer country-boy look to him. He and two brothers had all signed out of rural Brooksville, Florida, into the Brave organization. But after four years in the system, Garrett had the label of "nonprospect" until Bob Scheffing of the Mets saw something he liked. The Mets drafted him for $25,000 in the winter of 1968, and he hustled his way onto the team as a spare infielder.

The other new Met was Rodney Earl Gaspar, a bright-eyed native of Long Beach, California, who had batted .260 and .309 in two years of AA ball. He didn't have much power but he was fast and he could play the outfield well. On the new Mets, a young player who could help in a few categories was a positive addition. He was not expected to carry the whole ball club, the way some rookies had been burdened in the past.

After that five-game losing streak, the Mets went on the longest winning streak in their history. It started on May 29, when Koosman struck out fifteen in ten innings in a scoreless tie with San Diego. McGraw stopped the Padres in the top of the eleventh, and an error and Harrelson's single won it in the bottom of the inning.

The amazing victories just kept happening.

May 30—The Mets scored three in the eighth and Taylor saved Seaver's seventh victory, 4–3, over the Giants.

May 31—Charles hit a homer and drove in all the runs as Gentry and McGraw beat the Giants, 4–2.

June 1—Swoboda and Grote were the hitting stars as the Mets beat the Giants, 5–4, with a run in the ninth.

June 2—Koosman struck out eight to beat the Dodgers, 2–1. The Mets were at .500 again but still no champagne.

June 3—McGraw protected Seaver's 5–2 victory over the Dodgers to put the Mets above .500 for the first time this "late" in the season.

June 4—Willie Davis let a base hit get past him in center field as Agee raced all the way around the bases in the fifteenth inning as the Dodgers went down, 1–0.

Then the Mets went West with their seven-game winning streak.

June 6—Agee had three hits as Gentry beat San Diego, 5–3.

June 7—Koosman struck out eleven as Gaspar had three hits in a 4–1 victory over San Diego.

June 8—Seaver and Taylor beat the Padres, 3–2.

June 10—Taylor saved Cardwell's 9–4 victory over the Giants.

The next day the streak ended after eleven victories, but the rest of the league had been warned. The spurt gave the Mets only six losses more than the Chicago Cubs, who had taken the early lead in the Eastern Division. The Cardinals, the defending champions, already had six losses more than the Mets.

Even at this early stage, the Cubs' good start was a break for the Mets. Many people had expected the Mets to finish ahead of Pittsburgh, Philadelphia, and Montreal, and there was even some sentiment about battling the Cubs for second place. But hardly anybody expected the Mets to catch the Cardinals.

The Cardinals had too much ability for the Mets. They had Bob Gibson, Lou Brock, Tim McCarver, Curt Flood. But they had also won two straight pennants and had begun to enjoy very big money. The lowest salary among the regulars, it was written, was the $37,500 paid to the weak-hitting shortstop, Dal Maxvill.

In the spring of 1969, Gussie Busch had jolted the Cardinals in a public message that they owed a great deal to the fans and that their financial interests should not be placed ahead of team and civic spirit. Nobody quite knew what Busch had in mind but some people inferred that he was warning his players against becoming "fat cats." Everyone agreed that the key Cardinal players were not the type to become complacent.

When Trader Bing shipped Orlando Cepeda to Atlanta in spring training in return for Joe Torre, the Cardinals took it casually. They would miss Cha-Cha and his phonograph and his cheerleading, but they were receiving equal value in Torre. The Cardinals expected no slump at all, but they lost their first three games to Pittsburgh and they were in trouble right from the start.

Thus the Mets could look over their shoulders—far over their shoulders—and see the Cardinals. And when they looked ahead —far ahead—all they could see were the Cubs.

The Mets were not afraid of the Cubs. Going into 1969, the Mets had more victories against the Cubs than against any other club, having beaten them fifty-five times in seven seasons. A few veteran Mets even remembered humiliating the Cubs, 19–1, back in 1964 and sweeping entire weekends from the Cubs when they were going through their "head coach" lunacy. They remembered Leo Durocher saying in 1966: "This is no eighth-place team," and then proving it by finishing tenth—thereby getting the Mets out of the dungeon for the first time in history.

Sure, the Cubs had Ferguson Jenkins, Ken Holtzman, and Billy Hands, a fine starting trio of pitchers. The Cubs had an inspirational star in Ron Santo, a fine hitter in Billy Williams, and the soul of the franchise in Ernie Banks. They had three excellent young players in Glenn Beckert, Don Kessinger, and Randy Hundley. The Cubs had a fine ball club but the Mets just were not awed by them. This is a gut feeling that dogs and little boys experience, a special sense that tells whom they can beat and whom they can't beat. The Mets had no particular gut feeling that they couldn't beat the Cubs.

For the first time in their lives, the Mets began grabbing newspapers at odd hours to check how the Cubs had done. For the first time in their lives, the Mets were chasing somebody in a pennant race. They wouldn't admit it publicly, but it was happening.

Something else happened on June 15 to persuade the Mets they were in a pennant race. John Murphy came up with the kind of trade that clubs make when they are chasing for a pennant.

The general manager sent Kevin Collins and three young pitchers from the farm system—Steve Renko, Jay Carden, and Dave Colon—to the Montreal Expos in return for Donn Clendenon.

Clendenon was a thirty-four-year-old law student from Atlanta's Morehouse University. He had been the first baseman at Pittsburgh from 1962 to 1968, hitting homers and striking out frequently.

When the Pirates let him be chosen by Montreal in the expansion draft, Clendenon decided to play. But when Montreal traded him to Houston, Clendenon decided not to play. He had already heard Houston manager Harry "the Talker" Walker's lectures on batting when both were with the Pirates. Besides, Clendenon had been offered an executive job with Scripto in his hometown of Atlanta, and he also had a restaurant opening down there, so he figured it was time to retire.

However, Monte Irvin, the former Giant star, now an assistant to the commissioner, urged Clendenon to come out of retirement. Bowie Kuhn, the new commissioner, ruled that Clendenon still belonged to Montreal, and Clendenon went north, only to fall into an early slump.

The Mets had been searching for an experienced power hitter all year. Now they were willing to give up four young fringe players for that older player who might help them make that run at the first-place Cubs.

22

THE FIRST BIG GAME

◆

ERNIE BANKS TRIPPED GAILY into the noon sunlight. Ernie liked sunshine, and he had seen a lot of it in his seventeen summers with the Chicago Cubs, playing only day baseball in Wrigley Field.

Now Ernie was in New York for the opening of a three-game series in July, a series that was being treated with World Series intensity by the fans and by the reporters. The Mets had won five straight games and the Cubs had lost three straight, giving them only three losses fewer than the Mets. But if Ernie was nervous about these three games in Shea Stadium, he was not showing it.

"I like New York in June, how about you?" he crooned. "I like a Gershwin tune, how about you?"

Ernie had been singing to us ever since the Mets came into the league. He was the sunniest man in baseball, a flower child among the many dour players who trudge out to the ball field every day. Ernie loved to put on his Cubbie uniform with the No. 14 and go out and greet the New York writers. But mostly he loved to sing to us.

"East Side, West Side, all around the town," he sang, doing a little tap dance in the on-deck circle.

Then he got as serious as any man ever sees Ernie Banks. In

a conspiratorial tone, he revealed to the writers: "The Cubs are gonna shine in sixty-nine." We all nodded. Years before, Ernie had told us: "The Cubs are due in sixty-two."

So this was the kind of atmosphere that prevailed on the field of Shea Stadium on July 8 as 55,096 fans—unable to hear Ernie Banks singing—packed the ball park. And the reporters spilled in from magazines and from newspapers around the country, giving the game a World Series feeling. Of course, who can knock a few days in New York at any time?

Mrs. Joan Payson could not make the game because she had enrolled at the Elizabeth Arden health farm in Maine for the week. So she did the next best thing. She arranged for the games to be televised over a Maine station that would ordinarily not carry the Mets.

Frank Graddock was having television problems too. The laborer from Queens County was trying to watch the Mets in his living room this afternoon but his wife kept insisting on watching *Dark Shadows,* a program about supernatural beings. Blows were struck, according to police, and Mrs. Graddock went upstairs and lay down and died later that night. Graddock would have to follow the rest of the series from jail.

Not everybody was as excited as Frank Graddock about the first game. Manager Hodges set the tone for his players by droning: "I don't believe you can have a big series in July. Sure, we want to win today. We want to win tomorrow. But our season will not end regardless of what happens. I'm sorry I can't make it more exciting, but that's how I feel."

The pitchers for the first game were Koosman, bogged down with a 5–5 record, and Ferguson Jenkins, the tall right-hander with an 11–5 record.

Nobody scored until the fifth inning when Ed Kranepool whacked a homer with nobody on base. But then Banks did the same thing in the top of the sixth and lazed his way around the bases, basking in the sunshine as usual.

In the seventh Glenn Beckert broke the tie with a single. Then in the eighth, old Hilly-Billy Hickman—the last original Met himself—hit a homer to give the Cubs a 3–1 lead.

Going into the bottom of the ninth, Kranepool's homer was

still the only hit off Jenkins and the score was still 3–1. But the
fans, of course, were still screaming.

"A year ago I would have felt it was pretty helpless," Koosman recalled later. "But sitting on the bench, listening to that
crowd and all, I thought we could come back."

So the Mets came up for their last chance, and Ken Boswell,
not playing regularly because Hodges wasn't satisfied with his
effort, was sent up to pinch-hit. He clubbed a fly to shallow center that rookie Don Young could not reach, and it fell for a double.

Tommie Agee fouled out but Donn Clendenon lashed a long
drive to left center. This time Young raced back and got his
glove on the ball, just before bouncing off the green wooden fence.
The ball popped loose for a double, putting runners on second
and third.

The next batter was Cleon Jones, whose batting had gotten the
Mets this close to first place. Leo Durocher visited Jenkins at the
mound and told his best pitcher to "battle him." Durocher did
not want to walk Jones and put the winning run on base, but he
assumed that Jenkins would not give Jones anything good to hit.

Jenkins did not mean to do this, but he got a curve ball a little
too close to the plate and Jones smashed it into left field for a two-
run double that tied the game.

Now it seemed clear that at least for this one sunny afternoon
the Mets had magic working for them. The fans stood and cheered
as Jenkins walked Art Shamsky, and Wayne Garrett moved both
runners over with a grounder. With two outs, runners on second
and third, the batter was Kranepool.

Kid Kranepool. Frank Thomas had teased him in 1962. Casey
Stengel had played him in right field in 1963. In 1964 the banner
had asked: IS ED KRANEPOOL OVER THE HILL? Now in 1969, Kranepool was the fans' least favorite Met. He had become wealthy
through a job in the stock market and he played like a man with
money in the bank. The fans couldn't realize this as he stepped up
to bat, but Kranepool was not thinking of the money. He had
plenty of that. He was thinking of making up for all those losses
he had known.

Jenkins put a curve ball a little too close to the plate and
Kranepool reached out and tapped the ball over the shortstop,

too shallow for the left fielder, just right for a game-winning single as Jones scored the biggest run in Met history—so far, at least. After 439 victories and 771 defeats, the Mets had won themselves their big game.

The Mets had tried so hard to appear cool, but now they burst out of the dugout, pounding Kranepool on the back. In the clubhouse they shouted things like "attaboy," words that seemed out of place in a professional locker room. "We've got momentum now," Jones shouted.

Over in the Cub clubhouse, the players were not smiling. They were listening with amazement as Ron Santo, the spirited and mature captain of the Cubs, blasted the rookie, Don Young, for not catching the two fly balls in the ninth inning.

"The only reason he's in the lineup is for his glove," Santo growled, loud enough for everybody to hear.

The Cubs had not been prepared to brood over one little loss. But now their captain's words turned them silent and apprehensive. They dressed fast and scurried out of the stadium, many of them avoiding the team bus back to Manhattan. The next game was not until the following night. They now had twenty-four hours to think about this loss.

Santo thought about it all night. Then on Wednesday morning he called Young in the hotel and apologized for his outburst of the day before. Santo also called the Chicago reporters and publicly apologized for his blast. "It wasn't like me at all," he said.

It wasn't, either. Santo is one of the most considerate of all the stars. He seemed as amazed as anybody that he could have behaved like this. But somehow his public apology made people more aware of the tensions of a pennant race. Now people began watching the Cubs closely. The Cubs may even have started watching each other.

On Wednesday night the Cubs also watched Tom Seaver stretching and straining in the early innings. Seaver seemed to have some kind of shoulder stiffness and he took a few innings to get loose. But then the ball started blasting into Jerry Grote's mitt.

By the third inning, Rube Walker turned to Hodges on the bench and said: "Tom could throw a no-hitter tonight."

Walker must have known something, because at the end of eight innings Seaver had eleven strikeouts and the Cubs had put nobody on base. The Mets had a 4–0 lead, and the main reason for staying was to see if Seaver could complete the eleventh perfect game in baseball history.

When Seaver came to bat in the bottom of the eighth, the 59,083 fans gave him a standing ovation. It was as if seven years of sarcasm and defeat had never happened. For once, Met fans had a chance to root for sheer excellence.

"The fans were unbelievable," Seaver said later. "I grew up in Los Angeles where they clap softly when somebody hits a home run. The noise here gets into your system. I could hear my heart pounding, feel the adrenalin flowing. My arm felt light as a feather. It was like being in a dream."

The dream was tested in the top of the ninth, when the competitive Randy Hundley tried to bunt his way to base. Seaver pounced off the mound and threw Hundley out as the fans booed the Cub batter because they considered it unsportsmanlike for a man to try to break up a no-hitter with a bunt.

The next batter was Jimmy Qualls, a twenty-two-year-old rookie, playing in his eighteenth major-league game. Batting left-handed against Seaver earlier, he had hit a long fly to right and a grounder to first, indicating that he could "pull" Seaver's pitching. So Seaver tried to keep the ball outside this time. But an inch or two can make all the difference, and the pitch did not go far enough outside. Qualls slapped the ball sharply into the same zone that Kranepool had penetrated the day before. It fell for a single and the no-hitter was gone.

The fans stood and applauded anyway, needing to release the emotion they had felt. Grote rushed out to calm down his disappointed pitcher, and Seaver promptly retired the last two batters. Then the fans cheered again as Seaver left the field. He wondered how he should feel after his perfect game was broken up. He had just pitched a one-hitter to move his team only one game behind in the loss column. He decided to feel happy.

The next afternoon, there was nothing approaching perfection from the Mets, who made two errors and threw the ball around for a 6–2 defeat for Gentry. Somebody asked Leo "Nice-Guys-

Finish-Last" Durocher if the people had finally seen "the real
Cubs."

"No," Leo sniffed, "those are the real Mets."

The Cubs rushed out of town and the Montreal Expos came in.
On Friday night there was a letdown and the Expos stunned
the Mets, 11–4, as fans fought each other and spilled beer in the
aisles. It was the kind of night that demonstrated how ugly a
sporting mob can be at times.

The only good development of this steamy Friday night was
Bud Harrelson's return from his two weeks of army summer camp.
The little shortstop had spent his time refereeing softball games
and dashing out to an Italian restaurant to watch the Met game
on television in the evenings. He was released on Friday afternoon and barreled down the New York Thruway in time to put
on his favorite uniform with the No. 3 on it instead of sergeant
stripes.

On Saturday the Mets were rained out and Hodges said he
would not let Harrelson start a game until he had some practice.
The way Weis was playing, there was no rush to work Harrelson back into the lineup anyway. So Harrelson sat on Sunday and
watched Weis make three hits and drive in a run as the Mets
swept the Expos, 4–3 and 9–7.

The second game was marked by Cleon Jones being thrown
out when he protested being called out on an attempted steal
of second base. The umpire, Frank Dezelan, claimed that Jones
had called him that magic hyphenated phrase that is worth an
automatic ejection. Jones said: "I called him an angel," but the
outfielder agreed it might cost him a fine from league headquarters.

When the .350 hitter was thrown out of the game, the fans
began to boo and wave handkerchiefs and throw fruit toward
the umpires. They even booed poor Rocky Swoboda when he
chugged out to left field to replace Jones. Rocky had the perfect
answer for their boos, however. In the seventh inning he hit a
single that put the Mets ahead to stay.

Swoboda had arrived at a kind of unwanted compromise in
his career. He hadn't killed himself or anybody else in his adven-
tures in the outfield, but he had not become the next great slugger,

either. In 1969 he was a platooned right fielder, along with Art Shamsky, but he would always be a special Met. He was now married with two children and enjoyed working on his new house in Syosset, Long Island. His hands were calloused from digging dry wells and scratched from trimming trees. But there was more to Rocky than that. Rocky had volunteered to tour Vietnam in the winter of 1968. He had come back with questions about the war, but glad nonetheless that he had been able to cheer up the soldiers.

He was still capable of great failure on the field too. Early in 1969 he had struck out five times in one game as the fans booed heartily. Swoboda didn't mind.

"When you strike out five times, they should line up alongside the road and boo you all the way home," he said. "If we lost, I'd be eating my heart out. But since we won, I'll only eat one ventricle."

It was typical of Swoboda, after helping to win the game against the Expos, to praise Tommie Agee, who had hit a three-run homer, made a great catch, and scored the last two Met runs.

"Last year nobody thought of Tommie as being as strong as he was," Swoboda recalled. "Gil stayed with him a long time, longer than you might have expected. Well, you can see why now."

After the series with the Expos, the Mets flew to Chicago for another three-game series with the Cubs. Agee carried a .285 average with fifteen homers and forty-two RBIs and he gave all thanks to the manager.

"I can't describe how I felt last year," Agee recalled. "Sometimes it was so bad I felt like I was numb. I didn't know what to do, didn't know where to turn.

"I didn't get along with some of the fellows. It was my fault. I was irritable. Guys would ask me something and I might have barked at them instead of giving them a decent answer. I was depressed. A lot of times I didn't want to go to the park. Now I enjoy coming to the park. I owe that man a lot for staying with me."

Agee knew it would take a lot of courage to go to the park for the next three days, because he would have to play with his back to the bleachers in Wrigley Field, and expose himself to the missiles and the taunts of the Bleacher Bums.

The Bums were an instant tradition in Wrigley Field. Only a few years before, the bleachers had been the private solarium of a few hooky players and meditating hippies and elderly pensioners. But now that the Cubs were winning, the bleachers were suddenly packed with rough young men wearing yellow construction hats who liked to throw things at visiting players. The Cub management took no steps to calm these young hog-butchers from the city of broad shoulders. Cub players encouraged them.

Dick Selma, the former Met, had surfaced as a spare Cub pitcher and cheerleader. In his free moments in the bullpen, Selma would direct the Bums' cheering section. When the Cubs won a home game, Ron Santo treated the fans by kicking his heels together as he cavorted toward the clubhouse in the left-field corner. The Bums loved Santo's demonstrations and probably would have torn down the ball park if he had not done it.

Other clubs were not as thrilled by the Bums. Pete Rose had been called some uncomplimentary terms while Lou Brock had been showered with white mice and Mudcat Grant's handsome face was narrowly missed by a transistor radio battery. And Agee had been told that his wife was working the street—for dimes.

"Shows how stupid they are," Swoboda muttered. "Tommie isn't even married."

Agee's visit to Chicago did not begin well when he had to read a telegram to his roomie, saying that Jones had been fined $150 by league headquarters for cursing at umpire Dezelan on Sunday. The bad day continued at the ball park when Agee let Banks' single skip past him for a two-base error. Then in the seventh, he was called out on strikes and he flung his bat, striking Ken Boswell, who was kneeling in the on-deck circle. Agee didn't hurt Boswell, but he didn't hurt Billy Hands, either. Hands stopped Agee four times and beat Seaver, 1–0, on a single by Billy Williams in the sixth inning.

After the game, Santo did his heel-kicking act down the third-base line as the Bleacher Bums roared. Some of the Mets stood in their dugout and shouted "bush" and "horseshit" at the captain of the Cubs. They vowed to remind Santo of his insulting gesture as soon as possible.

They had their chance the next day when Dick Selma threw a fastball with two strikes, and Alfie Weis, all 165 pounds of him, swatted a three-run homer into the left-field stands. Weis had slugged four homers in his previous 1240-major-league at-bats, none of them as important as this one.

Gary Gentry and Ron Taylor protected the 5–4 victory and when it was over, Seaver and a few others kicked their heels in the dugout and called it to the attention of the retreating Cubs.

Then it was the third and final game on July 16. The Mets scored five runs off Jenkins, but Durocher let him take a pounding into the second inning. Cardwell and McAndrew gave the five runs back in a hurry but Cal Koonce—the former Cub bonus baby—pitched five shutout innings of relief, and then Taylor saved the 9–5 victory as heels kicked again in the Met dugout.

The Mets went into the Cub series five games behind. Now as they left Chicagoland (as the disc jockeys call it), they were 3½ games behind the Cubbies. They had come through the biggest ten days in their history in fine style, winning four of six from the first-place team. St. Louis was still far behind both of them. The Mets took off for Montreal, looking forward to the second half of the season and knowing that only a thorough collapse could keep them from having a very good year, pennant or not.

23

GROUNDED

◆

THEY ARRIVED IN MONTREAL LATE on July 16 and began a full day off. The tension of the Cub series was over and they anticipated an easy weekend against the expansion team. They would be surprised to learn that the most dangerous portion of the season was about to begin.

It started when they reached the ancient Windsor Hotel, formerly the showplace of the city with its high ceilings, great dining rooms, and ornate luxury of the Old World, but now it was merely a run-down old barn, dark in the corridors, musty in the rooms, dreary in the lobby.

The players knew they stayed at the Windsor because M. Donald Grant had grown up in Montreal and had relatives who had helped to run the hotel during its days of splendor. M. Donald Grant had long since sought his fortune south of the border, but now that he was bringing his team—*his team*—back to his native city, nostalgia impelled him to stay at the Windsor.

The Mets had suffered the hotel on their first visit, but now they knew better. Walking around this charming city—finding rare delight in being in a foreign land, checking out the highest hemlines in North America—they had seen three glittering new hotels towering over their dingy quarters. The players had explored the shopping arcades and the coffee shops and the brilliant lobbies, and when they returned to the scene of M. Donald Grant's youth, they became slightly sarcastic.

"I kept hearing this noise all night," Ed Kranepool said. "It was the wrecking ball."

"You know what the valet just brought to my room?" asked Rocky Swoboda. "Babe Ruth's suits."

Although the players knew that Lou Niss hadn't picked the hotel, they were inclined to question him about it anyway. Poor Niss. When the complaints got to be too much, he gave the players the inscrutable look of a road secretary and shuffled off in his well-known penguin walk that Casey used to imitate.

The free time in Montreal thoroughly unwound the players. When they reported to Jarry Park on July 18, Jerry Koosman fell behind early. In the fifth, two Met runs scored, and Cleon Jones tried to score from second on a single to right field. The throw arrived and catcher Ronnie Brand was waiting as Jones went into his slide. The umpire called Jones out as the runner and catcher became entangled over home plate. It looked like an accident for a few seconds as they scrambled to untangle themselves, but then Jones jumped up and without any discussion began punching Brand, one, two, three four times.

The little catcher went reeling backwards but recovered himself and charged forward. Just then the umpire, Billy Williams, stepped between them, and Brand hit Williams right in the face.

By this time both teams were milling around home plate in one of those typical baseball fights when everybody grabs somebody else. The one dangerous moment came when Seaver tried to pull Koosman out of the pile. One good block on both of them could have put the Mets right back in the Marvelous Marv era.

Finally the scramble was ended, and only Jones was thrown out of the game because the umpires ruled he had thrown the first punch. The Mets went on to win the game but people were more concerned with the fight. There was also some concern as to whether Jones was feeling the pressure of a pennant race, now that he had been in two incidents within six days.

"Sure, it looks bad getting thrown out twice in a week," Jones admitted after the game. "But why didn't they kick Brand out? I'd feel worse if I didn't protect myself. You know what he did to me? He kicked me in the arm when he started to get up. Sure, I came in high with my slide. He was blocking the plate. At least I didn't spike him."

Over on the other side of the stadium, Brand was reciting his version of it. "Jones came in high, which he always does. It's not dirty—but it's bush. What did he want me to do, walk around him? I admit it, I touched him with my knee. But he threw the first punch. It's his fault if he wants to get thrown out of the game."

Brand is a religious, hardworking little catcher who had never been in any scrapes in the league before. He admitted that he was still angry at the Mets ever since Agee and Jones had bowled over himself and Joe Morgan and a few other Houston Astros in 1968.

"Jones and Agee are safe because they play the outfield," Brand said. "You can't slide into them—and they know it. But they'll get one of their teammates killed if they're not careful."

The Mets didn't get killed the next day, but they had enough troubles when Seaver was blasted for seven hits and four runs by the third inning. After the game, trainer Gus Mauch gave Seaver some Butazolidin pills, the same drugs that are given to racehorses to treat their inflamed limbs. Seaver's shoulder had been stiff before that near-perfect game against the Cubs. Now he couldn't finish three innings in Montreal and he knew he had trouble.

The trouble continued in Sunday's doubleheader when Gentry gave up sudden homers to Mack Jones, Bob Bailey, and weak-hitting Bobby Wine, enough for a 3–2 Expo victory.

In the second game on Sunday, Don Cardwell held a 2–0 lead into the eighth inning. But then the Expos tied it up as Agee slammed into a fence post and dropped the fly ball he had chased so far. He hobbled off the field with a variety of aches and bruises.

The Mets went ahead again but the Expos tied it in the ninth when Tyrone Cline's strange grounder hopped off Donn Clendenon's glove for the tying single with two outs. The lusty Expo fans hooted Clendenon, who had not been very popular or productive in his two months in Montreal. As the game went into extra innings, this weekend in another country was getting down-right unpleasant for the aliens from New York.

But finally in the tenth, Rocky Swoboda replaced the weary Jones and doubled with two outs, sending a runner to third. Then Bobby Pfeil alertly dropped a bunt down the third-base line for a run-scoring single, having noticed that Coco Laboy was playing deep at third. The Mets finally won the game, 4–3.

Pfeil was a twenty-five-year-old infielder who had spent eight years in three different farm systems. By the spring of 1969, he was getting a little independent, and he insisted on keeping his job at the Walt Disney studios in California until two weeks before the Tidewater farm team opened its season. He reported in good shape and was batting .316 when the Mets purchased him to replace Harrelson for two weeks while Buddy was in the service. The reddish-haired rookie made himself useful and stayed with the club when Harrelson returned. This game-winning bunt seemed to assure him employment a little bit longer.

Jack DiLauro was credited with his first major-league victory because of Pfeil's bunt, so the two rookies had reason to smile as the Mets threw their uniforms into their duffel bags and anxiously jumped into the team bus. The team had a sore-shouldered pitching ace, a tired star hitter, an injured center fielder, and perhaps a good case of the collective staggers. The players had just gone through a weekend of trouble, and they were looking forward to the three-day All-Star game recess, which would begin as soon as the Mets got home.

There was one little problem, however. A little red light in the cockpit of their chartered 727 jet said there was something wrong with the oil system. It would be best, the little red light said, for this airplane to stay right here on the ground in Montreal.

How very typical. The Mets had done it again. For seven years they had been trying to find home plate. Now that they finally found it, they couldn't get back into their country to en-joy it. Amazing!

To make it worse, they were in the farthest lounge of the air-port on Sunday night, which is always the dreariest night in any

airport. In various stages and positions of dejection, they
slumped on the sofas in the waiting room. It was now 8 P.M.
Their wives were already leaving their homes on Long Island,
heading for Kennedy Airport to pick them up. It was too late
for the players to call their wives, because they knew that air-
lines rarely tell the truth about delayed flights to wives who call
to check arrival time.

The players could picture their wives and little children sitting
around the airport for hours waiting for a phantom flight while
some uniformed attendant insisted that it was due any moment.
Actually, the nearest available airplane was in Detroit. As soon
as it could be ferried over, the Mets could go home.

"Gentlemen," announced Lou Niss. "I have arranged for dinner for us all in the airport restaurant in an hour. Relax, have
a beer, there's nothing we can do."

The dispirited army trudged back a quarter of a mile to the
main terminal. Most of the players were carrying garment bags
with their extra suits inside. Others carried shaving kits or
attaché cases. Ed Charles carried a winter coat he had bought
for his wife. Cleon Jones carried his portable record player with
his Aretha Franklin records. Tom Seaver stopped at a water
cooler and popped another pill for his shoulder. Rocky Swoboda
patted Tommie Agee on the back as the wounded outfielder
hobbled down the endless corridor.

Back in the main terminal, the players filed into the bar
lounge. Only a few airport workers were sitting at the bar. The
last flights to Brussels and Vancouver and Mexico City had already departed. Only the Mets were left behind.

High up on the small colored television set, three other fortunate travelers had already reached their destination on this
evening of July 20. The players stared impassively at the flicker-
ing screen. There was no cheering and very little talking among
the Mets as Neil Armstrong, only a jumble of fluttery lines
on this television set, was edging down a ladder, about to take
man's first steps on the moon.

"How come we can send a rocket to the moon," mused Ron
Swoboda, "but we can't get our plane off the ground?"

Because, the answer seemed to be, because you are the Mets.

It is that simple. Things always screw up around the Mets sooner or later.

Jerry Grote, in his electric yellow suit, stared at the television set. The All-Star catcher of 1968 was in a slump this year, and he was currently brooding about a comment somebody had made a few days earlier. While the Mets were battling the Cubs in Chicago, the New York reporters had been asked to comment on the pennant race for the newspaper *Chicago Today*. Joe Gergen of *Newsday* had facetiously commented: "The Mets have about as much chance of winning the pennant as man has of landing on the moon."

Either Grote thought that was Captain Video on television for the past few days, or he missed the humorous aspect of Gergen's remark. Either way, the catcher was sure that Gergen had tried to "rip" the Mets.

The players stared remotely at the moon landing, then gulped down their steaks in the dining room. Around 1 A.M., their airplane arrived from Detroit. By 2:45 they were back at Kennedy Airport, hearing tales of woe from wives and tired children. The three-day vacation had begun.

Four Mets had no vacation, however, Cleon Jones was the starting left fielder, and he went 2-for-4 in the All-Star Game in Washington on Wednesday.

Seaver did not pitch because of his sore shoulder but Koosman worked one and two-thirds innings and gave up only one hit. Hodges was a coach for the Nationals and was given a big hand by his old fans in Washington.

Then it was time to start the second half of the season and take on the worst tormentors of all, the Houston Astros, who were also having their finest season. They had a 51–49 record and were only six games behind first-place Atlanta in the Western Division. But the Astros always played better than their record against the Mets.

On July 30 the teams began a doubleheader in swampy Shea Stadium. Koosman left after seven and the Mets were behind, 5–3. But then the Astros bombed Koonce and Taylor for eleven runs in the eighth inning, including grand-slam homers by Jimmy Wynn and Dennis Menke, the first time in ninety-three years of National League baseball that two grand slammers had been hit in the same inning.

When Hodges came out to remove Koonce, the fans booed. It was a hot, muggy day and the season was definitely turning nasty.

There wasn't even any suspense in the second game. Gentry was bombed for eight runs in the third inning before Hodges could even get Ryan warmed up. The fans booed again when the manager changed pitchers.

But the most critical event of the afternoon did not happen at home plate or the pitching mound. It happened in the marshland of left field as soon as Ryan replaced Gentry. John Edwards sliced a double into the left-field corner, and Jones chased after it carefully. Then he lobbed a throw that would later be described as a "balloon" (Vic Ziegel, New York *Post*) and "the finish of a parachute jump" (Joe Donnelly, *Newsday*). Whatever it looked like, it did not impress Gil Hodges.

The manager trudged out to left field, his hands in his hip pockets, his muscular body swaying side to side as if delaying the confrontation. When Hodges reached the left fielder, the manager did the talking and the outfielder looked down at his soggy shoes. Then Hodges did an about-face and plodded to the dugout, followed a dozen paces behind him by the only .346 hitter he had.

Now any impulsive person would have guessed that Hodges had hauled his best hitter out of the game for not hustling. The fans would have thought so, the reporters, the Astros, probably even the men on the moon. But a few minutes later, the trainer, Gus Mauch, made one of his rare voluntary admissions that Jones had in fact pulled a hamstring muscle sometime before coming out of the game. After the game, Hodges confirmed what the trainer had said.

"I saw him favor his leg that inning," Hodges said, staring blankly at the reporters. "I didn't think he should play if he was hurting."

Reporters tend to become extremely knowledgeable about the human body because of their frequent stories about players. So the learned scribes held a consultation and remembered that most hamstring muscles take seven to ten days to heal. However, Mauch was a little more optimistic.

"He could walk in here tomorrow and be able to play," the trainer said. "You never know."

The reporters were quite interested in this new hitherto unheard of miracle of modern medicine. But then they got a new version of the injury from Jones' main man, Tommie Agee.

"Any time it gets wet or it's raining, Cleon's feet start hurting," Agee said. "I know this from last year. He told me the second game his feet were starting to hurt, and he said, 'I don't know whether I can play this game.'"

Jones was not available to tell his version because he had left soon after the manager gave him the rest of the game off. He left a lot of questions in the clubhouse. Seaver's injury and the jinx to the Astros were now compounded by either an injury to their best hitter or bad feeling between manager and star—or both.

Also, the Mets could look over their shoulders and see the St. Louis Cardinals making their first good move of the season. The Cardinals were now only 2½ games behind the Mets, who were six games behind the Cubs. It was not a very good time for the best player to be sitting on the bench.

24

A TALE OF TWO MANAGERS

◆

CLEON JONES SAT IN THE BACK of the jet that was taking the Mets to Cincinnati, his portable phonograph playing soul music that only he could hear above the hum of the plane.

Gil Hodges sat in the front of the jet, next to his trusted coach, Rube Walker, discussing the rotation for the next two weeks. Their voices could not be heard, either.

Jones had not started a game since being hauled out of left field by Hodges five days before. It seemed like a good time for a reporter to find out how Jones was recuperating from his mysterious leg injury.

"I don't want to say anything," Jones said. "It's up to the manager when I'll play. Sure, I think I'm ready but it's up to him."

Then up at the front of the plane. "Did Mr. Jones say it was up to me?" Hodges mused, staring intently at the cloud formations over West Virginia. "Hmmm. Well, I would have to say that his leg is probably ready. You might see Mr. Jones any time now."

"Any time" turned out to be that night in Cincinnati. The name "Jones" turned up on the lineup card, a few inches above the signature of "Hodges." But any attempt to discuss the situation with the manager was met with cold rebuff. For most of the pregame practice, Hodges stood in shallow center field, far from the reporters in his dugout. He clapped his fist into his open palm a few thousand times. He yawned a few thousand times. He looked like the most relaxed man in the world.

Some of us who had grown up reading about this easygoing giant were finding there was a lot of steel underneath the bland façade. Hodges was managing a baseball team during a pennant race. He was not looking for good-guy awards or a lot of quotes in the newspapers. Also, he had no way of knowing what would come from the way he was handling Jones.

It seemed that the manager had indeed embarrassed his best hitter in public, making him an example to the whole team. Jones may not have been giving 100 per cent and his leg may have been bothering him, but Hodges could have chosen more tactful means of taking him out of that Houston game. Now it was possible that Jones might sulk the rest of the season, or he might play in a fury and carry the team for another two months. The players might be sparked by Hodges' show of power, or they might wither and die. Hodges was waiting to see how his strong stand worked.

In the first game in Cincinnati, Jones had no hits. In the second game, he had three hits. In the third game, he had one hit. And in the fourth game he beat out a dribbler to second base, then stole the base. We medical experts agreed that the leg was definitely better now.

Seaver was no better, however, as the Reds knocked him out in three innings. That night Seaver took a long walk through the deserted downtown area, finally rambling back to the hotel with a worried look to him. A pitcher never knows when an arm injury will heal, or if it will ever heal.

"I guess I'll go up and call my wife," he said to some of us in the hotel lobby. "She usually waits up after I pitch. I've got a great report for her tonight."

After winning one of four in Cincinnati, the Mets won three of four in Atlanta as Seaver struggled through seven and a third innings and said his shoulder felt better. But then they went to Houston where they predictably lost three straight. Now the

Cardinals were even with them in second place and the season was in danger of falling apart.

Fortunately, the pills Seaver had been taking did their job, because he opened a home stand on August 16 and shut out San Diego, 2–0. Grote won the second game of the doubleheader with a pinch single.

Sunday was Banner Day, the grandest old tradition the Mets had now that losing was going out of fashion. Laura Joss of New Hyde Park, Long Island, carried one of the winning banners: ONE SMALL STEP FOR HODGES, ONE GREAT LEAP FOR MET-KIND, a reference to the recent moon excursion.

The Mets also took two small steps in the Sunday doubleheader, beating the Padres twice by identical 3–2 scores.

The Giants came in for a three-game series. On August 19, Agee hit a homer off Juan Marichal in the fourteenth inning for a 1–0 victory as Gentry and McGraw shut out the powerful Giants in front of 48,968 fans.

On August 20, the shutout was 6–0 as McAndrew pitched a two-hitter in front of 48,414 fans. The winning streak was now six.

The streak ended on August 21 when Agee lost a fly ball for a triple, and the Giants won, 7–6, in the eleventh inning.

So Koosman and McGraw started another streak on August 22 when they combined for a 5–3 victory over the Dodgers as 50,460 fans celebrated.

The next afternoon, Maury Wills lost a pop-up in the sun in the bottom of the ninth as the Mets edged the Dodgers, 3–2, as 48,079 cheered.

On August 24, Swoboda hit a three-run double in the seventh for a 7–4 triumph over the Dodgers, and 48,435 went out of their heads.

It was about this time that Hodges began using a new catcher named Don Robert Dyer, called "Duffy" since birth because his parents liked the radio program *Duffy's Tavern*. The former Arizona State player had the pugnacious look of a popular Irish middleweight. He had hit a homer on opening day but then was dropped to Tidewater until midsummer. When Met pitchers began grumbling about Grote's temper and selection of pitches again, Dyer began getting more work. Also, the temporary insecurity helped prod Grote for the weeks ahead, which may have been Hodges' intention all along.

With four straight victories, the Mets went on their last Coast trip of the season. McAndrew shut out San Diego and Koosman won a two-hitter to stretch the streak to six.

On August 28, the Mets were back in the magic city of San Francisco, where some of them took a stroll from the old Palace Hotel and saw a sign in a store window: "This Is The Year. Go-Go-Go Mets." Imagine. Banner Day on Mission and Sixth.

The Giants won the first game of the series, 5–0. But it was the second game, on Saturday, that the Mets would remember for a long time to come.

That Saturday game was tied at 2–2 in the bottom of the eighth. A Giant runner tried to score from third on a pop-up down the right-field line but Grote tagged him out. It was to be a busy hour for Grote, who thought he had the third out and rolled the ball toward the pitching mound. Another runner broke for third, but Donn Clendenon alertly swooped over the ball and threw to third for the final out.

Still, the Giants threatened again in the ninth with a runner on first. The dangerous Willie McCovey screamed a line drive into the left-field center corner, an area he is not supposed to reach. Rod Gaspar, who had been inserted for defensive purposes one inning before, chased the ball down in the corner as the winning run raced for home. But Gaspar heaved an amazingly strong throw, considering his haste and the distance and the prevailing winds. The ball slashed through the winds and Bob Burda raced it home. Grote gave a tremendous fake to Burda, never once moving to indicate he expected the ball. No Giant shouted to warn Burda, who made a normal slide and must have been surprised when Grote caught the ball at the last second and pounced on top of him for the out.

After this reprieve, Clendenon hit a homer in the tenth for a 3–2 victory. But the Mets agreed that Gaspar's throw was the best play they had seen that day, or most any other day.

The Mets and Giants split a doubleheader on August 31, so the Mets went into September with a 76–54 record. The August

that had begun so ominously had finished with a successful
21–10 record. The Mets were playing well, but they knew they
needed some help from the Cubs.

"We knew we would stay hot after August," Ron Swoboda
would recall later. "We had faith in ourselves by now. But we
could have won a hundred games and finished second unless
the Cubs started losing."

The Cubs were not a happy club at this point. They had built
up a big lead with the help of the Cardinals' bad start. They also
had some fine players who were having the best years of their
lives. They had Dick Selma leading cheers for the Bleacher
Bums. They had Ron Santo kicking his heels together and playing excellent baseball. They had durable Billy Williams and lovable Ernie Banks. They had the best lights in baseball—"God's
own sun," as Ernie put it. And finally they had Leo Durocher.

Legend said that Durocher was best when goading a talented
team down the stretch drive. With a losing team, Leo was said
to lose interest in building character. But as a front-runner, with
unprecedented World Series shares awaiting the winners, Leo
was supposed to be in command. This was his kind of race.

But Leo had other interests in the summer of 1969. Early in
the season, he took a day off to marry Lynn Goldblatt, who had
previously been married to an owner of a Chicago department
store. When his young wife accompanied him on road trips, Leo
took an occasional day off because of ill health.

At sixty-three or sixty-four or sixty-five—depending on whom
you believed—Leo was entitled to an occasional sick day. The
players and coaches were not unhappy when their manager
missed a day's work. Even when they were far ahead, several
Cubs were grumbling that they would never win a pennant with
Leo in command.

After one of those absences, rumors began circulating that
Leo had been seen at Camp Ojibwa in Eagle River, Wisconsin,
accompanying his new wife on a visit to her son at camp. The
rumor even reached the Spearmint suite at the Wrigley Building.

Philip K. Wrigley has owned the Cubs for a long time out of
what must be pure civic pride, since he seems something less
than a baseball fan himself. He is the Howard Hughes of base-

ball. Every few years there is a rumor that P.K. has been seen in his ball park, sitting anonymously in the grandstands or quietly inspecting the movable ramps or the ivy on the walls or the gum dispensers that sell the opposition's brands.

However, Wrigley pays other people very well to work at his ball park, and one of those people was Leo Durocher. When Wrigley heard about Durocher's visit to Camp Ojibwa, he called the manager in for a friendly conference, and they decided that Leo would not go AWOL again in the very near future.

Now the Cubs were assured of Leo's pleasant company on every working day. They could look forward to his ordering pitchers to throw at enemy batters. They could look forward to his announcement whenever he got rid of a player: "Well, there goes horseshit."

Leo did reward excellence, however. When Kenny Holtzman was winning every start, Durocher invited him up to the front of the plane to play cards. But when Holtzman began losing on occasion, he was free to play solitaire in the coach section.

Leo liked to pamper his best players, the way he had coddled young Willie Mays back in the Polo Grounds in 1951. With the Cubs, he had praised a Panamanian named Adolfo Phillips, who also played center field and hit home runs. Durocher even held the team plane when Adolfo was half an hour late once. But when Phillips did not react well to enemy pitchers throwing close to him, Durocher lost patience with him. He criticized Phillips publicly, and the player crawled within himself and was of no value to anybody after that. Finally Durocher unloaded him to Montreal.

Chicago reporters are not the sort who ask tough questions or try to stir up controversy. But they began noticing that Leo was telling different stories to different reporters. By mid-season, Leo was not speaking to his reporters at all. He was hardly talking to announcer Lou Boudreau on their pregame show—and Leo was being paid handsomely for that little task.

Durocher's love of finances rubbed off on his players, who hired themselves an agent to handle their offers for public appearances. Soon their attention seemed to be divided between the games and their pool of endorsement money. The Mets, of course, began to be besieged by offers in August, but only after they had built up their momentum. The Cubs had been courted by the hucksters all year.

The Cubs also managed to antagonize most of the teams in the league. Earlier in the season, Durocher had squawked about the condition of the field at Montreal's Jarry Park. The Expos perked up whenever they played the Cubs, and they would finish with an 8–10 mark against the Cubs but only 5–13 against the Mets.

The Cardinals, who slumped back into third place again, saw they were not going to win the Eastern title. They had always conducted themselves with grace when they were champions, and they saw none of that in the Cubs.

"The Cubs are supposed to be professionals," said Bob Gibson. "I can see kids doing silly things but not a group as old as they are."

"Those fans say things about your mother that makes you want to get up in the stands and punch a few of them," said Mudcat Grant.

The Cardinals got mad when the Bleacher Bums called artist-center fielder Curt Flood a derogatory phrase. Against the Cubs they would have a 9–9 record in 1969. Against the Mets they would be 6–12.

While the Cubs were having internal and external problems, the Mets stuck close together. Jones returned to the lineup without any outward resentment toward Hodges, regardless of what his private feelings were.

The season careened into September and the recuperated Seaver beat the Phillies for his twentieth victory, the first Met ever to reach that special figure.

On September 7 the Mets won their second straight, and the Cubs lost their fourth straight. And on the morning of September 8 the Cubs flew into New York to open a two-night stand. After leading by as many as nine and a half games, the Cubs were now only two and a half games ahead of the Mets.

25

GOD ALMIGHTY DAMN

◆

IT WAS A COLD, NASTY NIGHT in Shea Stadium, with winter only a few hundred miles away. The players wore wool sweat shirts under their flannel uniforms. It was fall, money weather, the time of year when the old Yankees or the old Dodgers or the recent Cardinals would have known how to rip off a good victory. But what did the Cubs and the Mets know about big games?

The 43,274 fans watched the game start in chilly darkness as Jerry Koosman opposed the Met-beater, Billy Hands.

The first Met batter was Tommie Agee, who was getting a reputation for leading off games with a home run. Agee had been playing beautiful baseball for months, the timidity and the terror of 1968 all but forgotten. But an old man in the Cub dugout wanted Agee to remember what it was like to be scared.

Leo Durocher had signals when he wanted his pitcher to throw at a batter. Sometimes a towel would move ominously in a corner of the dugout. Sometimes an index finger would be pointed at the cranial cavity. Or sometimes a harsh voice would be heard saying: "Stick it in his ear."

Whatever Leo's signal was this time, Billy Hands got the message because the first pitch sailed directly at Tommie Agee's handsome dark brown head. Only because of his exceptional reflexes did Agee escape being knocked unconscious by Hands. He fell to the dirt and lay there while 43,274 fans began booing Hands and the old man who had ordered the knockdown pitch. The Mets stood up in their dugout; Tom Seaver shouted challenges across to the Cubs.

Only one man in the ball park did not seem to know what Hands had just tried to do. The home-plate umpire dusted off the dirt that Agee had unintentionally kicked. Then play resumed, and Agee grounded out and the Mets did not score.

Then it was the top of the second inning and Ron Santo, the Cubs' inspirational cleanup hitter, was the first batter. Jerry Koosman, the rosy-cheeked farm boy from Minnesota, who would laugh if you just grabbed him by the collar, went out to the mound. No harsh voices called "Stick it in his ear," but Koosman knew what had to be done.

The first pitch of the inning hit Santo on his right forearm, sending him into the dirt where Agee had sprawled a few minutes earlier. Rolling in the dust, Santo looked like one of the distorted beasts in Picasso's *Guernica*. Life is like this. Old men sit in dugouts and send young men into battles. But the Mets were willing to fight on Leo's terms. They put their feet on the steps of the dugout and waited.

But there was no trouble. The Cub trainer sprayed the sore area with pain-killer, and Santo veered toward first base. No Cubs swarmed over the top step. Nobody shouted "Stick it in his ear." In the Met dugout the players relaxed. Now they could get down to business and play baseball.

The next time Agee batted, there was a runner on base—but not for long. Agee blasted a two-run homer off Hands for the first score of the game.

The Cubs tied the score at 2–2. Then in the seventh inning, Agee dunked a fly onto the outfield grass and hustled into second with a double. Then Wayne Garrett, the $25,000 draft choice, slapped a single to right field, and Agee raced for home. Randy Hundley applied the tag and the umpire leaned over to inspect the play, finally spreading his palms outward. Hundley leaped into the air like Apollo 11. He raged at the umpire until

Durocher dashed out to add his advice. But Agee stayed safe, and the Mets had a 3–2 lead.

After seeing Santo drilled by Koosman's fastball, the Cubs backed away from home plate and struck out thirteen times. Koosman held on for a 3–2 victory, bringing the Mets within a game and a half of the Cubs.

The next night the Mets did it again, 7–1, as Clendenon and Shamsky homered, Boswell hit a two-run double, and Seaver beat Jenkins. The Cubs lost their sixth straight, the Mets won their fourth straight, and the lead was only half a game.

And in Shea Stadium that night, the song was "Good-Bye, Leo" to the tune of "Good Night, Ladies." It was probably the first time that Met fans had ever gloated over victory, but Durocher made people react that way.

"Leo has never left a good taste with anyone he has beaten," Ron Swoboda said. "He does this to you." And Swoboda ground his heel into the floor.

But there wasn't much time for gloating in the clubhouse because Mrs. Payson decided to pay a visit. The players all pulled their clothes back on as the chunky little lady entered from the lobby.

"We're all so sentimental," she said, shaking hands with Hodges and some of the players she recognized. Then she realized there were some young players, brought up at the end of their minor-league seasons, so she asked M. Donald Grant to introduce her to them.

"New boys, new boys," Grant cried, waving his hands and summoning them forward. "Now boys, raise your hands and say your names," Grant commanded.

A few minutes later Mrs. Payson left and the players jumped out of their sweaty uniforms at last.

After sweeping the Cubs, the Mets reached a new and exhilarating peak the next night. They beat the Expos, 3–2, in the first game of a doubleheader and tied the Cubs for first place. Then at 10:13 P.M., word was received that the Cubs had lost down in Philadelphia.

The Mets were in *first* place. They had never been there before.

Then they beat the Expos, 7–1, in the second game and stayed in first place overnight. *The New York Times* thought that was so amazing it ran a headline on page one: METS IN FIRST PLACE.

On September 11 the Mets beat the Expos, 4–0, on a six-hitter by Gentry, their seventh straight victory. The Cubs lost their eighth straight, 4–3, down in Philadelphia. The Mets were now two games in first place.

As they slipped further and further behind, the Cubs began talking about retaliation. They decided that when they got their hands on the Mets in Chicago on the last two days of the season, they would really give the Mets what-for. Back in New York, the Mets chortled at that late development.

"On the last day of the season," said Ed Kranepool, "when we're two games ahead of the Cubs, I'm gonna tell Ernie Banks, 'Hey, Ernie, let's play two today.'"

Nobody would really use Ernie's favorite expression against him, but the Mets didn't mind giggling at the Cubs' belated aggressiveness. The Cubs had had their chances in New York. Now they would just have to wait, along with their Bleacher Bums.

On September 12 the Mets played in Pittsburgh and added to their new thrills when they won both ends of a doubleheader by the minimum 1–0 score. Both runs were driven in by pitchers —Koosman, the celebrated nonhitter, and Cardwell, a good hitter for a pitcher. The Cubs broke their eight-game losing streak, thereby falling only two and a half games behind.

The next night the Mets were in a tight game in Pittsburgh when Swoboda batted in the eighth with the bases loaded. In eleven previous swings against the Pirates in 1969, Rocky had failed to get the ball out of the infield nine times. But this time he got the ball out of spacious Forbes Field, as outfielders Willie Stargell and Matty Alou turned around admiringly but never even bothered to take a backward step.

The Mets won that game as a fan held a banner proclaiming: MET BRUTALITY.

The Cubs started a new losing streak in St. Louis to fall three and a half games behind. The Cardinals started Bob Gibson after only three days rest against the Cubs. Although manager Red Schoendienst said it was to give Gibson a better chance at twenty victories, many people interpreted this as an attempt to knock off the Cubs.

"If we can't win, I hope the Mets do," Gibson said. "The Cubs shot off their pops, flipped their bills, ran off at the mouth."

The Mets lost in Pittsburgh on the fourteenth, then flew to St. Louis. On the night of the fifteenth, left-handed Steve Carlton set a major-league record for most strikeouts in a nine-inning game when he struck out nineteen Mets. The Mets made four errors in that game, and the Cardinals stole three bases off Grote.

There was only one satisfying note for the Mets that night. In the eighth inning, Agee singled and Swoboda hit his second homer of the evening, giving the Mets a 4–3 victory over the record-breaking pitcher. The Mets had given reporter Jack Lang a new negative statistic—but they had also won the game.

On the sixteenth the Mets were rained out while the Cubs beat the Expos. Some of the Cubs started talking about chipping away at the Mets' lead and even Durocher was communicative again. Ever since the Met series he had been answering questions with: "No comment. No bleeping comment." Now he was suddenly sweet again, and old Durocher-watchers said this was a sure sign Leo had given up. When beaten, Leo turned pleasant to keep the critics away from him and perhaps shift the blame elsewhere.

As the Mets left for St. Louis, they read stories that the Cardinals were rooting for them instead of the Cubs. With this backlog of affection, the Mets arrived in Montreal and found they were quartered like champions this time in the modern Hotel Queen Elizabeth. Koosman and Seaver reacted by pitching shutouts in two straight victories.

"It's so much fun to know the game has meaning," Seaver said. "It's more than salary. It's a team accomplishment. The game has never been so much fun. Where is the pressure? I don't know. How does pressure manifest itself? Maybe we're too inexperienced at winning in the major leagues to know what pressure is. Maybe this is pressure and we're mistaking it for excitement."

Seaver's teammates certainly didn't seem to feel any pressure when he finally dressed and joined them on the bus. "Let's hear it for the pitching staff," Seaver announced. His teammates booed him, of course.

Ed Kranepool drove in both Met runs in the final game in Montreal. Now he sat quietly in the dark of the bus as the new players heckled Seaver.

"Kranepool is only nine days older than Seaver," Bob Lipsyte wrote in his column in *The New York Times* the next day. "Yet the tall first baseman's eyes seem middle-aged and he carries himself with something of the spirit of the ancient mariner."

"I thought they'd win it a lot faster," Kranepool told Lipsyte. "If I could have seen ahead in 1962, I would have signed with another club. It was a lot of fun playing in the majors but a lot of frustrations, too. But I'll tell you something. I would have died if they traded me last winter and then I saw them win."

Kranepool said he was not even thinking about the $5000 for the Eastern title.

"I've made more than that in one day in the stock market," he said. "And lost it in the next day. What's $5000 these days?"

But many of the Mets were thinking about the money, of course, as they rampaged through the final weeks. Since that triple loss in Houston, they had won twenty-nine of thirty-six games. They had trailed the Cubs by nine and a half games on August 13. In five weeks they had made up fourteen and a half games. Seaver had won seven straight since recovering from his shoulder trouble, and Koosman was 6–1. And now they were flying home—and this time they didn't have to sit around the Montreal airport like the last time. Several hundred cheering fans were waiting for them at two in the morning as they arrived at Kennedy Airport. The players signed autographs on the run. They had a twi-night doubleheader in a few hours.

The doubleheader came up too fast. Before they knew it, they had lost, 8–2 and 8–0, to Pittsburgh. And after going 221 innings without the staff yielding a homer, McAndrew gave up a long blast to Willie Stargell.

The Cubs split a doubleheader, so the lead fell to four games.

The doldrums continued on Saturday as young Bob Moose of Pittsburgh pitched a no-hitter and the Pirates won, 4–0. But the Cards beat their friends, the Cubs, by a 4–1 score to bring the

Mets a little closer to a pennant. Not even old-fashioned Met ineptitude could delay them for long.

Finally on Sunday the Mets snapped back, sweeping the Pirates as Koosman and Cardwell pitched complete games. The Cubs won, but it hardly mattered any more.

The next visitors were the Cardinals, who had just been officially eliminated from the pennant race. Joe Torre looked forward to driving in from his home on Long Island to watch the play-offs and maybe the World Series.

"My wife's a Met fan," he noted. Mrs. Torre must have cheered on Monday night because Seaver won his twenty-fifth game against her husband's team.

On September 23, the Mets beat the Cards, 3–2, in the eleventh inning on singles by Swoboda, Grote, and Harrelson. The Cubs lost to the Expos in a drizzle in Chicago.

Then it was September 24, and 54,928 people came to see if the Mets could clinch the division title. If they came late, they missed most of the action because Clendenon hit a three-run homer and Charles hit a two-run homer, both in the first inning, for a 5–0 lead over the Cardinals. Then it was just a matter of waiting, as Gentry ticked away the innings with a four-hitter.

There was an interested spectator at this momentous game. Rod Kanehl, now in the insurance business in Los Angeles, had paid his way to New York just to see his old team clinch the pennant. He was visiting with his old friends in the press box as the innings passed.

At 9:07 P.M., Joe Torre bounced into a double play that ended the 6–0 victory and brought the Mets their first championship ever. The fans leaped onto the field and shouted the familiar "We're Number One," some of them clawing home plate out of the dirt, others stealing the bases, others ripping out hunks of sod from the outfield grass. But mostly they just milled around in happy delirium. Larry Merchant discovered six happy twenty-year-olds passing a peace pipe stuffed with some bliss-giving substance.

"It was an urban Bethel," Merchant wrote, referring to the music festival in upstate New York.

Rod Kanehl dug this scene too. He peered out of the press

box at the descendants of the fans who had discovered him in
the prehistoric past. "Gentlemen, there it is," Kanehl pronounced
to his reporter friends. "There is the gratitude and the riches
of it all—and you can quote me. It's that profound, I say. Look
at it. Times Square and World War Two. The people."

"Rod, Rod, what do you really think?" Bob Lipsyte asked.

"God Almighty damn," Kanehl exclaimed.

Down in their dressing room, the Mets found champagne waiting for them and began squirting it at each other. Seaver, the
star, was the instigator, daring to douse Ralph Kiner and Gil
Hodges while they were talking into a television camera.

The Mets' television network carried almost an hour of this
hilarity, showing the players getting progressively bolder and
drunker as they splashed each other with shaving cream, ice water,
and champagne. The honest joy in the clubhouse was one of
the most absorbing studies ever seen on television, proving once
again that the media is at its best when presenting events as they
happen.

Seaver's champagne dried in Hodges' hair, turning it slick and
heavy. It was a year to the day since Hodges had suffered the
heart attack in Atlanta while the Mets clinched ninth place. Now
they had clinched first place, and he seemed completely calm and
healthy.

"They're a great bunch of boys," Hodges said. "They showed
confidence, maturity, togetherness—and pitching. They proved it
could be done. Oh, yes, I'm excited, thrilled, very happy—not
quite as much as when I was a player, maybe, but all of those
things."

Mrs. Payson was not present at this celebration because she
had scheduled a trip to Europe for this time, and she was too
superstitious to change her plans. Casey was back in California,
preparing to travel east for the play-offs. But M. Donald Grant
was all over the clubhouse, telling anybody who would listen:
"Our team finally caught up with our fans. Our fans were winners
long ago."

The players soaked Grant, too, as they soaked newsmen and
other visitors to the clubhouse. Two big visitors got drenched
along with everybody else. One was Kanehl and the other was

Craig Anderson, who was remembered for his epic nineteen-game losing streak and was now working as a college administrator.

The two old Mets, both in their early thirties, chatted together as pandemonium raged around them. Finally Kanehl felt the urge to visit with some of the new Mets.

The Hot Rod, the Barracuda, the Mole who rode the subways, strode up and shook hands with Tommie Agee.

"Tommie . . . Rod Kanehl," he said.

Later, after Kanehl was farther down the row of lockers, Agee turned to a friend, and he said: "Who is that?"

26

BAD HENRY

◆

Lou Niss shuffled through the Met clubhouse, seemingly in imitation of the penguin walk that Casey had imitated so long ago. For eight years the wise old road secretary had been passing out itineraries, but the one for the final road trip of the season was the most joyous, the most obscure, of all.

"Destination Paradise—Site Unknown," was the heading.

When Niss had typed up his itinerary (pay all incidentals!), four teams were still competing for the Western Division title. Therefore, Niss had called, written, begged, and bargained for hotel rooms in Los Angeles, Cincinnati, San Francisco, and Atlanta.

Now the Mets had to play out the final week and wait to see who their opponent was going to be. It was strange for them to be winners, and it was just as strange to be planning for an opponent they could not name.

But 1969 was a very strange season. With the addition of expansion teams in San Diego and Montreal, the league was too bulky for one pennant race. Who would patronize a game between the eleventh and twelfth teams in September? So baseball's rulers had taken a suggestion—made years before by newspapermen—and split each league into two divisions.

This division was supposed to create four fascinating races, but Baltimore and Minnesota had won easily in the American League, and the Mets had roared past the faded Cubs in the National League East. Only in the National West was there a tight race.

So now the Mets sat on the sidelines and watched the Western race and meditated. What had they accomplished so far? How far could they go? Whom did they want to play? Was this all really happening?

In a philosophical sense, the Mets had reason to wonder if they were champions like all the other champions before them. They had put together one of the most surprising and inspirational seasons a team could have. They had won their first objective, the division title. But if they should lose in the league championship round, could they go home and call themselves "champions?" Or would they go home feeling the way a second-place team usually felt?

In fact, a check with league headquarters showed there was no plan to issue pennants for the division champions. "But I'm sure we can work something out," said a league spokesman.

The Mets, in effect, were in a never-never land where no team had ever been before. They puzzled over this as first Los Angeles was eliminated and then Cincinnati.

Most of the Mets did not care to open a series in the Giants' Candlestick Park with Willie McCovey and Willie Mays hitting baseballs up into the jet stream, and Juan Marichal and Gaylord Perry firing the ball at them. The Mets would take their chances in Atlanta with Henry Aaron & Co. They had won eight and lost four against both Western teams. (The only team that beat the Mets in the season series was, of course, Houston, which won ten of twelve. The Mets had reason to give thanks they were not playing the Astros in the play-off.)

While they were waiting, there were other matters to take care of. The afternoon following the clinching of the pennant, M. Donald Grant and Johnny Murphy visited Mayor Lindsay's office to plan a celebration. Afterward they sat on the fence outside City Hall and agreed that Hodges deserved a reward for winning the pennant. So they sent Grant's chauffeur to Hodges'

home in Brooklyn and brought the manager to Grant's office at
110 Wall Street.

It wasn't the biggest deal ever made at Fahnestock, but it
made Hodges happy. He was in the second year of a three-year
contract for $57,000 a year. Grant and Murphy gave him a new
three-year contract at $70,000 a year. There was also a bonus
for 1969.

"I never saw a better job of managing," Murphy said.

The next morning Hodges reported to Shea and found a telegram from his old manager with the Brooklyn Dodgers, Leo
Durocher.

"Congratulations to you and your fine ball club for the terrific
season you had this year," the wire said. "Please give my best
wishes to your club and tell them I thought they played great
ball all year. My best personal regards to you and your family.
Leo Durocher, manager."

As Hodges joined the team bus for the ride to Philadelphia,
there were already one hundred young fans standing on line for
play-off tickets. As they rode, Hodges and Rube Walker set up
a rotation of Seaver-Koosman-Gentry for the first three games of
the play-off. They also discussed letting Jones lead off in the final
games, to give him an extra at-bat to regain his batting form. A
hand injury and torn muscle in his side had put him out of the
lineup earlier in the month.

"I'm trying to find what I lost and I still haven't got it," Jones
said. "Every pitcher looks like Bob Feller. No, you better make
that Bob Gibson, because I never went against Feller."

Jones made only two hits in Philadelphia but the Mets won
three straight shutouts to run the pitcher's scoreless streak to
forty-two innings.

"Oh, it's only a club record," said Hodges, who likes to put
people on. "We're out to shoot for league records, not club
records."

By this time the Mets knew they were going to open in Atlanta,
which had outdistanced San Francisco in the West. Jones and
Agee—the boys from Mobile, Alabama—began receiving phone
calls from friends and relatives who were eager to see them play.

The next stop was Chicago, where Ernie Banks smiled and offered his congratulations and nobody, not even Kranepool, dared say, "Let's play two" to the beaten, beautiful man.

Ron Santo was in a reflective mood as he talked to reporters. "I learned a lot this year," he said. "I learned a lot about people —and I don't mean just fans. Well, there will be other times. I still have my health."

The scoreless streak ended in the first inning when Koosman gave up two runs to the Cubs. But the Mets won their one hundredth game when Shamsky singled in the twelfth inning, beating the Cubs, 6–5.

The Bleacher Bums were quiet on the first day, but they ran rampant on the final afternoon of the season, throwing a smoke bomb into center field, charging into the Cub dugout to praise their idol, Leo Durocher, and chanting and raging at the fates. The Mets' nine-game winning streak was broken, 5–3, but the club was happy to get out of town, particularly after Gentry was hit on the right arm with a line drive. Fortunately, nothing was broken.

The Mets finished the season with one hundred victories and sixty-two losses, eight games ahead of the Cubs. They had won thirty-eight of their last forty-nine games in one of the greatest finishes in sports history.

Then they took their chartered airplane to "Destination—Paradise," the city that General Sherman had leveled a century before, now a modern center of industry and culture in the South, and also the home of Bad Henry.

Sandy Koufax had labeled Henry Aaron as "Bad Henry"—because he was so good. The Mets could appreciate the irony. Bad Henry had batted .325 against them in twelve games in 1969, hitting five homers. But he drove in only six runs, which meant that the Mets were not letting him swing with men on base. They couldn't stop him from stealing bases and making great catches in right field but they could stop him from hitting homers with men on base.

"No matter who is batting behind him, you have to pitch around Henry in the clutch and take your chances," Hodges said.

The Braves had several good hitters before and after Bad Henry. They had Orlando Cepeda, who had brought his phono-

graph and a pennant with him from San Francisco to St. Louis
to Atlanta. They had Rico Carty, healthy again after missing
1968 because of tuberculosis. They had Felix Millan, a good,
young second baseman, and Tony Gonzalez, who had sparked
them in center field after coming over from San Diego. They also
had Clete Boyer, the old Yankee.

The pitching of Phil Niekro, Ron Reed, and Pat Jarvis was all
right, but it had been improved when Hoyt Wilhelm joined the
club in September. The ancient knuckle ball pitcher had come
too late to be eligible for the play-offs, however, and the only
other reliable pitcher was submarine pitcher Cecil Upshaw.

Over the previous years the Braves had been the Mets' third
toughest opponent, winning eighty-nine and losing only forty-
nine of their confrontations. But after the weird success of 1969,
the Mets were not afraid of the Braves—only of Bad Henry.

The manager of the Braves was Luman Harris, a former minor-
league pitcher who had been a quiet and unspectacular assistant to Paul Richards for many years. Harris had shown some
flexibility in 1969 when Orlando Cepeda arrived with his jazz al-
bums. Harris was not overly enthusiastic about music in the clubhouse until somebody reminded him that Cha-Cha had been the
life of the party in the Cardinal clubhouse. Harris let Cepeda
have his music, and Orlando batted .257 with eighty-eight RBIs.

The Mets assessed their chances as they arrived in Atlanta.

"All we've got to do is win one game here, just split, and we'll
go back to New York in good shape," Tommie Agee said. "We
could win two here but we don't have to. If we win just one,
I think we go back to New York with an 80 per cent chance of
winning."

Agee was looking forward to playing against the Braves, partially because he batted .341 against them during the season.

"Hank and Tommie Aaron, they're both from Mobile," he said.
"Last year, when they beat us pretty good, every time I saw Tommie or Hank, they kidded me about it. And Tommie and me live
only a block apart. We hit the ball around during the winter."

There was one sad note as the Mets arrived in Atlanta. They
had twenty-six eligible players and could use only twenty-five in
the series, so Bobby Pfeil was dropped from the roster. But he

was carried with the squad, with full privileges. The only thing he couldn't do was play.

Then it was the morning of October 4, the day of the Mets' first postseason game ever. The front office was in full delegation, including the seventy-nine-year-old vice-president, Casey Stengel, who trotted around the field before the game, chatting with Clete Boyer and Yogi Berra.

Mrs. Payson flew into town in the morning, arriving only fifteen minutes before game time. The last time she had been to Atlanta was in 1938 when she and her brother, Jock, had invested in a film called *Gone With the Wind.*

The premiere had been in Atlanta, and Clark Gable and Vivien Leigh had been there. Now Mrs. Payson was back, thirty-one years later, rooting for Tom Seaver instead of Clark Gable.

Gable must have had a better premiere than Seaver, because the twenty-five winner was rocked for five runs and eight hits by the team that had illegally signed him back in 1966. He gave up homers to Gonzalez and Bad Henry.

The Damnyankees were losing 5–4, going into the eighth inning and Phil Niekro, the twenty-three game winner with the knuckle ball, seemed to be getting tougher. But as the Mets batted in the eighth, Rod Gaspar and Al Weis began throwing in the bullpen. These two men were normally used as defensive replacements when the Mets were ahead. Did Hodges know something the rest of the world did not know?

Maybe he did. Wayne Garrett, the former Brave farmhand, opened the inning by flicking a ground double past Boyer at third. Then Cleon Jones dumped a pop single to left to tie the game, and Art Shamsky singled Jones to second.

Ken Boswell was the next batter and he was supposed to bunt, but he missed. Catcher Bob Didier tried to pick Jones off second, but the alert runner dashed for third and slid in safely. Boswell hit a grounder, and the Braves held Jones at third, settling for one out instead of trying for a double play.

With runners on first and third, Kranepool bounced to Cepeda, who saw Jones caught between third and home. But Orlando made a bad throw into the dirt, and Jones skipped home as the Mets took the lead, 6–5. Gaspar and Weis kept throwing.

An intentional walk loaded the bases with two outs and made Hodges decide whether to keep his twenty-five game winner in the game. The manager decided to go for some runs and called on J. C. Martin, the quiet Virginian who had batted .209 during the season.

Martin lashed Niekro's first pitch to center for two runs, and a third run scored on an error by Gonzalez. Gaspar and Weis kept throwing.

In the bottom of the eighth, Gaspar and Weis trotted out to right field and second base, respectively, and Ron Taylor replaced Seaver. Taylor finished up the 9–5 victory, and the Mets were winners in the first "championship round" game ever.

Seaver rejoiced in the victory but said he was upset about his bad showing, his worst outing since Montreal in July.

"It rubs me, it frustrates me," Seaver said. "I know what I can do but I just couldn't do it. It happens to me all the time, except that the tension dissipates itself after my first pitch usually. Today it stuck right with me well into the second inning."

On the second day, Mrs. Coretta King threw out the first ball, and 50,270 fans waited to see Met pitching battle Brave hitting again. But the Met hitters were unusually powerful, scoring eight runs in four innings, including two-run homers by Boswell and Agee.

Koosman could not last through the sixth inning and by the time Taylor got the side out, the Braves had narrowed the score to 9–6, with the help of another homer by Bad Henry.

In the seventh, the Mets' two Mobile natives nearly staged a beheading at home plate. Agee decided to steal home while Jones was lashing a foul line drive. Jones' drive missed Agee by only a few inches and the two men needed a minute of rest before they were calm enough to resume play.

The next time Jones swung, he lashed a two-run homer to make the score 11–6. Tug McGraw protected the victory to put the Mets two games ahead, but the postgame conversation was mostly about the near-accident at home.

"That's my buddy," Agee said. "He tries to miss and he hits the ball. That's how good a hitter he is."

"It wasn't really that close," Jones said. "It just seemed close."

Agee gave him a funny stare. "If that ball hit me, it would have been all over," he said.

So Agee escaped with his life and the Mets escaped with a two-game lead when they would have been willing to split the first two games.

"What we need," said the astute Clete Boyer, "is a day off."

The Mets flew home to Kennedy Airport after the game and were greeted by around two hundred fans, many of them teeny-boppers who looked like they should be following a rock band.

One spotted Tom and Nancy Seaver. "Forget her, Tom, I love you more and I'm prettier than she is," the teeny-bopper shouted. Another one kissed Stengel, which he enjoyed immensely.

There was no day off for the Braves, however, as the play-off series resumed the following morning. At 11 A.M., Tommie Agee was tying his baseball shoes when he heard a familiar voice.

"Congratulations," Gil Hodges said. Then the manager returned to his office.

"What does that mean?" somebody asked.

"We were supposed to be on the field at ten minutes to eleven," Agee replied. "That just cost me $25."

"He'll give it back if you have a good day," somebody said.

"No," Agee said. "Everybody on this club knows the rules."

By the time Agee got out to the field, the fans were already filing in. Some new faces were evident in Shea Stadium this October, smiling faces of politicians.

Mario Procaccino, the Democrats' mayoral candidate, was there, announcing: "It's the year of the Moon, the Mets, and Mario."

Former Mayor Wagner was also present. Blamed for letting the Dodgers and Giants leave during his administration, he had later become a true Met fan, attending some of their dreariest games after he left office.

Frank Smith and Sanford Garelik, the two opponents for City Council President, were also at this game.

And, of course, there was the handsome mayor of New York, John Lindsay, on one of his rare journeys to Queens. During the previous winter, Lindsay had been vilified by Queens residents when the city did not clear the streets fast enough after a severe snowstorm. Now fighting for his career as an Independent-Liberal candidate, Lindsay was back in Queens, undeniably basking in the warm glow of the Mets.

After the politicians had been shown where home plate was, Gary Gentry showed them what a home run was. First he gave up a single to Gonzalez, and then Bad Henry smashed a homer off the center-field flagpole, 410 feet away, his third homer in three play-off games.

Gentry was celebrating his twenty-third birthday, but Bad Henry was having all the fun. In the third inning, Gonzalez singled again and Aaron clouted a double to left-center.

The Met bullpen was working fast as Gentry pitched to the dangerous Rico Carty. When Carty golfed a line drive off the left-field wall, foul by only a few feet, Hodges began walking slowly toward the mound.

Gentry saw the manager striding toward him like Gary Cooper in *High Noon*. The pitcher looked like he wanted to draw first, or at least to stomp around on the mound to show his displeasure. Hodges saw the pitcher staring angrily at him and asked: "What are you looking at?"

"I'm watching you walk out," Gentry said.

"All right," Hodges said. "I'm going to take you out. You're not throwing right today."

Gentry very politely left the mound as Hodges signaled for a right-hander to pitch to Carty with one ball and two strikes. Most of the fans craned their necks to watch Nolan Ryan come in from the bullpen, but Carty didn't care who the new pitcher was. The huge man from the Dominican Republic, a former boxer who wore several rings on each hand, felt he could hit anybody when he was healthy. Carty had spent 1968 in a tuberculosis sanitarium and Ryan had not pitched against the Braves in 1969 because of injuries and military service.

"Sliders," somebody said laconically.

Poor Carty did not appreciate the irony until too late. When he stepped up to face Nolan Ryan, he was not ready for the 100 MPH fastball that roared over the plate. Carty stared at the pitch, and he was out.

Next Ryan walked Cepeda intentionally to load the bases before throwing a third strike past Boyer, who shook his head. Didier popped to Jones. The inning was over.

The Mets perked up immediately. Agee slammed a homer in the third. Boswell whacked a two-run homer in the fourth which landed in the bullpen where coach Joe Pignatano dropped it. Later Boswell would tell him "Hey, Piggy, you've got hands like me."

Cepeda put the Braves ahead, 4–3, in the fifth with a two-run homer. But in the bottom of the fifth, Ryan—who had only three hits all season—bounced a single through the infield.

The next batter was Garrett, the redheaded country boy who had seen himself and his two brothers waste their years in the Braves farm system. Garrett had not hit a homer since May, but he lofted one off the right-field foul pole to put the Mets ahead again, 5–4.

The Mets scored two more runs in the seventh as Dr. Dominic Principato, the radiologist from Flushing in his yellow slicker and pith helmet, carried signs that said: ON TO MINNEMORE and ON TO BALTISOTA.

Ryan's flamethrower struck out seven Braves in seven innings until 3:34 P.M., when Gonzalez grounded to Garrett for the final out of the National League season. The Mets were the champions in three straight victories. They had won a real pennant—not just a division pennant, but the real thing.

Once again, just as on September 24, the fans erupted from the grandstand, tearing out chunks of sod, trying to hug the players who ran for the dugout. In New York City, people applauded and honked their horns.

In the clubhouse, the Mets went through the champagne ritual again. The brand was imported this time, and so was the mood.

"It was as if we had to do what was expected of us, especially with the television cameras there," said Tom Seaver. "The other time it was more spontaneous."

There was one spontaneous moment in the clubhouse when the tall mayor of New York strode in. Two bright-eyed Californians, Seaver and Gaspar, doused the sculptured features of the mayor, who smiled under the shower and looked for the television cameras.

"This will get him thousands of votes," one reporter noted.

"It has probably crossed his mind too," another reporter said.

Some of the players even abstained from the champagne squirting. Art Shamsky had batted .538 in the play-offs, the highest average, and some people were joking that it was his reward for missing a game in September because he would not work on Rosh Hashanah.

"It's ironic," Shamsky said. "When I think of how I was hurting in spring training and thinking my playing days might be over and now this—and a World Series coming up—and I'm only twenty-seven—it's ironic and it just shows you.

"But you know what I'm glad of the most? That finally the fellows like Boswell and Garrett, who did so much all year, can get the recognition they deserve, because it came up for them to have the big hits when everyone was watching. We've been that way all year—if one guy didn't, another did."

One man seemed to feel more of a thrill in the play-off than in the divisional championship.

"This meant much more to me because it's more important," Gil Hodges said. "This is the championship of the whole league, not just one division. As I said then, you go one step, and then you go another step, and this step is further than the other one. And the next one would be bigger still."

"They won the pennant," Luman Harris said, "but I just don't believe they can hit our pitching like they did. I admire Gil Hodges. To me, there's no question he's the manager of the year. But I still believe if we played 'em three more games, we'd beat 'em three straight."

Jarvis seemed most perplexed by the man who hit the winning homer. "It's different if he's a McCovey or a Stargell or a hitter like that. But Wayne Garrett?"

While the Braves were dressing for the trip home, they were visited by M. Donald Grant, the chairman of the Mets. M. Donald introduced himself to Henry Aaron and said: "We were lucky and you were great."

Aaron had three homers and seven RBI's, records for the first series, but he was now finished for the season.

"I don't know what I'm going to do in the next few days,"

Bad Henry said. "I had planned on playing in the World Series. But the Mets messed me up."

The Mets were just starting to mess people up.

Outside Shea Stadium, Super Fan Karl Ehrhardt was holding his last banner until the World Series.

BRING ON THE BIRDS, it said.

27

SOMEONE WAS GOOD
TO US

◆

ONLY A FEW MINUTES AFTER the Mets polished off the Braves, a
flock of Baltimore Orioles repeated the ever-popular champagne
bath in the clubhouse in Minnesota.

The Orioles had knocked off the Twins three straight times for
the American League pennant. The final game was 11-2, and
it was such a laugher that certain Orioles sneaked back into the
clubhouse to watch the late stages of the Met game on the tube.

One of the things they noticed on television was a dripping
Met player predicting—for all the world to see and hear—that
the Mets would beat the Orioles in four straight. That player
was . . .

"Bring on Ron Gaspar," shouted Frank Robinson, the dynamic
leader of the Orioles.

"Rod, stupid," screamed Merv Rettenmund, another Oriole.

"Bring on Rod Stupid," the undaunted Robinson replied.

The Orioles had every reason to make jokes in their champagne mood. They had frolicked through the season, winning
109 games in the only major-league division without an expansion
club. They were a team with experience, with skill, with character. In 1966 they had polished off the Dodgers of Sandy Koufax

and Don Drysdale in four straight games in their first Series. Injuries had hurt the Orioles in 1967 and 1968, but now Frank Robinson was healthy again and they were the top team of the American League.

Mainly the club got its drive and character from the two Robinsons, Frank and Brooks, who were as varied in temperament as they were in color.

A native of Oakland, California, Frank was talkative and aggressive, a good needler. He had been a young star outfielder in Cincinnati but had been traded to Baltimore in 1966 by Bill De-Witt, who had allegedly called Robinson "an old thirty-one." Playing in a rage against the whispers, Robinson had led the Orioles to the 1966 World Championship.

In his early days, Frank had a reputation as a vicious base runner, a modern-day Ty Cobb. Some white players had been delighted when Don Drysdale and others threw at his head and body, trying to drive him out of his crouched stance over home plate. But Robinson never gave an inch and, in the long run, became respected by all players.

In 1967, Robinson suffered a concussion and double vision when he crashed into a White Sox infielder while trying to break up a double play. The infielder, Al Weis, had suffered a torn knee and missed the rest of the season. In 1968, players whispered that Robinson still could not see the ball well.

In the fall of 1968, Frank had taken a job as nonplaying manager of the Santurce Cangrejeros in the Puerto Rican Winter League, frankly stating that he was hoping to become the first black manager in the major leagues. He was quickly accepted by Latins as well as the U.S. whites and blacks and he won a pennant. Then, in 1969, his eyesight recovered completely and he was a superstar again.

Brooks Robinson did not profess the same goals as Frank. The greatest third baseman of his generation—of perhaps any generation—said he looked forward to running his restaurant and sporting goods store in Baltimore. He probably could be elected mayor on any ticket.

A native of Little Rock, Arkansas, Brooks had been a fixture in Baltimore since 1957, scooping up impossible grounders, driving in important runs, making friends wherever he went. He had overcome the prejudices of his southern upbringing to a point where sensitive black players said they did not think of color when they thought of Brooks Robinson. Brooks and Frank also were two of the most co-operative and intelligent subjects for the press, putting demigods like Mays and Mantle to shame.

In the Orioles' Kangaroo Court, the two Robinsons held opposite roles. Frank was "De Judge"—wearing a mop over his head, cajoling fines from players, officials, and reporters for a special charity fund. Brooks was "The Victim"—the family man who wanted to dress quickly and get home after a game and was willing to pay Frank the $1 or $2 fine for the privilege. A black played the leader and a white played the butt in the slapstick clubhouse comedy, and the Orioles drew closer together.

The Orioles were also drawn together by their playing ability. Frank had driven in a hundred runs with his .308 average while Brooks was still the finest third baseman in the world. Massive Boog Powell hit thirty-seven homers in 1969 while Paul Blair, who had broken in with Cleon Jones in the Met instructional team in 1962, was now a lithe center fielder who batted .284 with twenty-six homers and seventy-six RBI's. Other Oriole stars were shortstop Mark Belanger, left fielder Don Buford, and second baseman Davey Johnson, the Texan who had played on the same All-Star team with Jerry Grote so many years before.

The Oriole pitching was solid with Mike Cuellar (23–11), Jim Palmer (16–4), Dave McNally (20–7), and Tom Phoebus (14–7), backed up by a good bullpen and secondary.

The manager was a chunky little guy named Earl Weaver who had kicked around the Cardinal farm system as a second baseman before winding up managing in the Oriole system. Weaver was bright and aggressive, and he bothered the traditionalists in the Brother-in-Law League by arguing every point in his gravelly voice. Weaver looked like Mickey Rooney and acted like Eddie Stanky-Solly Hemus-Alvin Dark and all the other spiritual children of Leo Durocher.

Under the frank regime of Weaver, the Orioles were casual enough to admit they didn't know much about the Mets. They didn't know who played third base, for example.

"No idea," Frank said.

"Couldn't tell you," Brooks said.

"I remember the Mets," said Pete Richert, a breezy relief pitcher from Floral Park, Long Island. "When I pitched for the Dodgers, I remember they never used to hit a cutoff man. That's what I remember about them. Yeah, I remember we used to laugh a lot."

"We're not laughing at them now," Buford said. "They must have been lucky or good or something. All we know about them is that they used to be funny. We don't think they're funny any more."

If the Orioles didn't think the Mets were funny any more, many people didn't know the Mets had ever been funny.

Fans in the American League had probably never been properly briefed on Casey's old amazing Mets. When the Old Man had popped up with the Mets in 1962, he was remembered mostly as the manager who had swamped the American League for ten pennants with the Yankees. What was so funny about that?

Then the first Met folk hero had been Marvelous Marv Throneberry, and the American League had already caught his act.

"Throneberry?" harrumphed old sportswriters from Kansas City and Baltimore. "He was a bad ball player for us."

Baseball was not the same zesty spectacle in the American League, where everybody seemed to be related or just plain cozy together. Traditionally, runners did not slide as hard and pitchers did not pitch as tight in the American League. Managers did not yell as much and fans did not scream as loud. Part of the reason was the stranglehold the Yankees had on the league from the 1920s to the 1960s. Having lost for so many years, most American Leaguers couldn't see the humor in the Mets.

"How can you stand covering the Mets?" American League reporters used to ask us. "Isn't it awful to lose all the time?"

"It's history," Dick Young or Leonard Shecter might reply. "Besides, the Mets are nice people and we get to see the National League again."

So the Met mystique had never been properly explained to millions of fans in the Brother-in-Law League. They did not know about Choo Choo Coleman and Grover Powell and Banner Day.

All they knew was that the Mets used to lose but somehow in 1969 they suddenly won.

In Baltimore, there was some trepidation when a New York team qualified for the World Series. Baltimore had been having a tough year in 1969. In January, their beloved Colts had been upset in the Super Bowl by a bunch of characters from Shea Stadium called the New York Jets. In March, their first-place Bullets had been upset in the first round of the National Basketball Association play-offs by the New York Knicks.

Baltimore had already developed a New York complex from finishing behind the Yankees for so many years. This complex was heightened by the disproportionate publicity given to New York players because the communications media were centered in New York.

The Orioles saw the Mets pop up on national television commercials. They grumbled when Frank Robinson was introduced on the *Johnny Carson Show* as "Frank Robinson of the Baltimore Colts." And they became more indignant when Robinson was practically ignored by Carson while Seaver got all the attention.

"I think you could say that Baltimore and the Orioles have been pretty much overlooked by the people of New York," Brooks said.

A few months later, this theory about the concentration of power in the Eastern Establishment would be adapted by a frustrated Baltimore Colts fan named Spiro Agnew, who had taken on a new job in Washington, D.C.

New York politicians quickly discovered the Mets. Governor Nelson Rockefeller invited the players and their wives to a cocktail party at his Fifth Avenue apartment overlooking the Children's Zoo. The governor stood on a marble coffee table in front of a Matisse painting and said: "Ladies and gentlemen, join me in a toast to Joan Payson and the Mets. It's as good as landing on the moon."

"Better than the moon," Joe Pignatano corrected.

"I want to amend that," Rockefeller echoed. "Better than the moon landing."

The governor and his wife were so charmed by the Mets that

they asked if they could visit Shea Stadium—like, say, for the first Series game there. Jim Thomson, the Mets' capable business manager, was immediately deputized to come up with a few extra boxes for the governor's party.

Rockefeller's favorite mayor was also very concerned with the Mets in October. As the team prepared to fly from LaGuardia on Thursday, Lindsay saw them off with a dixieland band and a button that said WE'RE NO. 1. Fun City never seemed more together. Policemen politely asked for autographs, the mayor read a parody of "Casey at the Bat," and Hodges gave the "V" for victory sign, producing squeals of delight from the teen-agers who use the sign in their antiwar crusade. Hodges was talking about a forceful victory in his particular war, of course.

When they arrived in Baltimore, the Mets discovered that the newspapers were playing the World Series very straight, with no hometown rooting, just a front-page headline announcing: METS' MIRACLE STORY NEARING END.

While for everyone else on the club this was alien and hostile territory, for Rocky Swoboda this was home, where he had played on a sandlot team for the head Oriole scout. The man had expressed interest in Rocky, but had then given the big bonus to pitcher Wally Bunker.

"As a kid, I was just like the rest of the people in Baltimore," Rocky recalled. "I never went to the ball games."

In 1969, the Orioles did not reach a million paid customers until the last home game, despite having a team that won 109 games. Now the fans were clamoring for tickets and Swoboda was feeling the pressure. He spent $1000 for tickets for friends and relatives in Baltimore, including his Chinese step-grandfather, a cook who had written out a list of dishes for Swoboda to order in Chinese restaurants around the league.

Swoboda was looking forward to playing against the Orioles' left-handed pitchers.

"I'm tired of that cheerleading," he said. "I have no gripes about it because the guy ahead of me is doing a good job. But I'm getting anxious. I want to play."

Donn Clendenon, Al Weis, and Ed Charles also looked forward to playing on the right-handed platoon. Charles had told his friends that he was retiring after the season, and he wanted to finish his eighteenth season by helping to win a World Series.

"The worst feeling is not to be part of things, not to feel you've made a contribution," Charles said.

Two other men were happy to learn their contributions would finally be read about by their friends and family. While Jones and Agee had been wrecking the Atlanta Braves, their native city of Mobile had paid little attention, except at their old County Training School. The white newspapers and the white government and the white school system couldn't have cared less, or written less, about Jones and Agee.

On October 10, the day before the Series opened, reporter Roy Reed of *The New York Times* visited Mobile to see if the city was excited about having two native sons playing in the World Series. He found that white officials at City Hall had never heard of the pair.

Taking their cue from Reed's story, the New York *Daily News* volunteered to fly copies of its paper to County Training School, whose classes were being halted during the games so the 1200 students could watch their two famous alumni. Now the *Daily News* was going to "tell it like it is" for the blacks of Mobile.

Meanwhile, the Mets found themselves quartered at the Sheraton-Belvedere, an ancient establishment where George and Martha Washington had probably slept. When the players grumbled, they were told there was only one modern hotel in Baltimore—and it was booked solid. The only thing they could do was win the Series in five games to avoid a return trip to the musty old hotel.

On Saturday morning, Tom Seaver woke up for his first World Series game. He hadn't been sure if he could eat because of his excitement, but he was glad to see he was hungry.

Seaver dressed and went down to the coffee shop at 9:30 A.M., only half an hour before the team bus left. He decided he was very hungry. After ten minutes, he was still staring at the menu.

"Forget it," Bud Harrelson told him from the next table. "I've been here fifteen minutes and they haven't looked at me yet."

What had happened was that the bookkeepers or computers that run hotels had not foreseen the unusually large group of hungry people who would want to eat breakfast at 9:30 on this "typical" Saturday in early October. So the hotel was understaffed and could not handle the rush. By 9:45 A.M., the starting pitcher in the World Series gave up any hope for breakfast. "I'll get something at the ball park," he said.

When the bus reached Memorial Stadium, Nick Torman, the Mets' swinging traveling clubhouse man, sent out for some sandwiches for his hungry troops. Tom Seaver wolfed down a roast beef on white with mayonnaise, then went out to face the Orioles.

After all this, the game itself was an anticlimax. The first batter Seaver faced was chunky Don Buford, who cracked a homer. Buford also hit a two-run double in the fourth. The Mets did not score off Mike Cuellar until the seventh, and the Cuban lefty beat them, 4–1, on a six-hitter.

For the first time in a month, the Mets were behind. Seaver had not lost a game since that gloomy night in early August when he walked the streets in Cincinnati. He said it wasn't the lack of breakfast that hurt him, but the calf muscle he had pulled while running a few days earlier.

"I wasn't able to run for a few days and I need to run to be effective," he said. "So today I figured I'd run out of gas sometime—maybe in seven or eight innings, but certainly not four."

The Mets hadn't figured on that, either. Now they were down a game, and Koosman went against Dave McNally on Sunday, October 12.

Koosman did not allow a hit until the seventh inning as his wife, seven months pregnant, rooted for him in the right-field stands. Clendenon gave the Mets a 1–0 lead with a homer in the fourth. But in the seventh, Motormouth Blair singled and stole second, and Brooks Robinson singled to tie the score.

As the Mets went to bat in the eighth, they heard a commotion in the stands. World Series crowds are usually pretty quiet because the customers are expense account types and VIPs, not the true fan. However, the Mets could sense something familiar about this particular commotion. When they located the disturbance, the players saw four pretty girls carrying a banner. The banner said, of course, LET'S GO METS. Oriole fans pelted the four pretty girls with peanut shells.

The Mets recognized, behind the hail of peanut shells, Ruth Ryan (miniskirt, brunette), Nancy Seaver (miniskirt, blonde), Lynn Dyer (pants suit, blonde), and Melanie Pfeil (pants suit, brunette).

"Win it for the wives," the players said, laughing.

Columnists Larry Merchant and Stan Isaacs, always delighted to find an alternative to interviewing muscular athletes, dashed out to get the story of this pretty parade.

"We wanted to do something to show our support and make it seem a little like Shea Stadium," said Lynn Dyer, the mother of two children. "It was so quiet here yesterday and there were so few fans cheering for the Mets. So I stole a bedsheet from our hotel—I don't think you ought to tell anybody that—and I got some black shoe polish and I made up that sign. We didn't go out with it earlier because Jerry Koosman had a no-hitter and we didn't want to jinx him."

After stirring up some excitement, the Met wives returned to the seats the Oriole management had so thoughtfully provided them in deepest right field. And the players commenced to win it for the wives.

In the ninth inning, Clendenon and Swoboda swung for the fences but struck out. Then old Ed Charles rapped a single past Brooks Robinson at third. Charles was trying to steal second when Jerry Grote singled past short, so Charles steamed on to third.

That brought up Al Weis, the little infielder whose career had almost ended in a collision with Frank Robinson two years before. Weis hit the first pitch for a single and the Mets were ahead, 2–1.

In the ninth, Koosman got two outs before walking Frank Robinson and Powell. Once again Hodges trudged out to the mound.

"You did a fine job," Hodges said, signaling for a new pitcher.

On the way back to the dugout, Koosman thought to himself: "If I did a good job, I'd still be out there pitching."

But Ron Taylor got Brooks on a grounder to Charles, and the

Mets won, 2–1, and now the Series was all tied up. Out in the right-field boondocks, the Met wives hugged each other.

"If I were you," one of the wives told Lavonne Koosman, "I would have had the baby in the seventh inning."

In the clubhouse, the Mets joked about their gallant wives.

"I was just hoping Nancy would get back alive," Seaver said.

But the Mets were very much alive now as they headed for home. The next three games were in New York. If they won them all, they wouldn't have to return to Baltimore. Of course, if they lost them all, they wouldn't have to come back, either.

The two teams held a workout in Shea Stadium on Monday, a day off. The Orioles were snickering about all the stories about the Met wives. Nancy Seaver, they noticed, was even writing a column (with the help of various ghosts) in the New York *Post*.

"Man, that's really wild," said Pete Richert, the cocky Long Islander. "Where do they get this stuff about wives winning ball games? I haven't seen one wife throw a pitch yet. The other day I read where Seaver's wife said every time somebody gets a hit off Tom, she feels like a pin's been stuck into her. If my wife felt that way about me, she'd be walking around with more holes than a pin cushion."

On Tuesday, the politicians—all wearing their campaigning smiles—piled into Shea for the first Series game there: Governor Rockefeller, Mayor Lindsay, and candidate Procaccino. Candidate John Marchi had to cancel out because of a virus. None of these grinning, handshaking newcomers got as much attention, however, as Mr. and Mrs. Aristotle Onassis and her two children, who quietly appeared in the field boxes behind home plate as their body guards shooed away the gaping fans.

Even the Onassises were soon overshadowed by Tommie Agee, who opened the bottom of the first inning with a homer, the fifth time he had led off with a homer this year.

The Mets made it 3–0 in the third on Gentry's two-run double over Blair's head. Gentry had gone hitless in his previous twenty-eight at-bats and had driven in only one run all year.

It was Agee's turn again in the fourth, with two outs and two men on base, when left-handed Elrod Hendricks lashed a drive to left-center. Agee broke to his right, toward the green fence, running for forty yards, until he snared the ball in the very edge of his webbing, just before crashing into the fence. He rebounded with the ball still trapped at the end of the glove, a "snow cone" as the players call it. He dashed all the way to the infield with the ball bulging white, for all to see.

People were still saying that they'd never see a catch like that again, when Agee did it again—within the hour. Gentry loaded the bases on walks with two outs in the seventh, so Hodges brought in Nolan Ryan, the man who had blown his fastball past the Braves a week before. This time Paul Blair connected with a fastball and rocketed it down the right-center field alley, seemingly good for a three-run triple.

But Agee took off after that ball with all the power of one of those jets taking off from LaGuardia behind the ball park. Agee seemed to correct his course once or twice, the way a pilot will do while landing in a wind, and then Agee more or less caught up with the line drive, catching the ball as he dove headfirst, just before his body crashed into the turf. He skidded fifteen feet, and the ball was still in his glove when he came to a stop.

Paul Blair, who might have been the Met center fielder under different circumstances, rounded first base and stared soulfully at Tommie Agee and his little white souvenir.

Kranepool hit a homer in the seventh, and Jacqueline Onassis and her two children stayed until the final out of the 5–0 victory that put the Mets ahead in the series. As she and Caroline and John joined her husband in the limousine, they were probably talking about Tommie Agee. Earl Weaver certainly was.

"Listen," the losing manager said. "I saw him do it in 1963 in Charleston, West Virginia. He could always play that center field. That man has ability."

"The second one was easier," Agee said, "because it was away from my glove and I didn't have as far to go, but the wind kept taking it away and I had to dive."

Somebody asked Agee if he thought the Mobile newspapers and officials would recognize him and Jones now.

"Oh, people hear about us," Agee said. "They get clippings from out of town."

Then it was Wednesday, October 15, a beautiful day in New

York, with crisp air and blue skies and bright sun, a day for affirming the joy of being alive. It was also the day of the first Vietnam Moratorium, the nationwide protest against the war. The Mets and Tom Seaver soon found themselves right in the middle.

Several weeks before, Seaver had made some statements that caught the attention of some Moratorium people who asked Seaver if the Met players would mind an advertisement that said: "If the Mets can win the pennant, why can't we end the war?"

Seaver did not object to that sentiment.

"What is so unpatriotic about being against such a terrible war?" he reasoned.

Gradually, his sympathies were examined by members of the press. The younger reporters tended to be against the war and joked that it would be a magnificent gesture if Seaver should pitch and win on Moratorium Day. The older reporters—who didn't seem to object to the war—said that Seaver should not get involved.

On October 15, Seaver drove to the ball park and was handed a radical newspaper with his picture on the cover. In it he was quoted as saying:

"I think it's perfectly ridiculous what we're doing about the Vietnam situation. It's absurd. When this series is over, I'm going to have a talk with Ted Kennedy, convey some of my ideas to him, and then take an ad in the paper. I feel very strongly about this."

The patriot from the *Daily News*, Dick Young, approached Seaver brandishing a copy of this antiwar newspaper. Young often uses his articles and columns to criticize protest marches, players' unions, black consciousness, long hair, and other developments of the present outspoken generation. Apparently, Young did not want Seaver to take a stand on the Moratorium—at least, not for it.

Pressed for a statement, Seaver said: "The people are being misled by that (literature) and I resent it. I'm a ball player, not a politician. I did not give them permission to use me. I have certain feelings on Vietnam and I will express them as a U.S. citizen after this series is over."

While Seaver was talking in the clubhouse, over a hundred college students continued to picket outside. A few fans chatted with the young people but most of the well-dressed, well-fed, middle-aged World Series customers herded past with eyes on some distant turnstile.

The Met management got involved in the Moratorium controversy when Mayor Lindsay ordered the American flag flown at half-mast on all public buildings, in honor of the dead in Vietnam.

Since Shea Stadium is a city building, the Mets were technically obliged to follow this order, although firemen and policemen were disobeying the mayor at their stations. The Met officials would probably have flown the flags at half-mast except for 250 wounded veterans who had been invited to watch the game. These young men let it be known they would resent seeing the flag at half-mast on Moratorium Day. After a huddle between Mayor Lindsay and the baseball commissioner, Bowie Kuhn, it was agreed to raise the flag to the top.

This development was duly noted in the next day's newspapers. However, little mention was made of the college students who had stood outside, trying to jar a few consciences. A few young fans inside did remain seated during "The Star-Spangled Banner," but the mood in the stadium was "baseball, gentlemen, baseball."

Seaver put aside the controversy and tried to make up for his two bad starts in Atlanta and Baltimore. Clendenon hit a homer off Cuellar, in the second, and Seaver held a 1–0 lead going into the ninth.

But in the ninth, Frank Robinson hit a single to left and Boog Powell bounced a single through the right side with one out. Brooks Robinson hit a line drive to right, the kind of sinking line drive that should have been a base hit and maybe a lot more if Swoboda misplayed it. Rocky thundered in, no more graceful than in his early days under Casey, but this was 1969 and he dove headfirst, catching the ball a few inches from the ground. Some people would later say that Rocky should never have taken a chance on catching the ball. Others would say it was even better than Agee's two catches the day before, considering the score and the situation. But for the time being, a run scored on the "sacrifice fly," and the game went into extra innings.

In the bottom of the tenth, Grote led off with a fly to left. Buford started backward, then tried to reverse himself but the ball fell for a lucky double. Hodges sent in a runner for Grote. The Orioles knew him as "Who the hell is Ron Gaspar?"

Gaspar stayed at second as Weis was intentionally walked. Then Hodges pressed the J. C. Martin button again, which had been worth three runs in the first Atlanta game. This time Hodges was not asking Martin to swing—just to bunt Gaspar over to third.

The Orioles brought in left-handed Pete Richert, the man who remembered laughing at the old Mets when they botched up plays in the field.

Martin did his job. He plunked the bunt down in front of the plate and catcher Hendricks sprung out to make the only play at first. But Richert beat Hendricks to the ball and tried to whirl and throw at the same time.

The next thing J. C. Martin knew, the ball hit him on the left wrist and ricocheted toward second base. Martin saw nobody was near the ball and he knew the game would be over as soon as Ron Stupid raced home. Martin started jumping up and down like a sheep in an animated cartoon, and Gaspar landed on home plate and was greeted by a dozen teammates. The Mets were now two games ahead in the Series. They might not have to go back to Baltimore, after all.

Mrs. Joan Payson, wearing a gold numeral No. 1 on her wool suit, waved one finger in the air as she was escorted through the crowd. "What a beautiful bunt," she told people. "What a beautiful bunt."

The losers had the bunt on their minds, too.

"Maybe Ellie called something to me," Richert said. "But with 57,000 people screaming, I just couldn't hear. I decided to make the play because, if we both stand there, it's a bases-loaded situation.

"Hell, I've made that play dozens of times before but I would like to see a video tape of that play. Maybe that Martin ran out of the base line, maybe just a bit."

Two hours later, back in the offices of *The New York Times*, the meticulous Leonard Koppett asked to see photographs of the disputed play. Sure enough, Koppett noted, Martin's two feet were both in the base line, where a runner is not supposed to be. Rule (6.05 k) says that a runner must stay outside the base line when a pitcher or catcher is throwing to first base to avoid exactly what happened. Koppett realized that Martin should have been called out for interference, and the game continued with one out and Mets on second and third.

Koppett wrote a story to that effect, with accompanying photographs proving his point. A few blocks uptown, baseball people were eating dinner at the World Series headquarters in the Americana. When *Times* reporters confronted them with the pictures, the officials went into an emergency session.

"I don't know what the answer is," Bowie Kuhn said. "Now that I have been asked the question, I'll have to pursue it."

Soon afterward, plate umpire Shag Crawford told Kuhn that pictures did indicate that Martin's feet may have been "on" the base line. But since it was a judgment call, nothing could be done, so Kuhn told the anxious world that the result was now official.

While the officials pondered the pictures, several of the Orioles went to see *Hello, Dolly*, perhaps not knowing that Pearl Bailey is one of the true Met fans. Miss Bailey noticed the Orioles and introduced them from the stage, setting them up for her punch line: "Why aren't you home rehearsing?" Even the Orioles had to laugh.

Pearl was at Shea on Thursday, wearing her brown pants suit outfit and matching brown derby. She sang the anthem and began rooting for her favorite team. She had spent many a dreary Sunday watching the Mets lose, often with her friend Joan Hodges. She didn't seem to be doing much for the Mets this day, either.

McNally, the pitcher, hit a two-run homer off Koosman in the third and Frank Robinson unloaded a tremendous homer to make it 3–0. That was still the score in the sixth inning, and it was obvious that the Mets were either going to stage some unusual rally—unusual even for them—or else go back to the Sheraton Belvedere.

The only excitement had come when Frank Robinson was obviously hit in the leg by a pitch but the home-plate umpire, Lou DiMuro, missed it, touching off a long argument.

Then in the sixth, Cleon Jones hopped away from an inside pitch, pointing at his foot. DiMuro disagreed and ordered Jones back to the plate, seemingly in a reply of the Robinson incident a few minutes before.

Then out of the dugout came Gil Hodges, slow and deliberate, Gary Cooper all over again, plodding toward home plate carrying a baseball in his hand. The ball had skittered into the Met dugout after hitting—or not hitting—Jones on the foot. Now Hodges was carrying a ball.

The manager could have quickly antagonized the umpire with the wrong word or the wrong motion. But Hodges was impassive as he reached home plate. Then he extended his giant paw, still wrapped around the baseball. "Lou," Hodges said slowly. "The ball hit him."

DiMuro looked up at Hodges. DiMuro was willing to be reasonable. After all, Hodges was being so polite about it, the least DiMuro could do was inspect the ball. And when Hodges plunked the ball into DiMuro's hand, sure enough, there was a smudge of shoe polish.

This was a moment of high drama in the ball park. Everybody knew that Earl Weaver, who had been losing arguments all week, was poised in the dugout, ready to explode if the decision went against him. Everybody knew that the easiest thing for DiMuro to do was not accept the polish mark. But hadn't this whole insane year conditioned people for this moment? Wasn't it predetermined that DiMuro should now be staring, as if hypnotized, at this silly little white baseball with the silly little black smudge?

DiMuro was alone, terribly alone, the hero in history, faced with a momentous decision. The last sound he had heard was the solemn voice of Gil Hodges. The words may still have been ringing in his ears.

"Lou, the ball hit him. . . ."

DiMuro began some minor contortions, his body preparing itself for action, his right hand beginning to twitch like Dr. Strangelove going into a well-remembered salute. Then the umpire's hand, as if on its own volition, pointed to first base like a magnet pointing to the North Pole. Cleon Jones trotted to first base as 57,000 people cheered, and Lou DiMuro braced himself for the invasion. The next voice he heard was that of Earl Weaver.

"Was it the same ball?" Weaver asked.

"Yes," DiMuro said. "I watched it roll into the Met dugout."

Weaver was a beaten man. He had been thrown out of Wednesday's game. He didn't want to make it two in a row. He moped back to his dugout as if he understood the inevitability of it all.

Up in the press box, reporters were chortling about the only other shoe polish episode in World Series history, in 1957, when umpire Augie Donatelli sent a Milwaukee player named Nippy Jones to first base with the eventual tying run. "We Joneses have to stick together," Cleon would say later. And the Mets, of course, would deny any chicanery with baseballs and shoe polish.

With Cleon on first base, the other predictable unpredictables began to happen. Clendenon hit his third Series homer into the second deck in left field. Now the score was 3–2.

It was still 3–2 going into the bottom of the seventh. Behind third base, Karl Ehrhardt held up a sign that said: BELIEVE IN MIRACLES? Then he answered his question with: BELIEVE.

When Al Weis whacked a 375-foot homer among the wounded servicemen in the temporary left-field stands, tying the score at 3–3 one had to *believe*. The millennium had arrived.

Weis' homer kept Koosman in the game, and the lefty got through the eight innings as the 57,397 fans began clapping for the rally they assumed was now coming.

Eddie Watt came in to pitch for the Orioles, and Jones blasted a double over the head of his old friend, Blair. Clendenon tried to bunt Jones to third but grounded out. That brought up Ron Swoboda, the earnest relic of the Casey Era. Rocky drove a soft liner down the left-field line. Any of the Mets would have dived for the ball, and in this crazy season probably would have caught it. But Buford tried to backhand the ball and could only trap it. Jones scored the go-ahead run and Swoboda raced to second. After Charles flied out, Powell fumbled Grote's grounder as Swoboda scored.

In the ninth, Frank Robinson walked but Powell grounded out and Brooks Robinson flied out, and then Dave Johnson hit a line drive toward Jones in left field.

Shea Stadium was quivering as Jones sighted the ball, and the whole city erupted as he caught it, and the fans poured onto the field, and the New York Mets were the champions of baseball.

There were a million exciting things happening and it was hard to focus on any one incident. But out in left field, if you had been looking there, you would have seen Cleon Jones, with fans racing over to pummel him, stop for a moment, drop quickly to one knee. Later he explained his brief genuflection. "Someone was good to us."

28

THE MORNING AFTER

♦

AND SO THEY STREAMED, thousands of them, the same mad ideal-ists who had adopted the Mets back in 1962, onto the playing field at Shea to celebrate this delicious moment.

The guards and ushers made no attempt to hold back the mob. There was just no point to it. Any attempt to restrain this strange "Oktoberfest" would have ended in violence. The people needed to express themselves.

"This is a historic moment," said Jack Ginsberg of Middle Village, Queens. "I'm a fan since 1930 and I'm going to save this (a piece of sod he carried under his arm). You never know what might happen next year. They might turn into schlumps again."

Scott Barry, sixteen and a half years old, drained the last bubbles from his six-ounce bottle of champagne and waved the bottle in the air. "Ever since I was a little kid," he shouted, "back in the Polo Grounds, I've waited for this moment. Now I don't know what to say."

Most of the champagne was being poured in the Met club-house, however. For the third time in three weeks, the players were dousing each other with the bubbly stuff, some of them even drinking a belt or two.

"This is the summit," shouted Ed Charles, who had the feeling he had just played his last game. "We're Number One in the world—and you just can't get any bigger than this."

In the manager's office, Joan Hodges glanced solicitously at her huge puma of a husband. Only a year before he had been recovering from the heart attack. Now he seemed calm and healthy as reporters shouted questions, and players interrupted to congratulate him.

"You know what we are?" Mrs. Hodges squealed as she hugged her husband. "We're champions of the world."

In another part of the clubhouse, Mrs. Joan Payson kept repeating "Oh my, oh my, oh my" as she greeted the players.

Johnny Murphy permitted himself just the slightest bit of a gloat when he spotted Hodges in his office. Murphy remembered Paul Richards' crack about the Met "untouchables" in spring training, and now Murphy said: "Tell Richards we've started to win those pennants."

Then another visitor—seventy-nine-year-old Casey Stengel—dropped in to give Hodges a big husky embrace. The Met executive had been writing an exclusive article in the New York *Daily News* each day during the series. Casey said "amazing" about fifty times, and then he announced: "I gotta finish now that I'm goin' to Mrs. Payson's banquet, and I'll drink eight drinks, the first one for my fellow reporters, the next for the Amazin' Mets."

While the Met party moved slowly from the clubhouse to the Diamond Club upstairs, an instant party developed in the city. The people who had suffered for seven years were piling into the street to celebrate.

On East Forty-fourth Street, between Third and Lexington avenues, it was like V-E Day, like Lindbergh's homecoming, like New Year's Eve used to be. But it was even better because it was spontaneous. No Commissioner of Civic Celebrations engineered this display. It just happened, and the streets belonged to the people.

In one circle, holding hands, there was a Chinese man with sleek black hair, a young man with a razor haircut and turtleneck shirt, a chunky Puerto Rican girl with smoked glasses, a Negro man in a jacket and bow tie, a very tall girl in a very short skirt, a short black girl in an Afro haircut, a husky middle-aged

salesman with floppy cuffed trousers. They had come together
in an outpouring of happiness. It was the kind of afternoon when
anything was possible. The Mets had delivered a miracle to the
fans who had kept the faith.

Now it was the morning after. Some of the Mets had headaches from the night before. New York was full of headaches and
sore throats and sore feet. The Department of Sanitation had its
own headache—the 1010 tons of scrap paper that had been
dumped out of windows on Thursday afternoon.

It was time for the world to get back to normal again. Some
hardworking newspapermen even had to ring up Shea Stadium
for one reason or another. The phone rang. A voice at the other
end said:

"Good morning, World Champions."

What could you say? What could you possibly do except
giggle? World Champions? Is this the right number? Is this one of
the boys from the office? I was trying to get the New York
Mets. . . .

"World Champions, hello. . . ."

Yes, life would go on. But the Mets were World Champions
and life would never be quite the same.

Shea Stadium might not be the same for a long time anyway.
The ground crew was trying gallantly to repair the field, which
looked like a Vietnamese village after the U.S. Air Force has
passed over. The fans had turned the field into rubble, and the
ground crew was replacing 6500 square feet of grass because the
New York Jets—the World Champions of football—were due to
play Houston on Monday night.

"The big problem," explained head grounds keeper John
McCarthy, "is that it's all patchwork. It's very time-consuming
this way. Yesterday was a lot worse than the first two times."

While McCarthy's crew struggled over the weekend, the Mets
celebrated and appeared on the *Ed Sullivan Show* and City officials planned a Mets Day for Monday.

Mets Day was gorgeous, with temperatures in the low seventies, the kind of October day that New York does so well. The

Mets started in open cars at the Battery, as thousands of fans clogged the narrow old streets. They were greeted at City Hall by the omnipresent Mayor Lindsay. They were greeted at Bryant Park by Pearl Bailey. At every stop, Metropolitan Opera star Robert Merrill sang "The Star-Spangled Banner."

At Bryant Park, Ed Charles recited a poem he had written in 1961 after being traded to Kansas City following ten long years in the minor leagues:

> Author of my talents, only You have I praised,
> To Thee only shall my hands be raised.
> For when I'm burdened with the weight of my team,
> To my rescue You come, it will always seem.
> For outstanding is my play on any given day
> When You intervene and help lead the way.
> Grateful to You I'll always be
> For exploiting my talents for the world to see.

One of the cars in the motorcade was graced by Karl Ehrhardt, the little old sign maker, who was recognized by many fans. The parade continued to Gracie Mansion, the mayor's residence, where the players frolicked with neighborhood children as fireboats on the East River sprayed salutes.

At 7 P.M. the Mets went by bus to Flushing Meadow Park for another rally. Then, as fireworks exploded in the sky over Queens, the Mets sat in Shea Stadium and watched the other World Champions defeat the Houston Oilers, 26–17. It was nice to see that one World Champion could defeat Houston.

The Mets rooted for the Jets, but the football players did not have many nice things to say about M. Donald Grant and his team. M. Donald had a special arrangement with the city by which he kept the Jets off the Shea Stadium field until the Mets' season was over. So the Jets had been forced to shift their schedule while the Mets unexpectedly extended their season. And when the Jets finally got onto the field, it had been mutilated by the Met fans that stadium ushers and guards had not attempted to hold back, even if they could. Ironically, of course, M. Don-

ald's reason for not letting the Jets on the field in September was
to protect the grass.

"Wasn't it disgraceful?" asked middle linebacker Al Atkinson
of the Jets. "I mean, guys were just reaching down and picking
up huge chunks of dirt."

The sod didn't have anywhere near enough time to adhere to
the ground. So the Jets picked their way through the potholes
and cursed the city officials who let M. Donald Grant play dog-in-
the-manger with municipal property.

However, Mayor Lindsay had nothing bad to say about the
Mets. On the first Tuesday in November, he overcame his two
challengers and was reelected for another four years. His comeback would have been the biggest miracle of almost any year,
but in 1969 he had to rank second in the rally department.

The men who had helped return the mayor to office began
receiving their own awards. Hodges was named Manager of the
Year by every press organization that gave such an award.

Donn Clendenon was voted the outstanding player of the
World Series by *Sport Magazine*, and he received a Dodge
Challenger for his three important home runs. Little Alfie Weis,
whose .454 Series batting average led all hitters, didn't get a
sports car. But the efficient little fellow was given a new car by
the Volkswagen people in a masterful publicity stunt.

Back in Morris, Minnesota, Jerry Koosman was given the key
to the city as most of the 4199 residents welcomed him home.
He and his wife told their friends that they were planning to keep
their home in Morris rather than move to New York. "You can
take the boy out of the country," Koosman said, "but you can't
take the country out of the boy."

Wonder of all wonders, Tommie Agee and Cleon Jones were
honored by the city fathers and mothers back in Mobile. And Ed
Charles was amazed by the civic delegation when he got off the
airplane in Kansas City.

"I've been slipping in and out of town for years and nobody
particularly cared. Now we're winners and suddenly I'm a
celebrity."

Hodges was honored in his adopted hometown, too. In
Brooklyn, on October 22, Jackie Robinson, Ralph Branca, Gene

Hermanski, and Roy Campanella appeared at ceremonies at Borough Hall in honor of their old teammate. Pete Reiser, Mickey Owen, Carl Furillo, and Tommy Brown—other old Dodgers—sent telegrams.

"Is this the start of a Met dynasty?" somebody asked Hodges.

"I'd rather have it the start of the old Dodger days," Hodges said. "Just one happy family."

The family was spread all over the country but the biggest concentration was in Las Vegas, where Agee, Jones, Koosman, Clendenon, Kranepool, Shamsky, and Seaver were paid $10,000 apiece for appearing for two weeks in an act with Phil Foster at the Circus Maximus.

"They rendered (*render*, verb, to tear apart) 'The Impossible Dream' without once conjuring up memories of Richard Kiley," wrote the critic, James Tuite, in *The New York Times*.

Charles and Swoboda had also been invited to appear in the Vegas act, but both of them had already promised to join baseball-sponsored tours of military bases in Asia. Charles had announced his retirement from baseball after the last Series game, and this was his last chance to make big money as an athlete. The $10,000 would have bought a lot of therapy for his little boy, who was struggling with cerebral palsy. But Charles had agreed to tour Vietnam for free, and he did not back down.

"That's show biz," Charles said.

All the Mets had a stake in show business, with a record they made in October. The album of ten songs was called "The Amazing Mets," and it was reportedly selling quite well in New York but nowhere else. The players were paid $500 a man and their fund received twenty-two cents for every record sold.

But bigger money would be coming in for some of them, particularly the biggest names who had gotten agents for themselves.

Seaver was the hottest commodity because, as Bob Lipsyte pointed out, "he was somewhat more verbally polished than Jerry Koosman, his pitching partner, and considerably whiter than Donn Clendenon, the batting hero of the Series.

Seaver's company took newspaper advertisements that said: "Now Available: Tom Seaver, America's top athlete and sports personality, plus Nancy Seaver, Tom's lovely wife, for those situations that call for young Mrs. America or husband-and-wife sales appeal." This advertisement brought some obscene mail and phone calls.

The pitcher took a little longer to take that other advertisement he has promised, the one deploring the war in Vietnam. No doubt Met officials, agents and friends warned how financially damaging it might be for his image. However, on December 31, in *The New York Times* there appeared this gentle five- by seven-inch message: "On the eve of 1970, please join us in a prayer for peace." It was signed Nancy and Tom Seaver.

The Seavers did enjoy a vacation in the Virgin Islands before Tom returned to make an appearance on the *Kraft Music Hall*, where he took a pie in the face. His value on the market went up further when he was voted the Cy Young Award, as the best pitcher in the National League. He also finished second to Willie McCovey of San Francisco for the Most Valuable Player Award; two of the twenty-four voting reporters did not include him among the top ten because they did not think pitchers deserved the award.

"Oh, well, I'm only twenty-four," Seaver sighed. "Maybe I'll win it some other year."

The pitcher's disappointment was tempered a little when the Commissioner's office announced the breakdown of the World Series money. Because of the new division play-offs in 1969, the championship fund was the largest in history. Each player on the Mets received $18,338.18, as did the coaches, the managers, the two trainers, Gus Mauch and Joe Deer, clubhouse man Nick Torman (the man who polished Cleon Jones' shoes), and John McCarthy, the grounds keeper who repaired the field each time the Mets won a championship.

The Mets were delighted to know that their share was higher than the $12,794 that the 1963 Dodgers had received in the previous high pay-off. The losing Orioles of 1969 took home $14,-904.21 per man. The Cubs, who had been nine and a half games ahead of the Mets on August 13, got $574.94 per man because they got caught.

The players also voted Amos Otis, their "untouchable" of

spring training, a half share although he batted only ninety-three times after failing his early trial.

That was the last profit Otis would receive from the Mets. On December 3 he was traded to the Kansas City Royals, along with a young pitcher named Bob Johnson, in return for a New York-born third baseman, Joe Foy. After a World Championship, Otis wasn't exactly an "untouchable" any more.

"After the kind of year Tommie Agee had in center field," Murphy said, "we finally felt secure enough to trade Otis."

The acquisition of Foy made all those Met third basemen expendable. Wayne Garrett and Bobby Pfeil were right back where they had been a year before, fighting to stay out of the minor leagues, while old Ed Charles was given his unconditional release.

The Mets insisted that Charles had a future in their organization, and he began moving his family to New York in early December. But he and Murphy had a disagreement over $5000, which Charles claimed the Mets had promised him for moving expenses. On December 11, Charles had the moving van turned around in Buffalo, New York, and he flew his family back to Kansas City. Murphy said the job was still open, but by the end of the year it appeared that Charles had gone from "the summit" to unemployment in two quick months.

Another career ended with a more voluntary retirement. Gus Mauch, the trainer for all eight seasons with the Mets, announced that he was retiring to Treasure Island, Florida, to play more bridge with his wife, Mary. Gus had kept the Yankees healthy enough for them to collect twelve pennants in eighteen seasons. Now he had seen the Mets win the Series and he decided to retire while on top.

Johnny Murphy never got to retire. The general manager suffered a heart attack in late December and died on January 14, 1970, of a massive coronary. Three days later, Bob Scheffing was promoted from troubleshooter to general manager, and life went on.

The new executive was inheriting one of the most promising young organizations in sports. It wasn't just the Seavers and the Koosmans. It was the young players with names like Jon Matlack and Jim Bibby and Mike Jorgensen who helped the Mets' farm teams at Tidewater and Memphis win pennants in 1969. Bob Scheffing was inheriting the Youth of America, conceived by Stengel, begun by Weiss and Devine, matured under Hodges and Murphy. But the Met management quivered when it heard the word "dynasty."

"We're not in any such category," John Murphy had said in one of his last press conferences. "We realize it took hard work and spirit and luck—and that's what it will take again."

Again? Again what? What really happened in 1969, anyway?

Pitchers *(seasons with Mets)*	CAREER games	won–lost
Anderson, Craig (1962–64)	82	7–23
Arrigo, Gerry (1964)	189	35–37
Bauta, Ed (1963–64)	97	6–6
Bearnath, Larry (1963–66)	171	13–21
Bennett, Dennis (1967)	182	43–47
Bethke, Jim (1965)	25	2–0
Cardwell, Don (1967–69)	378	100–135
Cisco, Galen (1962–65)	192	25–56
Connors, Billy (1967–68)	26	0–2
Craig, Roger (1962–63)	368	74–98
Daviault, Ray (1962)	36	1–5
Denehy, Bill (1967)	18	1–7
DiLauro, Jack (1969)	23	1–4
Dillon, Steve (1963–64)	3	0–0
Eilers, Dave (1965–66)	81	8–6
Estrada, Chuck (1967)	146	50–44
Fisher, Jack (1964–67)	400	86–139
Foss, Larry (1962)	8	1–2
Friend, Bob (1966)	602	197–230
Frisella, Dan (1967–69)	36	3–10
Gardner, Rob (1965–66)	69	4–12
Gentry, Gary (1969)	35	13–12
Graham, Bill (1967)	6	1–2
Grzenda, Joe (1967)	94	5–5
Green, Dallas (1966)	185	20–22
Hamilton, Jack (1966–67)	218	32–40
Hendley, Bob (1967)	216	48–52
Hepler, Bill (1966)	37	3–3
Hillman, Dave (1962)	188	21–37
Hinsley, Jerry (1964, 1967)	11	0–2
Hook, Jay (1962–64)	160	29–62
Hudson, Jesse (1969)	1	0–0
Hunter, Willard (1962, 1964)	69	4–9
Jackson, Alvin (1962–65, 1968–69)	302	67–99
Johnson, Bob (1969)	2	0–0
Jones, Sherman (1962)	48	2–6
Koonce, Calvin (1967–69)	285	44–42
Koosman, Jerry (1967–69)	76	36–23
Kroll, Gary (1964–65)	71	6–7
Labine, Clem (1962)	513	77–56
Lamabe, Jack (1967)	285	33–41
Lary, Frank (1964–65)	350	128–116
Locke, Ron (1964)	25	1–2
MacKenzie, Ken (1962–63)	129	8–10
McAndrew, Jim (1968–69)	39	10–14
McGraw, Tug (1965–67, 1969)	98	13–22
Miller, Bob G. (1962)	86	6–8
Miller, Bob L. (1962)	466	44–62